STATISTICS
THE
EASY
WAY

Douglas Downing, Ph.D.
Jeff Clark, Ph.D.

BARRON'S

New York / London / Toronto / Sydney

Dedication

This book is for Jenny in gratitude for her affectionate support.

Acknowledgments

Our thanks go to Mark Yoshimi for his help with the probability experiments, Marlys Downing for photographic help, and Liz Ashburn for providing experimental data.

© Copyright 1983 by Barron's Educational Series, Inc.

All inquiries should be addressed to:
Barron's Educational Series, Inc.
250 Wireless Boulevard
Hauppauge, New York 11788

Library of Congress Catalog No. 83-15627

International Standard Book No. 0-8120-2666-7

Library of Congress Cataloging in Publication Data
Downing, Douglas.
    Statistics the easy way.

    Includes index.
    1. Statistics. 2. Probabilities. I. Clark, Jeff.
II. Title.
QA276.12.D68 1983   519.5   83-15627
ISBN 0-8120-2666-7

CONTENTS

*optional sections that require the use of more advanced mathematics

INTRODUCTION

Statistics is the study of how to acquire meaningful information by analyzing data, such as lists of numbers. This book teaches you how statistical methods work and how to use them.

You're probably wondering whether statistics is a hard subject. The answer to that question is "yes and no." Many of the important ideas in statistics can be understood even by someone with only a slight mathematical background. However, there are also parts of statistics that are hard. Many require the use of advanced mathematical methods such as calculus. For this reason, many of the important results in statistics have remained inaccessible to the general reader. The purpose of this book is to make these important results understandable by everyone. Many books attempt to simplify the material by presenting you with all the formulas that you need to know, making it possible for you to plug in numbers mindlessly and crank out results without understanding what you are doing. If you follow that method, you will sooner or later run into a situation where your lack of understanding could get you into trouble.

In this book we explain why everything works. However, the subjects that require the most mathematics are left as exercises or as optional mathematical sections. (You can peek in the back of the book if you wish, since the answers to most of the exercises are given there.) A star marks the exercises that require advanced math, and the optional mathematical sections are clearly labeled with warnings to prevent nonmathematicians from inadvertently straying into them. However, if you know calculus you will find that these sections of the book provide valuable explanations of the underlying theory.

You will need to know a little bit of algebra to use this book; for example, you will need to know what exponents are. We will use some set notation, but we will develop all of that from scratch. We also use some Greek letters. You can get to know them by checking the "Cast of Greek Characters" section at the beginning of the book. [We use Greek letters for two reasons: (1) Everybody else does it; and (2) it's easier to keep track of which symbol stands for what when more symbols are available.]

To understand statistics it is necessary to understand probability. Probability, the study of chance phenomena, is also an interesting subject in its own right. There are many fun aspects of probability, since it includes the study of dice, cards, and related games. There are also many important practical applications of probability, and the important concepts of statistical inference are based on the ideas of probability. The first few chapters cover the ideas of probability that you will need to know.

In both probability and statistics you will face the need to apply long and complicated formulas. That is the kind of work that is best left to a computer, so this book takes advantage of the fact that many people today have access to a small computer. You can still learn from this book even if a computer is not available to you, but it will be much easier for you to come up with numerical answers if you do have a computer. Answers expressed as numbers are far more satisfying than answers expressed as complicated formulas.

Many of the exercises ask you to write computer programs to perform the calculations discussed in the text. The computer exercises are clearly marked with a box: ❑. In the back of the book there are answers to many of these exercises written in the BASIC computer-programming language. BASIC is available on almost any small computer. You could also write your own programs in your favorite computer language. If you don't like to write your own programs but still would like the computer to do your work for you, you can just copy down the programs from the back of the book and type them into your computer. (We won't regard that as cheating.)

CAST OF GREEK CHARACTERS (AND OTHER SYMBOLS)

Here are the main Greek letters that you will have to know:

μ (lower-case mu), pronounced *mew;* μ stands for the mean of a random variable.

σ (lower-case sigma); σ stands for the standard deviation of a random variable.
σ^2 (sigma squared) represents variance.

χ (lower-case chi), pronounced like *kite,* but without the *t* at the end. χ^2 (chi squared) represents an important random-variable distribution.

π (lower-case pi), pronounced *pie;* π represents a special number about equal to 3.14159 that is used extensively in mathematics.

Φ (capital phi), pronounced *fie;* Φ is used for the cumulative distribution function for a standard normal random variable.

Σ (capital sigma); Σ represents summation. In other words, ΣX means "Add up all the values of X."

X INTRODUCTION

These Greek letters also appear:

λ (lower-case lambda); λ is used for the parameter in the Poisson and exponential distributions.

Δ (capital delta); Δ represents "change in."

ψ (lower-case psi), pronounced *sigh;* ψ represents a moment generating function.

ε (lower-case epsilon); ε represents a small positive number.

Γ (capital gamma); Γ represents the gamma function.

Other symbols that will be used are:

∪ union

∩ intersection

| given that

$\sqrt{n}$ square root

‖ absolute value

e 2.71828 . . .

ø empty set

> greater than

< less than

$\int_a^b f(x)\, dx$ area under the curve $f(x)$ from $x = a$ to $x = b$

CHAPTER 1

INTRODUCTION TO PROBABILITY

If you flip a coin, the result will be either heads or tails. It would be very useful if you could predict exactly how the coin will turn up when it is flipped (especially if you are the captain of a football team meeting the referee for the opening coin toss). However, it is practically impossible to do this. You could, in theory, calculate the path of the coin by using the laws of mechanics, if you knew the initial force that was applied to it and the other forces acting on it, and thus determine which side would be up when the coin comes to a stop. This would be very hard, though, so for practical purposes a coin toss is a good example of a random event: There is no accurate way to predict what the result will be.

If you toss a coin more than once, though, you can make some interesting predictions about what will happen. This is a general feature of random events, and it is one of the foundations of probability: You can't say what will happen in one occurrence, but if you watch the same thing happen many times you will be able to predict some patterns. For example, if you throw a dart at a phone book and try to guess the height of the person whose name is hit by the dart, you will probably be wrong. If you select 100 people at random and try to guess their average height, you will be much more likely to get it right.

If you flip a coin twice, there are four possibilities for the result: head-heads, heads-tails, tails-heads, and tails-tails. (After this, H will be used for heads and T for tails.) There are two possibilities for the first flip, and for each possible result of the first flip there are two possibilities for the second flip.

Now, if you need to know whether you will see no heads, one head, or two heads in the two flips, you can make a prediction. Assuming that the coin is a fair one, not biased toward head or tail, each of the four possible outcomes (HH, HT, TH, TT) is equally likely. You will see two heads if outcome 1 (HH) occurs, and you will see no heads if outcome 4 (TT) occurs. So you have just as much chance of seeing no heads as you do of seeing two heads. However, you will see exactly one head if either outcome 2 (HT) or outcome 3 (TH) occurs. So your best bet is to guess that one head will appear on the two flips. Of course, you still have a 50 percent chance of being wrong. But you have a much better chance of being right than if you had guessed no heads or two heads.

Here is an example to see whether this is right. We flipped a coin twice and wrote down the result. Then we repeated this same procedure 33 more times. (In probability theory, this would be called performing the *experiment* of flipping two coins a total of 34 times. One of the fun parts of probability is that you can say you are conducting scientific experiments while you are tossing coins and doing other amusing things.) The results were:

HT, TT, TH, HT, TT, HT, HH, TT, TT, HH, TT, TH, TT, TT,
TH, HH, TH, TH, HT, TT, HH, HH, HT, TH, HT,
TH, TH, HT, HT, HT, TT, TH, HH, TH

Adding up these results gives:

Result	Number of occurrences
No head	9
One head	19
Two heads	6

If you had been watching this experiment you definitely would have done better by guessing one head each time than by guessing either of the other two possibilities, although you might have begun to doubt it after the first 14 pairs of flips.

You probably could have figured this much out for yourself without knowing anything about probability theory. Now, we'll use the same ideas to figure out how many heads are likely to appear if you toss a coin any number of times. If you toss a coin 92 times, then intuitively you will guess that the number of heads that show up will most likely be about 46. At the opening of the play "Rosencrantz and Guildenstern Are Dead," Guildenstern tosses 92 heads in a row, thereby losing a lot of money to Rosencrantz. Intuitively, you know that this is extremely unlikely to occur.

In general, if you tossed a coin n times, n being a large number, you would expect that the number of heads would most likely be close to $n/2$ and that you would be unlikely to get n heads in a row. First, let us consider the case of flipping the coin three times. There are eight possible outcomes:

HHH, HHT, HTH, HTT, THH, THT, TTH, TTT

That is the first step in computing a probability: Find out how many possible outcomes there are. Then find out how many of those outcomes lead to the event that you are interested in. The *probability* of that event occurring is equal to the number of ways of getting that event divided by the total number of possible outcomes. For example:

Event you're interested in	Outcomes that lead to that event	Number of outcomes	Probability of event
No head	TTT	1	1/8
1 head	HTT, THT, TTH	3	3/8
2 heads	HHT, HTH, THH	3	3/8
3 heads	HHH	1	1/8

If you are forced to guess how many heads will appear, you should guess either 1 or 2. You clearly shouldn't guess 0 or 3.

We can follow the same method if we need to make a prediction about the results of four flips: list all the outcomes, and then count how many outcomes have no heads, how many outcomes have one head, and so on. This method would get a bit tedious, though, and it would be very difficult if we tried it for a large number of flips. What is needed is a way to count the outcomes without having to list them all. That concept is one of the important ideas in probability.

First, we need to count all the possible outcomes from four flips. There are two possibilities for the first toss, then for each of those possibilities there are two for the second toss, then for each of these combinations there are two possibilities for the third toss, and so on. Altogether, there will be $2 \times 2 \times 2 \times 2 = 2^4 = 16$ possible outcomes. You should be able to convince yourself that if you flip a coin n times, there will be 2^n possible outcomes. Now you can see why the listing method doesn't work. If you flip a coin 10 times, there will be $2^{10} = 1,024$ possible outcomes.

Next, we need to count how many outcomes have zero heads, how many have one head, etc., up to how many have four heads. The case of zero heads is easy, since there is only one outcome (TTTT) that has zero heads. To calculate the number of possibilities with one head, we need to figure out how many different ways we can write one H and three T's. Since there are four possible places for the H, there are four possibilities: HTTT, THTT, TTHT, TTTH. Now we need to figure out how many ways we can write two H's and two T's. There are four possible places to put the first H (call it H1):

H1 __ __ __ , __ H1 __ __ , __ __ H1 __ , __ __ __ H1

For each of these possibilities there are three places to put the second H (call it H2):

H1 H2 __ __ ,	H1 __ H2 __ ,	H1 __ __ H2,
H2 H1 __ __ ,	__ H1 H2 __ ,	__ H1 __ H2,
H2 __ H1 __ ,	__ H2 H1 __ ,	__ __ H1 H2,
H2 __ __ H1 ,	__ H2 __ H1 ,	__ __ H2 H1

(Note that we only have to worry about where to put the H's, since once we've done that it will be obvious where to put the T's.) There are 12 of these possible ways to arrange the H's. However, it doesn't make any difference which is H1 and which is H2; __ H1 H2 __ is the same as __ H2 H1 __. We must divide by 2 to avoid double-counting these duplications. That means there are six possible ways to get two heads:

$$\text{HHTT, HTHT, HTTH, THHT, THTH, TTHH}$$

Therefore, the results for four flips are as follows.

Number of heads (h)	Number of outcomes with h heads	Probability that h heads will occur
0	1	1/16 = .0625
1	4	4/16 = .2500
2	6	6/16 = .3750
3	4	4/16 = .2500
4	1	1/16 = .0625

(You should note that these probabilities are symmetric—that is, the probability that you will get *h* heads is exactly the same as the probability that you will get *h* tails.)

Now we need to figure out a general formula for the number of outcomes that have *h* heads in *n* tosses. In principle it is the same as what we did before: We need to figure out how many ways we can write *h* capital H's on *n* blanks. There are *n* possibilities for the first H that we write, then $n - 1$ places left for the second, $n - 2$ places left for the third, and so on. Altogether, there will be

$$n \times (n - 1) \times (n - 2) \times (n - 3) \times \cdots \times (n - h + 1)$$

ways of writing down all the H's. Then we must divide by

$$h \times (h - 1) \times (h - 2) \times (h - 3) \times \cdots \times 3 \times 2 \times 1$$

to eliminate the duplications caused by the different orderings. Therefore, if we flip a coin *n* times, the number of possible outcomes that have exactly *h* heads will be

$$\frac{n \times (n - 1) \times (n - 2) \times (n - 3) \times \cdots \times (n - h + 1)}{h \times (h - 1) \times (h - 2) \times \cdots \times 3 \times 2 \times 1}$$

The quantity $h \times (h - 1) \times (h - 2) \times (h - 3) \times \cdots \times 3 \times 2 \times 1$ is interesting. It turns out that there are many times in probability theory when we need to calculate the product of all the numbers from 1 up to a particular number. This quantity is called the *factorial* of the number, and it is symbolized by an exclamation mark (!). For example,

$$3! = 3 \times 2 \times 1 = 6, \quad 4! = 4 \times 3 \times 2 \times 1 = 24,$$

$$10! = 10 \times 9 \times 8 \times 7 \times 6 \times 5 \times 4 \times 3 \times 2 \times 1 = 3{,}628{,}800,$$

$$69! = 1.71 \times 10^{98}$$

As you can see, factorials become very big very fast. It should be obvious that $1! = 1$. There are also some formulas where we may need to find $n!$ for $n = 0$. These formulas only work if $0!$ has the value of 1, so we will make that definition.

Now we can use the factorial notation in the denominator to simplify the formula for the number of combinations with h heads:

$$\frac{n \times (n - 1) \times (n - 2) \times (n - 3) \times \cdots \times (n - h + 1)}{h!}$$

We can also write the numerator in a shorter fashion using the factorial function. Multiply and divide the numerator by $(n - h)!$:

$$n \times (n - 1) \times (n - 2) \times \cdots \times (n - h + 1)$$

$$= \frac{n \times (n - 1) \times (n - 2) \times \cdots \times (n - h + 1) \times (n - h)!}{(n - h)!}$$

$$= \frac{n \times (n - 1) \times (n - 2) \times \cdots \times 3 \times 2 \times 1}{(n - h)!}$$

$$= \frac{n!}{(n - h)!}$$

Therefore, we can write our formula in a very compact form:

$$\frac{n!}{h!\,(n - h)!}$$

(We will see this formula again in Chapter 5.)

To calculate a factorial it is best to use a computer. See the answer to Exercise 6 for an example of a computer program written in the BASIC programming language to calculate factorials.

What this all means is that we are now willing to predict that if we flip a coin n times the probability that we will get h heads is

$$\left[\frac{n!}{h!\,(n - h)!}\right]2^{-n}$$

Let's make sure that this formula works for $n = 5$ (2^{-n} in this case is 1/32):

TABLE 1-1

h	Number of combinations with h heads		Probability of h heads
0	$\frac{5!}{0!5!} = 1$	TTTTT	1/32 = .031
1	$\frac{5!}{1!4!} = 5$	HTTTT, THTTT, TTHTT, TTTHT, TTTTH	5/32 = .156
2	$\frac{5!}{2!3!} = 10$	HHTTT, HTHTT, HTTHT, HTTTH, THHTT, THTHT, THTTH, TTHHT, TTHTH, TTTHH	10/32 = .313
3	$\frac{5!}{3!2!} = 10$	TTHHH, THTHH, THHTH, THHHT, HTTHH, HTHTH, HTHHT, HHTTH, HHTHT, HHHTT	10/32 = .313
4	$\frac{5!}{4!1!} = 5$	HHHHT, HHHTH, HHTHH, HTHHH, THHHH	5/32 = .156
5	$\frac{5!}{0!5!} = 1$	HHHHH	1/32 = .031

We can also use the formula to see that the chance of getting 92 heads in a row is 2.019×10^{-28}.

Keep that in mind if you decide to try to break Rosencrantz and Guildenstern's record.

EXERCISES

1. Toss a coin 50 times and keep track of the results. Is the number of heads that appears close to the number that is predicted?

2. Toss five coins and write down the number of heads that appear. Repeat this process 50 times and then compare the observed frequencies to the probabilities.

3. Suppose you toss two coins. What is the probability that they will match?

4. Suppose you flip a coin n times. If you win a dollar every time the coin comes up heads and lose a dollar every time it comes up tails, what is the probability that you will win k dollars?

❑ 5. Write a computer program that lists all the possible results of tossing a coin six times.

❏ 6. Write a program that reads in a number n and then calculates $n!$.

❏ 7. Write a program that reads in the number of coin tosses (n), and then prints a table showing the probability of getting h heads, for all values of h from $h = 0$ to $h = n$.

8. If you flip a coin 50 times, what is the probability of getting 25 heads? If you flip a coin 100 times, what is the probability of getting 50 heads?

CHAPTER 2

INTRODUCTION TO HYPOTHESIS TESTING

In the last chapter we investigated a probability problem: If you toss a coin a certain number of times, how many heads are likely to appear? During that calculation we assumed that the coin was a fair coin—that is, during any particular flip there was a 50 percent chance of flipping heads and a 50 percent chance of flipping tails. Now we will consider an even more perplexing problem: How can we tell whether or not the coin is really fair? You will especially need to know the answer to this question if you are considering playing a coin-flipping game with an unkempt-looking stranger in a strange town. To put it formally, if we let p stand for the probability that the coin will come up heads, how do we know that $p = 1/2$?

This problem is a problem in *statistics*. Probability and statistics are very closely related, because they ask opposite types of questions. In probability, we know how a process works and we want to predict what the outcomes of that process will be. In statistics, we don't know how the process works but we can observe the outcomes of the process. We want to use the information about the outcomes to learn about the nature of the process.

In our coin example we should first, of course, make an obvious check. If the coin has two heads, then $p = 1$; if it has two tails, then $p = 0$. Once we've done that, though, it is very difficult to tell just by looking at the coin whether it is fair or not. Intuitively, we can't think of any reason why it might be more likely to come up heads rather than tails (or vice versa), but it might be unbalanced in such a way as to make one outcome more likely than the other. If we flip the coin once, we won't have a clue as to whether or not it is fair. However, if we flip the coin many times, then we will start getting some information that we can use to estimate how fair it is.

Problems of this sort are called *hypothesis testing* problems. First we decide on the hypothesis we want to test. In this case our hypothesis is that $p = 1/2$. The hypothesis that is to be tested is often called

8

the *null hypothesis* (for some obscure reason). The only other possibility is that the null hypothesis is wrong. The hypothesis that says, "The null hypothesis is wrong" is called the *alternative hypothesis*. In our case the alternative hypothesis is that the coin is not fair ($p \neq 1/2$). We know that either the null hypothesis or the alternative hypothesis must be true, since they are the only two possibilities. The question is: Do we accept the null hypothesis and say that the coin is fair, or do we reject the null hypothesis and say that the coin is unfair?

It is clear intuitively that we should flip the coin many times; let n be the number of flips. Then, if the number of heads that appears is close to $n/2$, we should accept the hypothesis that the coin is fair. If the number of heads is very far from $n/2$, we should reject the hypothesis that the coin is fair. For example, if we flip the coin 100 times and come up with 44 heads, it seems quite likely that the coin is fair. However, if we come up with only 10 heads in 100 flips, we can almost surely say that something fishy is going on and that the coin is not fair.

Therefore, our test procedure will work like this. We will pick a number c. If the number of heads (h) is between ($n/2 - c$) and ($n/2 + c$), we will accept the null hypothesis and say that the coin is fair; otherwise we will say that the coin is not fair. We can call the region from ($n/2 - c$) to ($n/2 + c$) the *zone of acceptance*. If h is not in the zone of acceptance, we will be very critical of the hypothesis and will reject it. Therefore, the zone for which the hypothesis will be rejected is called the *critical region*.

The main problem now is: How far away from $n/2$ can we let the number of heads get before we say that the coin is unfair—that is, how big should we make c?

We would like to make the right judgment about our null hypothesis. There are two ways we can be right: We can accept the hypothesis when it is true, or we can reject it when it is false. However, that means that there are also two ways we can be wrong: We might reject the hypothesis when it is really true, or we might accept the hypothesis when it is really false. The first kind of mistake can be called slip-up type 1 and the second kind can be called slip-up type 2. Table 2-1 shows the possibilities.

TABLE 2-1

	Accept hypothesis	Reject hypothesis
Hypothesis is true	right	slip-up type 1 (we want to avoid this)
Hypothesis is false	slip-up type 2	right

If we choose a large value for c, then we will have a wide zone of acceptance and we will be more likely to accept the hypothesis than we would with a small value of c. That means that there is less chance of committing slip-up type 1—that is, we're not likely to reject the hypothesis if it is really true. However, if we make the zone of acceptance large we are increasing the risk that we will accept the hypothesis even if it is really false, which means that we would commit a type 2 slip-up.

The other strategy is to choose a narrow zone of acceptance. If we do that, it is unlikely that we will commit slip-up type 2 (we're not likely to accept the hypothesis if it is really false) but we stand a much greater chance of committing slip-up type 1 (rejecting the hypothesis when it is really true). There is an inherent trade-off involved in hypothesis testing. We usually can't devise a single test procedure that will minimize the chances of committing both types of error.

Often we will be more worried about the possibility of incorrectly rejecting the hypothesis, so we will be more careful about avoiding type 1 slip-ups. If we're going to have the courage to tell the unkempt stranger that we think his coin is unfair, then we want to make almost certain that we're right. (Otherwise he might get nasty.) In scientific work, if we decide to accept the hypothesis, then we're likely to keep on searching for more evidence to see if we can make a convincing case for it. If we decide to reject the hypothesis, that means we're really convinced that the hypothesis is false, so we can stop.

What is often done in statistics is to set an upper limit to the probability of committing slip-up type 1. Usually this limit is set at either 10 percent or 5 percent. At first it can be confusing to remember the difference between type 1 and type 2. Just remember that our number one priority is to avoid slip-ups of type 1, which we do by being very polite and making sure that we don't reject the hypothesis unless we're pretty sure it's wrong. If we decide on a 10 percent test, that means we want to make sure there is only a 10 percent chance that our test procedure will say that the coin is unfair when it is really fair.

Once we've decided this, we need to figure out how wide to make the zone of acceptance. Let's suppose that the coin is fair. Once we make that assumption we know exactly what the probabilities are, using the principles we developed in the last chapter. If n is the number of flips and h is the number of heads, then the probability that h will equal a particular value k is

$$\frac{n!}{k!\,(n-k)!} \times 2^{-n}$$

Suppose that $n = 20$. Then we can make a table of the probabilities that $h = 0$, $h = 1$, $h = 2$, and so on. (See Table 2-2.)

These probabilities are shown in the graph.

We want to choose our zone of acceptance so that there is roughly a 90 percent chance that h will land in the zone and only a 10 percent chance that h will land outside the zone. If we add up the probabilities for $h = 7$, $h = 8$, $h = 9$, $h = 10$, $h = 11$, $h = 12$, and $h = 13$, we find that if the coin is fair there is a .8846 probability that h will have one of these seven values. So we'll design our test like this: We will flip the coin 20 times and count the number of heads (h). If h is between 7 and 13, we will accept the hypothesis and say that the coin is fair. If h is less than or equal to 6, or if h is greater than or equal to 14, then we will say that the coin is unfair.

In this way we can ensure that the probability of erroneously rejecting the hypothesis (slip-up type 1) is only about 12 percent. For

TABLE 2-2: Results of Tossing a Coin 20 Times

Number of heads	Probability	Number of heads	Probability
0	9.5×10^{-7}	11	.160179
1	.000019	12	.120134
2	.000181	13	.073928
3	.001087	14	.036964
4	.004620	15	.014785
5	.014785	16	.004620
6	.036964	17	.001087
7	.073928	18	.000181
8	.120134	19	.000019
9	.160179	20	9.5×10^{-7}
10	.176197		

example, suppose that there are 5 heads out of the 20 flips. Then we can say with a fair degree of confidence that the coin is not a fair coin. We cannot say this with absolute certainty, because there is a 1.48 percent chance that only 5 heads will turn up in 20 flips of a fair coin. So there still is a possibility that we might commit a type 1 slip-up by saying that the hypothesis is false when it is really true. However, we have made sure that the probability of this happening is less than 12 percent.

Of course, you can be still more cautious if you want to. Suppose you are very worried about erroneously rejecting the fair-coin hypothesis, so you want to make sure that the chance of that happening is less than 4 percent. Then you can change your test procedure so that you will accept the fair-coin hypothesis if h is between 6 and 14.

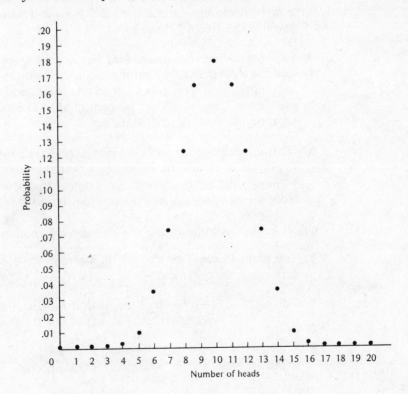

FIGURE 2–1

With this procedure, you are even more sure that you won't say that the coin is unfair if it is really fair. However, by widening the zone of acceptance you are increasing the chances of committing a type 2 slip-up—that is, saying that the coin is fair when it is really unfair. There is no way to calculate the probability of a type 2 slip-up, since you don't know what the probabilities are for the different numbers of heads if the coin is unfair. So even after you've decided to accept the hypothesis you're not sure that the coin is really fair. For example, suppose the probability of heads is .51. Then you are very likely to accept the fair-coin hypothesis even though the coin is not fair. The only way to improve on this situation is to increase the number of flips.

We'll talk a lot more about hypothesis testing later. (See Chapter 17.)

EXERCISES

Use the program you wrote in Chapter 1 to answer these questions:

1. What is the probability that you will get 44 heads in 100 tosses of a fair coin?

2. What is the probability that you will get 10 heads in 100 tosses of a fair coin?

3. Suppose you flip a coin 100 times and you want to test the hypothesis that the coin is fair, making sure that there is less than a 5 percent chance of erroneously rejecting the fair coin hypothesis. How wide should the zone of acceptance be? How wide should the zone be if you flip the coin 5 times? How wide should the zone be if you flip the coin 10 times?

4. Suppose a friend has tossed two dice, one blue and one red. You are told the total of the two numbers appearing on the dice but not the individual numbers. You want to test the hypothesis that the blue die shows 3, with only a 5 percent chance of a type 1 error. What should your testing procedure be?

5. (This one might take a while.) Flip a coin 20 times. Decide whether to accept or reject the hypothesis that the coin is fair, based on what we did in this chapter. Now repeat this procedure 100 times. How many times did you accept the hypothesis?

State the null hypothesis and the alternative hypothesis in these cases:

6. You want to see if cars made on Monday have more defects than cars made on other days.

7. You want to see if football teams that mostly run the football win more on the average than teams that mostly throw the football.

8. You want to see if people who drink coffee without caffeine are healthier than people who drink regular coffee.

CHAPTER 3

INTRODUCTION TO STATISTICS

Now we will look at some general statistical tools that will be useful later on. At first, many people think statistics is a dull subject that is not very much fun. However, think about how much *more* dull work you would have to do if you didn't know statistics. If you've just been given a large pile of numbers, you have no hope of understanding them unless you can figure out some way to summarize them. And that's what statistics is all about.

For example, suppose that you are interested in the height and weight of the human body, perhaps so you can give a general description of the human race to a friendly extraterrestrial. Suppose further that you have a wonderful computer called the Brain that can give you the height and weight of every person. How would you give the information to the extraterrestrial?

You probably wouldn't take the time to give him the 4 billion or so heights and weights. Instead, you would organize the information and tell him how many people weighed between 50 and 55 kilograms, how many between 55 and 60 kilograms, and so on.

Descriptive statistics is the study of ways to get meaningful information out of sets of numbers that are too large to handle. These numbers, called *raw data*, often give us more information than we really need. In the above example, the extraterrestrial really didn't need the raw data (the height and weight of every human being). Giving him the number of people in various height and weight categories was enough.

Suppose, however, that a power surge burns out some circuits in the Brain, and it can only provide you with the raw data for 100,000 people (randomly distributed). By seeing what fraction of the 100,000 people are in various categories, one might assume that the same proportions hold for all four billion people in the world.

It is usually the case that the raw data don't cover all of the cases that you want to cover. In statistics, the term *population* refers to all of the people or things in the group you are interested in. A *sample* is a group of items chosen from the population. Examples include:

- population: the 31 flavors of ice cream at a 31-flavor ice cream store
  sample: the five flavors that you have tested in order to determine whether this store sells good ice cream

- population: all voters in the United States
  sample: the 3,000 people who are interviewed as part of a Gallup poll

- population: all people in the United States with television sets
  sample: the people who are surveyed by the Nielson television rating firm

- population: all people in the United States
  sample: the 100,000 people interviewed in the Census Bureau's Monthly Population Survey

In these situations we use information about the sample to estimate the properties of the entire population. This process is called *statistical inference.*

You can make statistical inferences in some cases with more confidence than in others. If your raw data consist of one person of height 150 centimeters and weight 60 kilograms, then you probably don't want to assume that everyone in the world has height 150 centimeters and weight 60 kilograms. How large does a sample have to be before you can make accurate inferences about it? We will discuss that question in Chapter 18.

Let's look at another set of raw data. Suppose a history class consisting of 30 people has the following scores on a one-hundred-point test:

53 87 76 73 62 99
78 93 82 69 65 93
92 92 78 82 89 65
63 49 88 87 94 73
85 77 98 59 93 82

We can learn more about how the scores are distributed if we group the scores like this:

Interval	Number of scores in interval
41–50	1
51–60	2
61–70	5
71–80	6
81–90	8
91–100	8

To display these data in even clearer form we can draw a *frequency diagram*. Figure 3–1 shows a frequency diagram for these data.

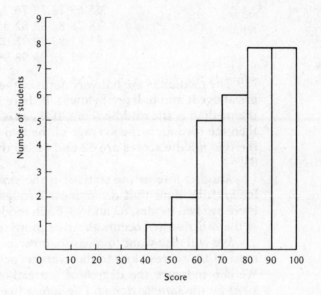

FIGURE 3–1

The height of each bar is the number of people whose scores are in that interval.

It often helps to compress the data even further and calculate the *average* value of all of the numbers. To calculate the average we just add up all the numbers and then divide by the number of numbers. The average is also called the *mean*. Let's suppose that we have n numbers. We'll call them $x_1, x_2, x_3, \ldots, x_n$. We'll use the symbol $\bar{x}$ (x with a bar written over it) to stand for the mean. Then we can write out the formula:

$$\bar{x} = \frac{x_1 + x_2 + x_3 + \cdots + x_n}{n}$$

The mean test score for the above data is 2376/30 = 79.2.

The average is an example of a *statistic*. A statistic is a single number that is used to summarize the properties of a larger group of numbers. We will talk about some other important statistics later.

We can save a little bit of writing by using *summation notation*. In summation notation we use a Greek capital letter sigma: Σ. The expression Σx means "add up all the values of x." The average can be written $\bar{x} = (\Sigma x)/n$. Sometimes the summation symbol is written like this:

$$\sum_{i=1}^{n} x_i$$

to indicate that we start with $i = 1$ and keep going until $i = n$.

Another useful statistic is the *median*. In order to compute this, we must place the scores in order:

$$49\ 53\ 59\ 62\ 63\ 65$$
$$65\ 69\ 73\ 73\ 76\ 77$$
$$78\ 78\ 82\ 82\ 82\ 85$$
$$87\ 87\ 88\ 89\ 92\ 92$$
$$93\ 93\ 93\ 94\ 98\ 99$$

The median is the halfway point of the data. Half of the numbers are above it and half are below it. If there is an odd number of scores the median is the middle score. If there is an even number of scores, then the median is the average of the two middle scores. In this case the two middle scores are 82 and 82, so the median is $(82 + 82)/2 = 82$.

Another interesting statistic is the *mode*. The mode (or modes) is (or are) the data that occur most frequently. In the above sample, there are two modes, 82 and 93. Each mode occurs three times. None of the other scores occurs three or more times.

We will also want to measure how spread out the scores are. Are most of the scores close to the average, or are they mainly far away? We can measure the degree of "spread-out-ed-ness" (called *dispersion*) by the *sample standard deviation* (we'll call it s_1):

$$s_1 = \sqrt{\frac{(x_1 - \bar{x}^2) + (x_2 - \bar{x})^2 + \cdots + (x_n - \bar{x})^2}{n}}$$

$$= \sqrt{\sum_{i=1}^{n} \frac{(x_i - \bar{x})^2}{n}}$$

It is usually easier to calculate s_1 from this formula:

$$s_1 = \sqrt{\overline{x^2} - \bar{x}^2}$$

where $\overline{x^2}$ is equal to the average value of the squares of all of the x's. There are also times when we will want to use an alternative standard deviation measure, which we'll call s_2:

$$s_2 = \sqrt{\frac{n}{n-1}}\ s_1$$

For the history scores, we can calculate that $\overline{x^2} = 6452$, so $s_1{}^2 = 6452 - 79.2^2 = 179.36$. Therefore, $s_1 = 13.39$ and $s_2 = 13.62$.

We'll also want to investigate the question of the relationship between two different sets of data. For example, suppose we want to investigate the question: Do the people who get high scores on history tests also get high scores on math tests? First, we need to look at the raw data (a set of math test scores, arranged in the same order as the history test scores were originally):

$$74\ 57\ 62\ 64\ 69\ 51$$
$$61\ 54\ 59\ 66\ 68\ 54$$
$$54\ 54\ 61\ 59\ 56\ 68$$
$$69\ 76\ 56\ 57\ 53\ 64$$
$$58\ 62\ 51\ 71\ 54\ 59$$

Then we can measure the relationship between the two sets of data with a quantity called the *sample correlation coefficient* (*r*). We'll call the two sets of numbers *x* and *y*, and we'll denote the standard deviation of *x* by s_{1x} and the standard deviation of *y* by s_{1y}; $\overline{xy}$ is the average value of the product of *x* and *y*. The correlation coefficient is defined this way:

$$r(x, y) = \frac{\overline{xy} - \bar{x}\,\bar{y}}{s_{1x}\,s_{1y}}$$

If the correlation coefficient is close to 0, then there is very little relation between a person's history scores and math scores. If the correlation coefficient is close to 1, then people who do well in history also tend to do well in math; if the correlation coefficient is close to −1, then people who do well in history tend to do worse in math. For the data presented here, the correlation coefficient is −.999.

Now we've introduced some important statistics, but we still have to figure out when to use which statistic and we have to determine what the statistics mean. For example, if we've gathered data on two different groups of rats that received different treatment, how can we tell how much difference (if any) the treatment made? If we have surveyed the opinions of a sample of people, how can we tell whether or not their opinions are representative of the population as a whole? If we have looked at the relation between national income and consumer spending in the past, do we think we can reliably predict the relationship between these two quantities in the future?

We'll cover all of these questions later. First we need to develop the main concepts of probability. Probability is an amusing subject itself. Historically, probability concepts were developed to help understand games of chance, and we will talk a lot about games. Probability also has important applications in fields such as insurance and decision-making.

NOTE TO CHAPTER 3

The frequency diagrams discussed in this chapter are examples of a more general type of diagram called a *histogram*. We considered only cases in which the classes were of equal width. You can draw a histogram even if the classes are of unequal width by drawing the diagram so that the area of each rectangle is proportional to the number of numbers in its interval.

EXERCISES

1. The temperatures in degrees Celsius each day over a three-week period were as follows: 17, 18, 20, 22, 21, 19, 16, 15, 18, 20, 21, 21, 22, 21, 19, 20, 19, 17, 16, 16, 17. Compute the mean, median, and mode of these raw data, and, using two-degree intervals starting with 15–16, draw a frequency diagram.

2. Calculate the same statistics as in Exercise 1 using all of the positive numbers that are perfect squares and that are less than 1,000. (For the frequency diagram use these intervals: 1–100, 101–200, etc.)

3. Calculate the mean and standard deviation for these numbers: 5, 10, 6, 11, 0, 0, 0, 10.

4. Here are the team earned-run averages for American League teams in 1982: Detroit, 3.80; California, 3.82; Chicago, 3.87; Seattle, 3.88; Toronto, 3.95; Milwaukee, 3.98; Baltimore, 3.99; New York, 3.99; Boston, 4.03; Kansas City, 4.08; Cleveland, 4.11; Texas, 4.28; Oakland, 4.54; Minnesota, 4.72. Draw a frequency diagram, and calculate the mean and standard deviation.

5. Here are scores on an English paper for the same students discussed in this chapter:

58 88 79 76 66 99
80 94 84 72 69 94
93 92 80 84 90 69
67 54 90 89 95 76
86 80 98 63 94 84

Calculate the correlation coefficient between the English scores and the history scores.
Here are some chemistry scores for the same students:

76 94 88 86 81 99
89 96 91 84 82 96
96 96 89 91 94 82
81 74 94 93 97 86
92 88 99 79 96 91

Calculate the correlation coefficient between the chemistry scores and the history scores.

6. In 1979 the mean U.S. household income was $19,620, while the median household income was $16,533. What do you think is the significance of the fact that the mean is greater than the median?

7. Calculate the correlation between the following sets of numbers:

0, 1, 2, 3, 4, 5, 6, 7, 8
0, 1, 4, 9, 16, 25, 36, 49, 64.

8. Calculate the correlation between these two sets of numbers:

0, 1, 2, 3, 7
0, 2, 4, 6, 14

9. Calculate the correlation between these two sets of numbers:

−1, 0, 1, 0
0, −1, 0, 1

10. Make a list of some of your friends and relatives, and then draw a frequency diagram showing the number of people whose first names start with a particular letter. Which letters seem to be the most popular for starting names?

❏ 11. Write a computer program to calculate the sample average x for a group of n numbers.

❏ 12. Write a program to calculate the sample standard deviation, s_1, and the alternate measure of the standard deviation, s_2, where $s_2 = s_1 \times \sqrt{n/(n-1)}$.

❏ 13. Write a program to calculate the sample correlation coefficient between two sets of numbers.

❏ 14. Write a computer program to sort a group of numbers and print them out in order.

❏ 15. Write a computer program to find the median of a group of numbers. (Use the results of the preceding exercise.)

❏ 16. Write a computer program to calculate the frequency distribution for a group of numbers (in other words, how many numbers in the group are between 0 and 1, how many between 1 and 2, etc.) The size of the classes you use will depend on the nature of the numbers you are considering. If you like computer graphics, you can even write a program that draws a graph of the frequency distribution.

CHAPTER 4

DEFINITION OF PROBABILITY

Interpretations of Probability

What exactly is probability? That is a tricky (and sometimes controversial) question.

Consider the statement, "If we flip a coin, the probability is 1/2 that the result will be heads." It is a difficult philosophical question to determine exactly what this statement means. According to the *relative frequency* view of probability, this statement means that the number of heads will be close to 1/2 of the total tosses if you toss the coin a large number of times. (We will show that this is indeed the case, but does that mean that the probability is nothing more than the relative frequency?)

There are some events for which the relative-frequency interpretation is difficult. The weather report often says, "There is a 20 percent chance of rain today." However, we can't have today repeat itself 100 times to see if it rains 20 of those times.

The *subjective* view of probability states that the probability is an estimate of what an individual *thinks* is the likelihood that an event will happen. In that case two individuals might estimate the probability differently. The subjective view makes it possible to talk meaningfully about the probabilities of a wider class of events, but the probabilities become more intangible because we can't objectively specify what the probabilities are.

We'll assume that we know the meaning of the statement, "The probability is 1/2 that a coin toss will result in heads." If this is true we can calculate what the probabilities will be for any number of coin flips, as we did in Chapter 1. We won't worry about the philosophy of probability any more here.

Random Events

We can state some characteristics of a *random event* in which each outcome is equally likely. Examples of such random events are the toss of a single coin, the roll of a fair die, and the selection of a single card from a well-shuffled deck. The main characteristic of a random event is that there is no way to predict the outcome that is any better than any other method.

For an example of a random event, let us consider tossing a coin again. If you're captain of a football team, you'll face this problem: How do you predict the outcome of a single toss? As we'll see, there is no accurate way to do this, even if you've spent a lifetime studying probability.

Here are the results for 100 flips of a coin:

H, T, H, T, T, T, H, H, H, H,
T, H, H, T, T, T, T, T, H, H,
H, H, H, H, H, T, T, H, T, T,
T, T, H, T, T, H, H, H, H, H,
H, T, H, H, T, T, H, H, T, H,
H, T, T, T, H, H, T, H, T, H,
H, H, T, T, T, T, H, H, T, H,
H, T, H, H, T, H, H, T, T, T,
H, T, H, H, H, H, H, T, T, T,
T, T, H, H, T, T, T, H, T, T

Now, let's compare several different prediction rules to see which one does best. One simple prediction rule is to guess heads every time. If you followed this rule you would be right 53 times and wrong 47 times in our example. This method would work better than guessing tails every time, but not much better.

Another method you might try is this: Since there will most likely be about the same number of heads as tails, why don't you arrange it so that you guess heads as many times as you guess tails? One way to do this would be to guess heads and tails on alternate tosses. If you first guess heads, then tails, then heads, and so on, you will get 52 right and 48 wrong, so this method is no better than the other.

You could adopt a strange rule, such as, "Guess heads four times in a row, then guess tails, and keep repeating that same pattern." This method would give you 55 right answers, making this method slightly better than the others, but not much better.

Not only is there no best method; there is also no worst method. Suppose that you want to guess wrong as often as possible. This is just as hard as guessing right, since if you could guess wrong on purpose you could also guess right by calling each toss the opposite way.

Probability Spaces

Now we will develop the formal method of determining the probabilities associated with a random experiment. First, we'll make a list of all the possible results of our experiment. We're going to use the technical name *set* for this list. *Set* is just a formal name for a collection of objects. Some examples of sets are:

{Richard Nixon, Gerald Ford, Jimmy Carter}
{Dallas Cowboys, Washington Redskins, New York Giants, St. Louis Cardinals, Philadelphia Eagles}
{1, 2, 3, 4, 5, 6}

Sets can be defined by either of two methods. We can use the listing method as we just did. That just means to write down all of the members of the set. The set members are surrounded by braces: {   }. Then it's clear what is in the set and what is not.

Sets can also be defined by stating a rule that makes it clear what is in the set. For example, the sets above could have been defined by these rules:

- the set of all U.S. presidents during the 1970's

- the set of all football teams in the National Football League National Conference East Division

- the set of all possible results of tossing one die

It should be noted that there need not be a rule that fits the set; {Richard Nixon, New York Giants, 4} is also a set (although one that is not likely to come up in practice).

With small sets, the listing method or the rule method will work equally well. However, with large sets the rule method works much better. For example, it would be very difficult to list all of the members of these sets:

- the set of all whole numbers from one to a million

- the set of all possible results of flipping a coin 12 times

We are especially interested in sets that contain all of the possible results of an experiment. The set of all possible results is called the *probability space* (or sometimes the *sample space*). Mathematicians like to use the term *space* for this type of set. Here are some examples of probability spaces:

- experiment: flip coin one time
  probability space: {H, T}

- experiment: flip coin three times
  probability space: {HHH, HHT, HTH, HTT, THH, THT, TTH, TTT}

- experiment: roll one die
  probability space: {1, 2, 3, 4, 5, 6}

- experiment: roll two dice
  probability space:

$$\{(1,1)\ (1,2)\ (1,3)\ (1,4)\ (1,5)\ (1,6)$$
$$(2,1)\ (2,2)\ (2,3)\ (2,4)\ (2,5)\ (2,6)$$
$$(3,1)\ (3,2)\ (3,3)\ (3,4)\ (3,5)\ (3,6)$$
$$(4,1)\ (4,2)\ (4,3)\ (4,4)\ (4,5)\ (4,6)$$
$$(5,1)\ (5,2)\ (5,3)\ (5,4)\ (5,5)\ (5,6)$$
$$(6,1)\ (6,2)\ (6,3)\ (6,4)\ (6,5)\ (6,6)\}$$

• experiment: draw one card from a deck of 52 cards
probability space:

{ace hearts, ace diamonds, ace spades, ace clubs,
two hearts, two diamonds, two spades, two clubs, etc.}

(There will be 52 elements if we list them all.)

In order to save us the bother of writing "probability space" each time, we'll use the letter S to stand for a probability space. (S is short for space. Or, if you like Greek letters, the letter Ω (omega) is often used to represent probability spaces.)

The important thing is that every single possible result of the experiment must be included in the probability space. We'll call each possible result an *outcome*. We'll use a small s to represent the total number of outcomes in the probability space S. In the examples above, the first probability space has two possible outcomes and the others have 8, 6, 36, and 52 outcomes, respectively. For now, we'll assume that each outcome is equally likely. (This is called the *classical approach* to probability.) Then, since there are s outcomes the probability of any one outcome is $1/s$.

Now we'll use a probability space to solve a practical problem. Suppose that we're playing Monopoly, and that our marker is on North Carolina Avenue. We already own Park Place, so we will have it made if we roll a 7 and land on Boardwalk. As we saw earlier, there are 36 possible outcomes for the experiment of rolling two dice. We want to get a 7, so it doesn't make any difference to us if we roll (1,6) or (2,5) or (3,4) or (4,3) or (5,2) or (6,1). We can put all of these outcomes together in a set. We'll often use capital letters to stand for sets, so we may as well call this one set A:

$$A = \{(1,6),\ (2,5),\ (3,4),\ (4,3),\ (5,2),\ (6,1)\}$$

We can also define set A by the rule method: Set A is the set of all possible outcomes from rolling two dice such that the sum of the numbers on the two dice is 7.

Set A contains 6 outcomes. If we roll the dice, we have an equal chance of getting any one of the 36 outcomes. Since 6 of these outcomes give us what we want (a total of 7 on the dice), the probability of getting a 7 is 6/36 = 1/6.

Set A is an example of what we will call an *event*. An event is a set that consists of a group of outcomes. In our case, (1,6), (2,5), (3,4), (4,3), (5,2), (6,1) are all outcomes, and the set {(1,6), (2,5), (3,4), (4,3), (5,2), (6,1)} is an event.

An event can also be defined this way: An event is a *subset* of the probability space. A subset is a set that contains some (or possibly all) members of another set. If set A is a subset of set S, that means that every outcome in set A is contained in set S. Here are some examples of subsets:

- set: all people living in New York State
  subset: all people living in New York City

- set: all Star Wars movies
  subset: {*The Empire Strikes Back, Return of the Jedi*}

- set: all whole numbers less than 10: {1, 2, 3, 4, 5, 6, 7, 8, 9, 10}
  subset: all odd numbers less than 10

- set: all possible outcomes from flipping a coin three times
  subset: all possible outcomes of three flips with one head: {HTT, THT, TTH}

Probability of an Event

Now we're ready to give a formal definition for the probability of an event A. First, count the number of outcomes in A. Call that number $N(A)$. (Read this "N of A," which is short for "number of outcomes in A.") Remember that s is the total number of outcomes in the probability space S. Then we can define the probability:

$$\text{Probability that event } A \text{ will occur is } \frac{N(A)}{s}$$

In other words, count the number of outcomes that give you the event A, and then divide by the total number of possible outcomes.

It would save a lot of writing to have a shorter way to write, "Probability that event A occurs." So we will use Pr to stand for probability, and write it like this:

Pr(A) means "probability that event A will occur"

Our result becomes:

$$\text{Pr}(A) = \frac{N(A)}{s}$$

EXAMPLE What is the probability of getting one head if we toss a coin three times?

In this case, there are $2^3 = 8$ possible outcomes, so $s = 8$. There are three outcomes that give one head (HTT, THT, TTH), so if A is the event of getting one head, then $N(A) = 3$. Therefore, Pr(A) = 3/8.

EXAMPLE What is the probability of getting a total of 5 if we roll two dice?

There are 36 possible outcomes, so $s = 36$. Let B be the event of getting a 5 on the dice, so B contains 4 outcomes:

$$B = \{(1,4), (2,3), (3,2), (4,1)\}$$

Then $N(B) = 4$, so $\Pr(B) = 4/36 = 1/9$. (So your chances of getting a 5 are worse than your chances of getting a 7.)

EXAMPLE What is the probability of drawing an ace if we draw one card from a deck of cards?

There are 52 possible outcomes, so $s = 52$. Let C be the event of drawing an ace, so C contains four outcomes:

{A hearts, A diamonds, A clubs, A spades}

Then $N(C) = 4$, so $\Pr(C) = 4/52 = 1/13$.

There are two special events that are interesting. Let us consider the probability that the event S occurs. Remember that S contains all of the possible outcomes of the experiment. Using the formula

$$\Pr(S) = \frac{N(S)}{s} = \frac{s}{s} = 1$$

That result should be obvious. All it says is, "The probability is 100 percent that the result will be one of the possible results." (Just ask yourself: What is the probability that the result will *not* be one of the possible results?)

Another possible event is the set that contains *no* outcomes. You should be able to convince yourself that this set has zero probability of occurring. This set is often called the empty set, because it doesn't have anything in it:

$$\Pr(\text{empty set}) = 0$$

The empty set is often symbolized by a 0 with a slash, /, through it, like this: $\emptyset$. So we can say:

$$\Pr(\emptyset) = 0$$

Now we can develop another important result that is fortunately very obvious. Many times we will want to know the probability that an event will *not* happen. For example, returning to our Monopoly game, suppose we are on North Carolina Avenue and our opponent has a hotel on Boardwalk. In that case we're mainly interested in the probability that we will *not* get a 7. It should be clear that if there is a 1/6 chance of getting a 7, then there is a 5/6 chance of not getting a 7. We can demonstrate that. Let A be the event of not getting a 7. Then A contains 30 outcomes:

$$
\begin{array}{llllll}
\{(1,1) & (1,2) & (1,3) & (1,4) & (1,5) & \\
(2,1) & (2,2) & (2,3) & (2,4) & & (2,6) \\
(3,1) & (3,2) & (3,3) & & (3,5) & (3,6) \\
(4,1) & (4,2) & & (4,4) & (4,5) & (4,6) \\
(5,1) & & (5,3) & (5,4) & (5,5) & (5,6) \\
& (6,2) & (6,3) & (6,4) & (6,5) & (6,6)\}
\end{array}
$$

Therefore $N(A) = 30$, so $\Pr(A) = 30/36 = 5/6$. In general, if p is the probability that a particular event A will occur, then $1 - p$ is the probability that the event will not occur.

We will give a special name to the set that contains all of the outcomes that are not in set A. It is called the *complement* of A, written A^c. (The little c stands for complement. Read the symbol as "A complement.")

Then:

$$\Pr(A^c) = 1 - \Pr(A)$$

This result is important for calculations, since sometimes it is easier to calculate the probability that an event will not occur than it is to calculate the probability that it will occur.

Here are some examples of complements:

- If the experiment consists of flipping a coin, and A is the event of getting a head, then A^c is the event of getting a tail.

- If the experiment consists of flipping four coins, and B is the event of getting four heads, then B^c is the event of getting at least one tail.

- If the total set is the set of all 52 cards in a deck of cards, and R is the event of drawing a red card, then R^c is the event of drawing a black card.

- If the total set is the set of all major league baseball teams, and A is the set {Yankees, Mets}, then A^c is the set of all major league teams that are not from New York.

Probability of a Union

Now suppose that nobody owns either Boardwalk or Park Place, and we would like to know the probability that we will land on either of them. If we're currently on North Carolina Avenue then we need to know the probability that we will get either a 5 or a 7. It often happens in probability that we need to find out the probability that either one of two events will occur. Let's say that A is the event of getting a 7. Then A contains the outcomes

$$\{(1,6), (2,5), (3,4), (4,3), (5,2), (6,1)\}$$

If B is the event of getting a 5, then B contains the outcomes

$$\{(1,4), (2,3), (3,2), (4,1)\}$$

Let's say that C is the event of getting either a 5 *or* a 7. Then C contains these outcomes:

$$\{(1,6), (2,5), (3,4), (4,3), (5,2), (6,1), (1,4), (2,3), (3,2), (4,1)\}$$

C contains 10 outcomes, so $\Pr(C) = 10/36$.

There is a special name for the set that contains all of the elements that are in either or both of two other sets. It is called the *union* of the other two sets. In this case, *C* is the union of set *A* and set *B*. You can think of it this way: set *A* and set *B* get together and join forces to form a union, and the result is set *C*. In mathematics the word *union* is symbolized by a little symbol that looks like a letter *u*: ∪. Therefore, we can write "*C* is the union of *A* and *B*" as

$$C = A \text{ union } B$$

or

$$C = A \cup B.$$

Here are some examples of unions:

- If *A* is the set of even numbers and *B* is the set of odd numbers, then $A \cup B$ is the set of all whole numbers.

- If *V* is the set of vowels and *C* is the set of consonants, then $V \cup C$ is the set of all letters.

- If *A* is the set {AH, KH, QH, JH, 10H}, and *B* is the set {QH, JH, 10H, 9H, 8H}, then $A \cup B$ is {AH, KH, QH, JH, 10H, 9H, 8H}.

There is another interesting fact that we can learn from the dice example. We said that (probability of getting a 7) = Pr(*A*) = 6/36, (probability of getting a 5) = Pr(*B*) = 4/36, and (probability of getting a 5 or a 7) = Pr(*A* or *B*) = Pr($A \cup B$) = 10/36. It looks as though you could just add the probabilities for the two events to get the probability that either one of them will occur, since 10/36 = 6/36 + 4/36. This amazingly simple rule will work a lot of the time:

$$\text{Pr}(A \text{ or } B) = \text{Pr}(A \cup B) = \text{Pr}(A) + \text{Pr}(B)$$

However, this result holds only when there is no possibility that event *A* and event *B* can occur at the same time. Here is an example of incorrect reasoning. "Toss a coin twice. Since the probability of getting a head on the first toss is 1/2 and the probability of getting a head on the second toss is 1/2, the probability of getting a head on either the first toss or the second toss is 1/2 + 1/2 = 1." Obviously, that is not the case. In the dice example we could use the simple formula because there is no way to get both a 5 and a 7 on a single toss of a pair of dice. Two events that can never occur together are called *disjoint* events.

Probability of an Intersection

Now we will consider an example in which two events can happen together. Suppose you are selecting one card from a deck and you want to know the probability that you will get a red face card. Let's say that F is the event of getting a face card. Then F contains these outcomes:

$$\{JH, \ JD, \ JC, \ JS,$$
$$QH, \ QD, \ QC, \ QS,$$
$$KH, \ KD, \ KC, \ KS\}$$

(Here we are using J to stand for jack, Q = queen, K = king, H = hearts, D = diamonds, C = clubs, S = spades.)

Since $N(F) = 12$, the probability of getting a face card is 12/52.

Let R be the event of getting a red card, so R contains the outcomes:

$$\{AH, \ 2H, \ 3H, \ 4H, \ 5H, \ 6H, \ 7H, \ 8H, \ 9H, \ 10H, \ JH, \ QH, \ KH,$$
$$AD, \ 2D, \ 3D, \ 4D, \ 5D, \ 6D, \ 7D, \ 8D, \ 9D, \ 10D, \ JD, \ QD, \ KD\}$$

R contains 26 outcomes, so $\Pr(R) = 26/52 = 1/2$.

Let C be the event that both event F and event R occur—in other words, C is the event that you get a card that is *both* a red card and a face card. Then C contains these 6 outcomes:

$$\{JD, \ JH, \ QD, \ QH, \ KD, \ KH\}$$

Therefore, $\Pr(C) = N(C)/s = 6/52$.

There is a special name for the set that contains all of the elements that are in both of two other sets. It is called the *intersection*. For example, in this case set C is the intersection of set F and set R, because it contains those outcomes that are in both set F and in set R. The symbol of intersection is the symbol for union turned upside down: $\cap$. Now we can write:

C = set that contains the elements in both A and B;
$C = A$ intersect B; or
$C = A \cap B$

Here are some examples of intersections:

- If V is the set of vowels and C is the set of consonants, then $V \cap C$ is $\{y\}$.

- If A is the set of hands with five cards in sequence, and B is the set of hands with five cards of the same suit, then $A \cap B$ is the set of all straight flushes.

- If you flip a coin twice, and A is the event of getting a head on the first toss and B is the event of getting a head on the second toss, then $A \cap B$ is $\{HH\}$.

There is no general formula for the probability of the intersection of two events, but Chapter 6 discusses a formula that can be used sometimes. For now, we'll have to count the number of outcomes in the intersection and calculate the probability directly from that.

If two events can't happen together (in other words, they are disjoint events) then their intersection is the empty set. For example, we can't get both a head and a tail on a single coin flip, so if H = event of getting a heads, and T = event of getting a tails, then $\Pr(H \text{ and } T) = \Pr(H \cap T) = 0$. In general, if A and B are disjoint, then $A \cap B = \emptyset$ and $\Pr(A \cap B) = 0$.

Now let us consider the possibility that we will get either a face card *or* a red card when we draw a card from the deck. If F is the event of getting a face card, and R is the event of getting a red card, then we want to know

$$\Pr(F \text{ or } R) = \Pr(F \cup R).$$

We can't use the simple formula $\Pr(F) + \Pr(R)$, because these two events can happen together. We can make a list of all the outcomes in $F \cup R$:

{AH, 2H, 3H, 4H, 5H, 6H, 7H, 8H, 9H, 10H,
JH, QH, KH,
JC, QC, KC,
AD, 2D, 3D, 4D, 5D, 6D, 7D, 8D, 9D, 10D,
JD, QD, KD,
JS, QS, KS}

Altogether there are 32 outcomes, so

$$\Pr(F \text{ or } C) = \Pr(F \cup C) = 32/52.$$

Now we can figure out a general formula for the probability of $A \cup B$. We know that

$$N(A) = \text{(number of outcomes in } A \text{ but not in } B\text{)}$$
$$+ \text{(number of outcomes in } A \text{ and in } B\text{)}$$

$$N(B) = \text{(number of outcomes in } B \text{ but not in } A\text{)}$$
$$+ \text{(number of outcomes in } A \text{ and } B\text{)}$$

If we add together $N(A) + N(B)$, we get:

$$N(A) + N(B) = \text{(number of outcomes in } A \text{ but not in } B\text{)}$$
$$+ \text{(number of outcomes in } B \text{ but not in } A\text{)}$$
$$+ 2 \times \text{(number of outcomes in } A \text{ and } B\text{)}$$

But we know that the number of outcomes in $A \cup B$ is

$$N(A \cup B) = \text{(number of outcomes in } A \text{ and not in } B\text{)}$$
$$+ \text{(number of outcomes in } B \text{ and not in } A\text{)}$$
$$+ \text{(number of outcomes in both } A \text{ and } B\text{)}$$

When we just add $N(A)$ and $N(B)$, we're counting the outcomes in $(A \cap B)$ *twice*. So in order to get the number of outcomes in $A \cup B$, we can subtract $N(A \cap B)$, like this:

$$N(A \cup B) = N(A) + N(B) - N(A \cap B)$$

Therefore,

$$\text{Pr}(A \text{ or } B) = \text{Pr}(A) + \text{Pr}(B) - \text{Pr}(A \text{ and } B)$$

or, written mathematically:

$$\text{Pr}(A \cup B) = \text{Pr}(A) + \text{Pr}(B) - \text{Pr}(A \cap B)$$

This formula is good for any two events, whether or not they are disjoint. Notice that, if A and B *are* disjoint, then $\text{Pr}(A \text{ and } B) = 0$, so we get the same formula that we had before: $\text{Pr}(A \text{ or } B) = \text{Pr}(A) + \text{Pr}(B)$.

EXAMPLE   Suppose, in the middle of a backgammon game, you want to know the probability that you will get either a total of 8 or doubles on the dice. Let's say that $E1$ is the event of getting an 8. Then:

$$E1 = \{(2,6), (3,5), (4,4), (5,3), (6,2)\}, \qquad \text{Pr}(E1) = 5/36$$

Let $E2$ be the event of getting a double. Then:

$$E2 = \{(1,1), (2,2), (3,3), (4,4), (5,5), (6,6)\}, \qquad \text{Pr}(E2) = 6/36$$

These two events are not disjoint, since you can get both an 8 and a double (if the dice turn up (4,4)). Then $(E1 \cap E2)$ is the event of getting (4,4), which has a probability of 1/36. So now we can use our formula:

Pr(getting either a double or an 8)

$$= \text{Pr}(E1 \text{ or } E2) = \text{Pr}(E1) + \text{Pr}(E2) - \text{Pr}(E1 \text{ and } E2)$$
$$= \quad 5/36 \quad + \quad 6/36 \quad - \qquad 1/36$$
$$= 10/36$$

EXAMPLE   What is the probability that you will get at least one 6 when you roll two dice?

We'll call $E1$ the event of getting a 6 on the first die and $E2$ the event of getting a 6 on the second die. Then the event that you will get at least one 6 is $E1 \cup E2$. We know that $\text{Pr}(E1) = \text{Pr}(E2) = 1/6$. Since $E1 \cap E2$ is the event of getting 6's on both dice, we know that the probability of that happening is 1/36. Therefore, we can use the formula:

$$\text{Pr}(E1 \cup E2) = \text{Pr}(E1) + \text{Pr}(E2) - \text{Pr}(E1 \cap E2)$$
$$= \quad 1/6 \quad + \quad 1/6 \quad - \qquad 1/36$$
$$= 11/36$$

So your chances of getting at least one 6 are 11/36.

Axioms of Probability

We've now discussed everything we need in order to develop the formal mathematical model of probability. Formal mathematics works like this. First, make some assumptions (which are called *axioms* or *postulates*). Then, use the postulates to prove *theorems*.

Start with a probability space S. We will adopt these axioms:

$$\text{Axiom 1: } \Pr(S) = 1$$

This axiom just says that we are absolutely positive that the result of an experiment will be one of the possible results.

Now, let X be any event. (In other words, X is any subset of the probability space S.)

$$\text{Axiom 2: } \Pr(X) \geq 0$$

This axiom just states the obvious fact that there is no such thing as a negative probability.

Axiom 3: If A and B are any two disjoint events, then $\Pr(A \cup B) = \Pr(A) + \Pr(B)$

Now we can use these axioms to prove theorems. (The proofs will be left as exercises if you're interested.)

Theorem 1: $\Pr(X) \leq 1$, for any event X

Theorem 2: $\Pr(A^c) = 1 - \Pr(A)$

Theorem 3: $\Pr(\emptyset) = 0$

Theorem 4: $\Pr(A \cup B \cup C) = \Pr(A) + \Pr(B) + \Pr(C)$ if A, B, and C are any three disjoint events

Theorem 5: $\Pr(A \cup B) = \Pr(A) + \Pr(B) - \Pr(A \cap B)$

This framework allows us to generalize our results further. So far we have only considered experiments where we could count the number of outcomes and each outcome was equally likely. We can still do probability outcomes even if the outcomes are not all equally likely. All we need to do is assign a probability to each outcome, and then make sure that all of the probabilities add up to 1.

Continuous Probability Spaces

We will also want to consider random experiments in which we can't count the number of outcomes. The probability spaces we have discussed up to now are called *discrete* probability spaces. Now we'll look at an example of a *continuous* probability space. For example, suppose we throw a dart at the dart board in Figure 4–1. (We won't count throws that don't hit the dart board, so the probability is 1 that any throw that does count will hit the dart board.) Suppose we have no idea where on the dart board the dart will land, one place being as likely as another. Then we can regard the dart throw as a random experiment, but we can't count all of the outcomes. For example, the position of the dart might end up being the point 1 inch down and 1 inch to the left, but it could also be at the point 1.5 inches to the left, or 1.25 inches left, or 1.00000002 inches left, etc. (assuming that we can measure the point where the tip of the dart hits with infinite accuracy). In this case we can't calculate the probability that the dart will hit a particular point, but we can calculate the probability that it will hit within a particular area. For example, the probability that we will hit the left half of the diagram (shown as the shaded region in

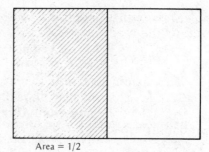

FIGURE 4–1

Area = 1/2

Figure 4–1) is 1/2. In general, if s is the area of the whole dartboard and a is the area of a particular region A, then the probability that the dart will hit the area A is a/s. In the case of continuous probability spaces, the events we're interested in can be represented as areas, and we'll often draw these dart board-like diagrams to represent continuous probability spaces.

For another example of a continuous probability space, consider this situation. Suppose your nosy neighbor is going to visit sometime between 12 noon and 5 P.M., but you have no idea when. Then, for example, you can say that the probability is 1/2 that the neighbor will arrive before 2:30, and the probability is 1/5 that the neighbor will arrive in the first hour, 1/10 that the neighbor will arrive in the first half-hour, and so on.

Unions of Three or More Events

There are times when we will be interested in the probability that any one of three events might occur. (Stated mathematically, we want to know the probability that the union of the three events will occur.) If the three events are disjoint, then we can just add the three probabilities (see Theorem 4), but the situation is more complicated if the three events are not disjoint. Consider the three regions A, B, and C on the dart board shown in Figure 4–2. Suppose that the area of the

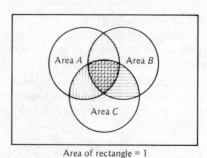

FIGURE 4–2

Area of rectangle = 1

whole dart board is 1. Then $\Pr(A \cup B \cup C)$ is the entire area enclosed by the circles. If we add together $\Pr(A) + \Pr(B) + \Pr(C)$, we will double-count the striped area and triple-count the checked area. We can eliminate the double counting by subtracting, like this:

$$\Pr(A) + \Pr(B) + \Pr(C) - \Pr(A \cap B) - \Pr(B \cap C) - \Pr(A \cap C)$$

Now, however, we are not counting the checkered area at all, so we need to add that area back in:

$$
\begin{aligned}
\Pr(A \cup B \cup C) = {} & \Pr(A) + \Pr(B) + \Pr(C) \\
& - \Pr(A \cap B) - \Pr(B \cap C) - \Pr(A \cap C) \\
& + \Pr(A \cap B \cap C)
\end{aligned}
$$

This formula tells in general how to find the probability that the union of three events will occur. For example, suppose you are in a group of three people who are holding a Secret Santa draw. Each person is going to select randomly the name of one person in the group to give surprise presents to. What is the probability that one of the three people will select his or her own name?

First, we can easily calculate the probability that *you* will select your own name. Since there are three names you might choose, and one of them is your own, there is a 1/3 chance that you will draw your own name. Now we need to know the probability that at least one person in the group will draw his or her own name. If we let $E1$ be the event that you draw your own name and $E2$ and $E3$ be the events that person 2 and person 3 draw their own names, respectively, then we want to know the probability of $E1 \cup E2 \cup E3$. To use the formula, we need to know $\Pr(E1 \cap E2)$. $E1 \cap E2$ is the event that both person 1 and person 2 get their own names. The probability of that happening is 1/6. There are $3! = 6$ total possible ways of drawing the names, and there is only 1 way for both of them to get their own names. By the same reasoning, $\Pr(E1 \cap E3) = 1/6$, $\Pr(E2 \cap E3) = 1/6$, and $\Pr(E1 \cap E2 \cap E3) = 1/6$. Then, using our formula, we have

$$
\begin{aligned}
\Pr(E1 \cup E2 \cup E3) = {} & \Pr(E1) + \Pr(E2) + \Pr(E3) \\
& - \Pr(E1 \cap E2) - \Pr(E1 \cap E3) - \Pr(E2 \cap E3) \\
& + \Pr(E1 \cap E2 \cap E3) \\
= {} & 1/3 + 1/3 + 1/3 \\
& - 1/6 - 1/6 - 1/6 \\
& + 1/6 \\
= {} & 2/3
\end{aligned}
$$

So there is a 2/3 probability that one of the three people will select his or her own name.

We could also have solved the problem by listing each of the six ways in which the names could have been drawn:

Name drawn by 1	Name drawn by 2	Name drawn by 3
1	*2*	*3*
1	3	2
2	1	*3*
2	3	1
3	1	2
3	*2*	1

Asterisks mark those locations where a person has picked his or her own name, and we can see that four of the possible drawings have at least one person picking his or her own name.

If we want to know the probability of the union of more than three events, we end up with an awful formula.

The basic pattern for the probability of the union of *n* events is:

1. Add the probabilities of all *n* events individually.
2. Subtract the probabilities of the intersections of all possible pairs of the events.
3. Add the probabilities of all possible intersections of the events taken three at a time.
4. Subtract the probabilities of all possible intersections of the events taken four at a time.

By now, you should have caught on to the pattern.

EXAMPLE   Suppose that, during a backgammon game, your opponent has put one of your pieces on the bar, and your opponent has points 5 and 6 covered. In order to get back on the board, you need to roll a 1, 2, 3, or 4 on your next roll. What is the probability that you will do so?

Let's say that $E1$ is the event of getting at least one 1, $E2$ is the event of getting at least one 2, and so on. Then we want to find the probability of $E1 \cup E2 \cup E3 \cup E4$. Using the method described above, we obtain

$$
\begin{aligned}
\Pr(E1 \cup E2 \cup E3 \cup E4) =\ & \Pr(E1) + \Pr(E2) + \Pr(E3) + \Pr(E4) \\
& - \Pr(E1 \cap E2) - \Pr(E1 \cap E3) - \Pr(E1 \cap E4) \\
& - \Pr(E2 \cap E3) - \Pr(E2 \cap E4) - \Pr(E3 \cap E4) \\
& + \Pr(E1 \cap E2 \cap E3) + \Pr(E1 \cap E2 \cap E4) \\
& + \Pr(E1 \cap E3 \cap E4) + \Pr(E2 \cap E3 \cap E4) \\
& - \Pr(E1 \cap E2 \cap E3 \cap E4)
\end{aligned}
$$

We know that $\Pr(E1) = 11/36$, since it must be the same as $\Pr(E6)$, which we have already calculated. By the same reasoning, $\Pr(E2) = \Pr(E3) = \Pr(E4) = 11/36$. The event $E1 \cap E2$ is the event of getting a 2 and a 1 on the dice. There are two ways for this to happen, so

$$\Pr(E1 \cap E2) = 2/36.$$

$E1 \cap E2 \cap E3$ is the event of getting a 1 and a 2 and a 3, which is obviously impossible since we are only rolling two dice. So, using the formula, we get:

$$
\begin{aligned}
\Pr(E1 \cup E2 \cup E3 \cup E4) =\ & 11/36 + 11/36 + 11/36 + 11/36 \\
& - 2/36 - 2/36 - 2/36 \\
& - 2/36 - 2/36 - 2/36 \\
=\ & 32/36
\end{aligned}
$$

EXERCISES

1. What is the probability of getting a prime number when you roll a die?

2. What is the probability of getting a 7 or an 11 when two dice are rolled?

3. Consider a roulette wheel that will stop on a number from 1 to 36, or 0 or 00. What is the probability that the wheel will stop at 7? Is this a discrete or a continuous probability space?

4. Consider a roulette wheel with a circumference of 38 inches. Assume that the wheel can stop at any point along the circumference. Is this a continuous or a discrete probability space? What is the probability that the wheel will land exactly on 7? What is the probability that the wheel will land between 7 and 10?

5. What is S^c? What is $\emptyset^c$?

6. Prove $\Pr(X) \leq 1$, for all events X.

7. Prove $\Pr(A^c) = 1 - \Pr(A)$.

8. Prove $\Pr(\emptyset) = 0$.

9. Prove $\Pr(A \cup B \cup C) = \Pr(A) + \Pr(B) + \Pr(C)$, if A, B, and C are all disjoint events.

10. Prove $\Pr(A \cup B) = \Pr(A) + \Pr(B) - \Pr(A \cap B)$.

11. The town of Wethersfield, Connecticut, has an area of about 14 square miles. What is the probability that a meteorite thrown randomly at the earth will hit Wethersfield? (The surface area of the earth is about 200,000,000 square miles.)

12. What is the probability that a meteorite thrown randomly at the earth will hit an ocean?

13. If you flip a coin five times, what is the probability that you will get heads on either the first, second, or third toss?

14. If you roll a die three times, what is the probability that you will get a 1 on at least one of the three tosses?

15. Seventeenth-century Italian gamblers thought that the chances of getting a 9 when they rolled three dice was equal to the chances of getting a 10. Calculate these two probabilities to see if they were right.

16. You're coach of a football team that has just scored a touchdown, so you are now down by 8 points in the fourth quarter. You expect to score one more touchdown in the game. Should you try for a two-point conversion now, or should you kick a one-point conversion now and then try a two-point conversion after your next touchdown? Assume that you have a 100 percent chance of making the one-point conversion but only a 50 percent chance of making the two-point conversion.

17. Each person receives an eye-color gene from each parent. For simplicity, assume that the only two eye colors are blue and brown. A person with two brown-eye genes will have brown eyes, a person with two blue-eye genes will have blue eyes, and a person with one blue-eye gene and one brown-eye gene will have brown eyes. Assume that a child is equally likely to inherit either of the two genes from the mother, and either of the two genes from the father. What is the probability that the child will have blue eyes if the parents have the different gene types shown below?

Mother	Father
Br–Br	Br–Br
Br–Br	Br–Bl
Br–Br	Bl–Bl
Br–Bl	Br–Bl
Br–Bl	Bl–Bl
Bl–Bl	Bl–Bl

Is it possible for two parents with brown eyes to have a child with blue eyes? Is it possible for two parents with blue eyes to have a child with brown eyes?

18. Suppose you know that all four grandparents of a child have one brown-eye gene and one blue-eye gene, but you don't know what gene types the two parents have. What is the probability that the child will have blue eyes?

19. Consider again the situation in the preceding problem. Suppose now that you are able to find out what color eyes the parents have, but you don't know what gene types they have. What is the probability that the child will have blue eyes if both parents have blue eyes? If both parents have brown eyes? If one parent has blue eyes and one parent has brown eyes?

20. If you were captain of a football team, how would you decide what to call at the opening coin toss?

21. If you toss a coin n times, what is the probability that you will get at least one head?

22. Assume that there are 21 one-hour slots for prime-time television shows during the week. Suppose that the networks select the time slots for their shows at random. If your two favorite shows are on different networks, what is the probability that they will conflict?

23. What is the probability that your two favorite shows will be on the same night?

24. What is the probability that your two favorite shows will both be on Monday?

25. Suppose your backgammon opponent has points 4, 5, and 6 covered, and you have two pieces on the bar. In order to get back on the board, you need to have both dice result in either 1, 2, or 3. What is the probability that both pieces will get back on the board?

26. Suppose you have a 40 percent chance of getting a job offer from your first choice firm, a 40 percent chance of getting a job offer from your second choice firm, and a 16 percent chance of getting a job offer from both firms. What is the probability that you will get a job offer from either firm?

27. Suppose 70 percent of the families in a certain town have children. 30 percent of the families have children under 6, and 60 percent of the families have children 6 or over. How many families have children both over 6 and under 6?

CHAPTER 5

CALCULATING PROBABILITIES BY COUNTING OUTCOMES

In the regular situation when we have a set of outcomes that are all equally likely, the probability that an event A will occur is given by

$$Pr(A) = \frac{N(A)}{s}$$

where $N(A)$ is the number of outcomes in A and s is the total number of possible outcomes. This means that if we can calculate these two numbers—$N(A)$ and s—then we're done. We can then directly calculate the probability. So an important part of probability involves figuring out how to count the outcomes corresponding to a given event. If there are not too many outcomes we can list them all; but for complicated situations the number of outcomes quickly becomes too large to list.

Multiplication Principle

Suppose we want to choose a car that has one of these four colors: red, blue, green, or white. We are interested in three different body types: 4-door, 2-door, or wagon. How many different types of cars do we need to consider? We can make a list:

red 4-door,	red 2-door,	red wagon
blue 4-door,	blue 2-door,	blue wagon
green 4-door,	green 2-door,	green wagon
white 4-door,	white 2-door,	white wagon

There are 12 possible types, since 12 = 4 × 3.

We can make a general statement of this principle. Suppose we are going to conduct two experiments. The first experiment can have any one of *a* possible outcomes, and the second experiment can have any one of *b* possible outcomes, and let's suppose that any possible combination of the two results can occur. Then the total number of results of the two experiments is

$$a \times b$$

This rather obvious result is sometimes called the *multiplication principle*. Here are some examples:

- If you flip two coins, each flip has two possible outcomes, so the number of total outcomes is 2 × 2 = 4.

- Suppose you toss two dice. Since each die has six possible outcomes, the total number of possible outcomes from the two dice is 6 × 6 = 36.

- Suppose there are 5 candidates in the Republican primary for a particular office, and 6 candidates in the Democratic primary. Then the total number of possible general-election matchups is 5 × 6 = 30.

- There are 12 teams in the National League and 14 teams in the American League, so there are 12 × 14 = 168 possible World Series matchups.

Sampling with Replacement

Now, suppose you have five sweaters in your drawer. Each morning you reach in and randomly select one sweater. In the evening you put the sweater back and mix the sweaters up again. How many different ways can you wear sweaters for the week?

We can use the same principle, only now there are more than two experiments. There are five possible sweaters for you to wear on Sunday. There are also five sweaters for you to wear on Monday, so there is a total of 25 possible different combinations of sweaters you can wear on Sunday and Monday. For each of these possibilities there are 5 more choices for Tuesday, so there are 25 × 5 = 125 possible sweater-wearing patterns for the first three days. In fact, for the first week there are

$$5 \times 5 \times 5 \times 5 \times 5 \times 5 \times 5 = 5^7 = 78,125$$

different ways of wearing the sweaters.

From this information we can calculate the probability that you will wear the same sweater every day. Since there are 78,125 possible outcomes, and only five outcomes in which you wear the same sweater every day, the probability of selecting the same sweater every day is

$$\frac{5}{78,125} = .000064$$

The sweater selection process described here is an example of what is called *sampling*. Sampling means choosing a few items from a larger group. The larger group is called the *population*. In this case the population consists of five sweaters. We are selecting a sample of one sweater on Sunday, one sweater on Monday, and so on, for a total of seven selections. This type of sampling is called sampling *with replacement*. It should be obvious why we use the words "with replacement," since we are replacing the sweater in the drawer each evening. (Later, we will discuss sampling without replacement.) In general, if you sample n times with replacement from a population of m objects, then there are m^n possible different ways to select the objects.

The key idea of sampling with replacement is that once an item has been selected it can still be selected again. Flipping a coin is an example of sampling with replacement. In this case the population is of size 2: heads and tails. Just because you've selected heads once that doesn't mean you can't select heads again the next time. So if you flip a coin n times there are 2^n possible results.

Rolling a die is another example of sampling with replacement. In this case the population is of size 6. If you roll a 5 on the die once, then nothing will prevent you from rolling a 5 the next time. Therefore, there are 6^n total possibilities if you roll a die n times.

Here are some more examples of sampling with replacement:

EXAMPLE Suppose you have to take a 20-question multiple choice exam in a subject you know absolutely nothing about. Each question has five choices. What is the probability that you will be able to get all of the answers right just by guessing?

In this case we are sampling 20 times from a population of size 5, so the total number of possible ways of choosing the answers is $5^{20} = 9.5 \times 10^{13}$. There is only one possible outcome in which you have selected all of the right answers, so the probability of getting all of the answers right by pure guessing is $1/(9.5 \times 10^{13}) = 10^{-14}$ (approximately).

EXAMPLE Suppose you are trying to guess the license-plate number of a friend's car. (You haven't seen the car, but you do know that it doesn't have vanity license plates.) Assume that each license plate consists of three letters followed by three digits, such as DGM 235. First, calculate how many different possibilities there are for the three letters. That is the same as sampling 3 times with replacement from a population of 26 (since there are 26 letters in the alphabet), so there are $26^3 = 17,576$ ways of selecting the three letters. Since there are 10 possible digits there are $10^3 = 1,000$ ways of selecting the three digits. Each possible letter combination can be matched with each possible digit combination to give a valid license plate, so the total number of license plates is $17,576 \times 1,000 = 17,576,000$. Therefore, your chance of guessing the license plate correctly is $1/17,576,000 = 5.69 \times 10^{-8}$.

EXAMPLE   Suppose you're with a group of 15 people and you are comparing birthdays. How many different possible patterns of birthdays are there in a group of 15 people?

First, ignore people born on February 29, so then there are only 365 possibilities for the birthdays. Then you're sampling 15 times from a total population of 365, so the total number of possible birthday patterns is $365^{15} = 2.7 \times 10^{38}$.

Sampling without Replacement

Now, consider a different situation. Suppose that you have seven T-shirts. Each morning you reach into the drawer and randomly select one T-shirt to wear that day. However, this time, instead of putting the T-shirt back in the drawer in the evening you put it in the bag of clothes to be washed. (The wash gets done only once per week.) How many ways can you select the seven shirts for the week?

On Sunday you have seven choices. However, on Monday there are only six clean T-shirts left, so you only have 6 choices. Therefore, there are $7 \times 6 = 42$ possible ways of choosing the T-shirts that you will wear during the first two days. On Tuesday there are only five shirts left, so there are $7 \times 6 \times 5 = 210$ ways of choosing the shirts for the first three days. Continuing the process for the rest of the week we can see that there are $7 \times 6 \times 5 \times 4 \times 3 \times 2 \times 1 = 5,040$ ways of selecting the T-shirts for the week.

We've already given a name to this quantity (see Chapter 1). $7 \times 6 \times 5 \times 4 \times 3 \times 2 \times 1$ is called 7 factorial and written 7!. In this case we know for sure that you will wear each shirt exactly once during the week, so the only question is: What order will you wear them in? In general, if you have n objects, there are $n!$ different ways of putting them in order.

EXAMPLE   How many different ways are there of shuffling a deck of 52 cards? There are 52 possibilities for the top card, 51 possibilities for the second card, and so on, so that altogether there are $52! = 8.07 \times 10^{67}$ ways of shuffling the deck.

EXAMPLE   Suppose you have five different dinner menus to choose from for five days: hamburgers, hot dogs, pizza, macaroni, and tacos. In how many different orders can you arrange these five meals so that you don't repeat any meals during the five days?

Since there are five meals, the number of different orderings is $5! = 120$.

EXAMPLE   Suppose that your team is part of a 12-team league, and during the season you play each of the other teams once. How many different possible ways are there to arrange your schedule? Since there are 11 opponents, and the only question is what order you will play them in, there are $11! = 39,916,800$ possibilities for the schedule.

EXAMPLE   Suppose you are having 20 people show up for a dinner party at your home. What is the probability that they will arrive at your house in alphabetical order?

Since there are 20 guests there are 20! = 2.43×10^{18} different possible orders in which they can arrive. Since there is only one way of putting them in alphabetical order, the probability that they will arrive in alphabetical order is therefore $1/(2.43 \times 10^{18}) = 4.12 \times 10^{-19}$.

EXAMPLE   Suppose an indecisive baseball manager decides to try out every possible batting order before deciding on the order that is best for the team. How many games will it take to test every possible order?

There are nine players (assuming that this league does not have designated hitters), so there are 9! = 362,880 different orders.

Permutations

Suppose now that you have ten T-shirts (and the T-shirts are still washed every week). How many different ways of selecting T-shirts are there during seven days? Note that in this case you will not wear every shirt every week.

There are 10 choices for the shirt you wear on Sunday, then 9 choices for Monday, 8 choices for Tuesday, and so on down to 4 choices on Saturday. So the total number of choices is

$$10 \times 9 \times 8 \times 7 \times 6 \times 5 \times 4 = 604,800$$

We'd like a shorter way of writing that long expression, so we'll write it like this:

$$10 \times 9 \times 8 \times 7 \times 6 \times 5 \times 4$$
$$= \frac{10 \times 9 \times 8 \times 7 \times 6 \times 5 \times 4 \times 3 \times 2 \times 1}{3 \times 2 \times 1}$$
$$= \frac{10!}{3!}$$

What we're doing is choosing a sample of size 7 without replacement from a population of size 10. It's obvious why we call this sampling without replacement, since this time we're *not* replacing the T-shirt in the drawer after it has been selected. Sampling without replacement means that once an item has been selected it cannot be selected again.

In general, suppose you're going to select j objects without replacement from a population of n objects. Then there are

$$\frac{n!}{(n-j)!}$$

ways of selecting the objects. Each way of selecting the objects is called a *permutation* of the objects, so the formula $n!/(n-j)!$ gives the number of permutations of n things taken j at a time.

EXAMPLE   Suppose you want to find out how many ways birthdays can be distributed among a group of 15 people so that none of them have the same birthday. This means that there are 365 possibilities for the first person's birthday, 364 choices for the second person's birthday, and so on. This is an example of selecting a sample of size 15 without replacement from a population of size 365. Therefore, there are

$$\frac{365!}{(365 - 15)!} = \frac{365!}{350!}$$

$$= 2.03 \times 10^{38}$$

ways of dividing birthdays among the 15 people so that no two have the same birthday.

EXAMPLE Suppose that you are attending an eight-horse race, and you are trying to guess the order of the top three finishers without knowing anything about the horses involved. What is the probability that you will guess right?

Since three horses are to be chosen from the eight horses entered, this situation is equivalent to choosing a sample of size 3 without replacement from a population of size 8. Therefore, there are

$$\frac{8!}{(8 - 3)!} = \frac{8!}{5!} = 8 \times 7 \times 6 = 336$$

possible finishes. Your chance of randomly guessing the correct order is 1/336 = .003.

Combinations

Suppose you are in a card game and you are going to be dealt a hand of 5 cards from a deck of 52 cards. There are 52 possibilities for the first card you will draw, then 51 possibilities for the second card, and so on. We can consider this an example of choosing a sample of size 5 without replacement from a population of 52 cards. (Once you've drawn a card, you can't draw that particular card again. If you do draw the same card again, something suspicious is going on.) Therefore, there are

$$\frac{52!}{(52 - 5)!} = \frac{52!}{47!}$$

$$= 52 \times 51 \times 50 \times 49 \times 48$$

$$= 311,875,200 \text{ ways of drawing the cards}$$

However, suppose you drew these cards:

5C, 8D, 6H, AH, AD

For practical purposes that hand means exactly the same as it would if you drew the cards like this:

8D, 5C, 6H, AH, AD

The second hand contains exactly the same cards, the only difference being that they were picked in a different order. In many card games, the order in which you draw the cards doesn't matter; it's only *which* cards you draw that matters. However, in the way we have been counting the hands, we have counted these two possibilities as separate hands, because they were drawn in different orders. There are, of course, a lot of different orders in which this hand could be drawn.

How many different orderings of these cards are there? We have already discussed that problem. Since there are 5 cards, there are 5! = 120 different ways of arranging the cards in different orders. In fact, for *every* possible hand there are 120 different orderings. Our formula 52!/(52 − 5)! has told us the total number of different orderings of all the hands, but in this case we are only interested in the total number of *different* hands, regardless of the ordering. Therefore, our formula gives us 120 times too many hands, so we have to divide by 120. Therefore:

(total number of distinct 5-card hands that can be drawn from a deck of 52 cards not counting different orderings)

$$= \frac{52!}{(52 - 5)! \, 5!}$$

$$= 2{,}598{,}960$$

In general, suppose we are going to select j items without replacement from a population of n items and we're only interested in the total number of selections, without regard to their order. Then the number of possibilities is given by the formula

$$\frac{n!}{(n - j)! j!}$$

The number of arrangements without regard to order is called the number of *combinations*. The formula $n!/[(n - j)! j!]$ is said to represent the number of combinations of n things taken j at a time. We will use the formula $n!/[(n - j)! j!]$ a lot in probability and statistics. (Remember that we already used it in Chapter 1.) We'd like a shorter way of writing this formula, so we will symbolize it like this:

$$\binom{n}{j} = \frac{n!}{(n - j)! j!}$$

This expression is also called the *binomial coefficient* because it is used in a mathematical formula called the binomial theorem.

Here is an example of the formula. Suppose we have 5 letter blocks and we are going to select 3 of them. In how many ways can we make the selection? If the blocks have letters A,B,C,D,E, then we can list all of the possible permutations:

```
ABC  ACB  BAC  BCA  CAB  CBA
ABD  ADB  BAD  BDA  DAB  DBA
ABE  AEB  BAE  BEA  EAB  EBA
ACD  ADC  CAD  CDA  DAC  DCA
ACE  AEC  CAE  CEA  EAC  ECA
ADE  AED  DAE  DEA  EAD  EDA
BCD  BDC  CBD  CDB  DBC  DCB
BCE  BEC  CBE  CEB  EBC  ECB
BDE  BED  DBE  DEB  EBD  EDB
CDE  CED  DCE  DEC  ECD  EDC
```

There are 60 permutations in this list, which agrees with the formula:

$$\frac{5!}{(5-3)!} = \frac{5!}{2!} = 60$$

However, if we look closely at the list we can see that all of the arrangements in a particular row contain exactly the same letters, only arranged in different orders. Each of the 10 rows has different letters in it, so there are 10 different combinations of the letters. That agrees with the formula for combinations:

$$\frac{5!}{(5-3)!3!} = \frac{5!}{3!2!}$$
$$= 10$$

EXAMPLE How many 13-card hands can be dealt from a deck of 52 cards? Using the formula for the number of combinations of 52 objects taken 13 at a time, we have

$$\frac{52!}{(52-13)!13!} = \frac{52!}{39!\,13!}$$
$$= 6.35 \times 10^{11}$$

Now we have all the tools we need to solve many probability problems. There's no sure-fire method that always works, because many problems contain subtle twists.

EXAMPLE Suppose you and your dream lover (whom you're desperately hoping to meet) are both in a group of 20 people, and five people are to be randomly selected to be on a committee. What is the probability that both you and your dream lover will be on the committee?

The total number of ways of choosing the committee is

$$\binom{20}{5} = 15,504$$

Next, we need to calculate how many possibilities include both of you on the committee. If you've both been selected, then the three other committee members need to be selected from the remaining 18 people, and there are

$$\binom{18}{3} = 816$$

ways of doing this. Therefore, the probability that you will both be selected is 816/15,504 = .053.

EXAMPLE   Suppose 18 people are going to be randomly divided up into two baseball teams. What is the probability that all 9 of the best players will be on the same team?

There are $\binom{18}{9}$ = 48,620 ways of choosing the team that will bat first. Therefore, the chance of all the best players being on the team that bats first is 1/48,620. However, there is just as good a chance that all the best players will be on the team that bats second, so the chance they will all be on the same team is 2/48,620 = 4×10^{-5}.

EXAMPLE   We can calculate the probabilities of the various hands that can occur in a poker game. We have already calculated that the total number of possible hands is 52!/[(52 − 5)!5!] = 2,598,960. We can assume that each hand is equally likely, which is reasonable as long as the deck is well shuffled and the dealer is not cheating. Next, we need to figure out the number of possible ways of getting each type of hand.

• royal flush
A royal flush must contain the cards 10, J, Q, K, A, and they must all be of the same suit. Since there are 4 suits to choose from there are 4 possible royal flushes.

• straight flush
A straight flush must contain five cards in sequence, and they must all be of the same suit. We'll assume that we're playing under rules that allow the ace to be the low card in a straight as well as the high card. Then there are 9 possible straights other than the royal straight. (The 9 possible straights start with A, 2, 3, 4, 5, 6, 7, 8, or 9.) There are 4 choices for the suit, so there are $4 \times 9 = 36$ possible straight flushes.

• four of a kind
There are 13 possible choices for the type of card that we will draw 4 of. The fifth card in the deck can be any one of the 48 remaining cards, so altogether there are $13 \times 48 = 624$ possible hands with four of a kind.

• full house
A full house has 3 of one type of card and 2 of another. We have 13 choices for the type of card of which we will have 3. Those 3 cards must be chosen from the 4 cards of that type, so there are $\binom{4}{3} = 4$ ways of choosing them. Altogether, then, there are $13 \times 4 = 52$ ways of choosing the 3-of-a-kind cards. There are 12 possible choices left from

which to choose the 2-of-a-kind type. Once we have chosen the type, there are $\binom{4}{2} = 6$ ways of selecting the cards of that rank, so there are $12 \times 6 = 72$ ways of choosing the 2-of-a-kind cards. That means that there are $52 \times 72 = 3,744$ hands that are full houses.

• flush

A flush is a hand in which all 5 cards have the same suit. If the hand is to be all hearts (say), we need to choose 5 cards from the 13 hearts, so there are $\binom{13}{5} = 1,287$ ways of doing this. Since a flush can be any one of the 4 suits, there are thus $4 \times 1,287 = 5,148$ total flushes. However, this total includes straight flushes, so we need to subtract 40 from this total to get 5,108 hands that are plain flushes.

• straight

A straight consists of any 5 cards in sequence. As we saw earlier, there are 10 possible runs of 5 cards in sequence. For each of these possibilities there are $4^5 = 1,024$ ways of selecting the suits for the cards, so altogether there are 10,240 possible straights. However, once again we need to subtract the 40 straight flushes, to get a total of 10,200 plain straights.

• three of a kind

There are 13 ways to choose the rank of the card that we will select 3 of. Then there are 4 ways of selecting the cards of that rank. Then we have 48 choices for the 4th card in the hand, and then 44 choices for the 5th card (since the 5th card cannot match the 4th card). However, we have to divide by 2 because we don't care in which order we draw the 4th and 5th cards. So altogether there are

$$13 \times 4 \times 48 \times 44 \times \frac{1}{2} = 54,912 \text{ possible hands with 3 of a kind}$$

• two pairs

There are $\binom{13}{2} = 78$ ways of choosing the ranks of the cards that will make up the pairs. For each pair there are $\binom{4}{2} = 6$ ways of choosing the cards of that rank. Then, for each possible set of two pairs there are 44 ways of selecting the 5th card. Altogether, there are

$$78 \times 6 \times 6 \times 44 = 123,552 \text{ hands with 2 pairs}$$

• pair

There are 13 choices for the rank of the card that will make up the pair. Then there are $\binom{4}{2} = 6$ ways of choosing the cards of that rank. Now we need to figure out the number of ways of choosing the remaining 3 cards, which can be any nonmatching cards. There are 48 choices for the 3rd card, 44 choices for the 4th card, and 40 choices for the 5th card. We also have to divide by $3! = 6$, because we don't care about the order in which we draw the last 3 cards. Therefore, there are

$$13 \times 6 \times 48 \times 44 \times 40 \times \frac{1}{6} = 1{,}098{,}240 \text{ hands with 1 pair in them}$$

• nothing

We have covered all of the ways to get a hand with something that counts. If we add up all of these possibilities we find that there are 1,296,420 hands with something. We can then subtract to find that there are 1,302,540 hands with nothing. We can make a table of these results to get the probability of each hand occurring:

TABLE 5-1: Probabilities of Poker Hands

Type of hand	Number of possible hands	Probability
Royal flush	4	1.54×10^{-6}
Straight flush	36	1.39×10^{-5}
Four of a kind	624	2.40×10^{-4}
Full house	3,744	.00144
Flush	5,108	.00197
Straight	10,200	.00392
Three of a kind	54,912	.02113
Two pairs	123,552	.04754
Pair	1,098,240	.42257
Nothing	1,302,540	.50118

(Notice that the ranking of the hands has been scientifically designed so that the hands with lower probability have higher rankings.)

In the interests of science, we decided to check these results by dealing out 400 five-card hands. (Sometimes science is a lot of work.) The results we got were: 222 nothings (.555), 157 pairs (.393), 17 two-pairs (.043), and 4 three-of-a-kinds (.010).

EXAMPLE   In Chapter 4, we found that there is a 2/3 probability that somebody will pick his or her own name if three people take part in a Secret Santa drawing. That isn't very good, since it's no fun to be your own Secret Santa. Let's add more people, so now there are n people participating in the drawing. First, what is the probability that *everybody* will draw his or her own name? There are $n!$ ways of making the drawing, and there is only one way where everybody draws his or her own name. So the probability of everybody drawing his or her own name is $1/n!$.

Second, what is the probability that you will draw your own name? Since you are picking from n names, the probability of that happening is $1/n$. Third, what is the probability that Andrew and Ann, the two people first in alphabetical order, will both draw their own names? If Andrew and Ann have both drawn their own names, then there are $(n - 2)!$ ways for the other $n - 2$ people to draw their names, so the probability is $(n - 2)!/n!$ that Andrew and Ann will draw their own names.

Fourth, what is the probability that the first j people in alphabetical order will all draw their own names? There is only one way for the names to be drawn by those j people, and then there are $(n - j)!$ ways for the other $n - j$ people to draw their names. Therefore, the probability that the first j people will draw their own names is $(n - j)!/n!$.

Finally, what is the probability that at least one of the n people will draw his or her own name? If we let Ei be the event that person i draws his or her own name, then we need to find the union of $E1, E2, E3, \ldots$ and so on, up to En. We have to use the horrible formula described in Chapter 4. First, we have to add up the probability of each event individually. $\Pr(Ei) = 1/n$, as we saw, and there are n of these events, so we get $n(1/n)$ as the first part of the sum. Next, we need the probabilities of all of the intersections of the events taken 2 at a time. We already saw that $\Pr(E1 \cap E2) = (n - 2)!/n!$. By the same reasoning we used for Ann and Andrew, we can show that $\Pr(Ei \cap Ek) = (n - 2)!/n!$ for any two people in the group (that is, for any values of i and k). How many possible intersections are there between two sets in a group of n? That is $\binom{n}{2}$.

Going on, we can see that there are $\binom{n}{j}$ ways of choosing groups of j from the set. The probability of the intersections of these events taken j at a time is $(n - j)!/n!$, as we saw. Therefore, we can use the formula:

$$\Pr(E1 \cup E2 \cup E3 \cup \ldots \cup En)$$

$$= \binom{n}{1}\frac{(n-1)!}{n!} - \binom{n}{2}\frac{(n-2)!}{n!} + \binom{n}{3}\frac{(n-3)!}{n!} - \binom{n}{4}\frac{(n-4)!}{n!} + \cdots$$

If we simplify this expression, it turns out to be equal to

$$\frac{1}{1} - \frac{1}{2!} + \frac{1}{3!} - \frac{1}{4!} + \frac{1}{5!} - \frac{1}{6!} + \cdots \frac{(-1)^{n-1}}{n!}$$

We can make a table of these results. (See Table 5-2.)

TABLE 5-2

Number of people in Secret Santa drawing	Probability at least one person gets own name
1	1.00000
2	.50000
3	.66667
4	.62500
5	.63333
6	.63194
7	.63214
8	.63211
9	.63212
10	.63212

Note that the probability that at least one person will draw his own name does not go to zero, as you might expect, as n becomes large. Instead, it approaches a constant value of about .63212. This is an interesting number for mathematicians, since it is about $1 - 1/2.71828$. The number $2.71828 \ldots$ is a very special number that is given the name e. We will run into it again later.

EXAMPLE Suppose that a group of 16 people is going to be divided into roommates with two people in each room. The group consists of 8 pairs of best friends. If the selection is made entirely at random, what is the probability that all of the best friends will be roommates?

First, we need to calculate the number of different ways a group of n people can be divided into roommates. If there are two people, then there is obviously only one way. If there are four people, then there are three ways. If the people are labeled A, B, C, and D, then we can list all of the ways:

$$\begin{array}{l} \text{AB, CD} \\ \text{AC, BD} \\ \text{AD, BC} \end{array}$$

Now, suppose that we have n people. Let's make up a function called Roommate, such that Roommate(n) equals the number of ways of dividing a group of n people into roommates. (Note that n obviously must be an even number, because there is no way to divide an odd number of people into groups of 2.) Then, we have seen that Roommate(2) = 1, and Roommate(4) = 3. Now, let's consider Roommate(n). There are ($n - 1$) choices for the first person's roommate. After the first person's roommate has been chosen, ($n - 2$) people are left; they can be divided into roommates in Roommate ($n - 2$) ways. Therefore

$$\text{Roommate}(n) = (n - 1) \times \text{Roommate}(n - 2)$$

From this rule we can figure out that Roommate(6) = 5 × Roommate(4) = 15; Roommate(8) = 7 × Roommate(6) = 105; and, in general:

$$\text{Roommate}(n) = 1 \times 3 \times 5 \times 7 \times 9 \times 11 \times \cdots \times (n - 1).$$

In particular, we are interested in Roommate (16), which is equal to 2,027,025. Therefore, there are 2,027,025 total ways for the 16 people to be divided into roommates, and there is only one way in which all of the pairs of best friends are together, so the probability of the best friends being together if the selection is made totally at random is $1/2,027,025 = 4.93 \times 10^{-7}$.

We can write our formula in a shorter form:

Roommate(n)

$$= 1 \times 3 \times 5 \times 7 \times 9 \times \cdots \times (n - 1)$$

$$= \frac{1 \times 2 \times 3 \times 4 \times 5 \times 6 \cdots \times n}{2 \times 4 \times 8 \times \cdots \times n}$$

$$= \frac{n!}{(2 \times 1) \times (2 \times 2) \times (2 \times 3) \times (2 \times 4) \times \cdots \times (2 \times n/2)}$$

$$= \frac{n!}{2^{n/2} (1 \times 2 \times 3 \times 4 \times 5 \times \cdots \times n/2)}$$

$$= \frac{n!}{2^{n/2} (n/2)!}$$

Multinomial Formula

This formula is an example of a more general formula called the *multinomial formula*. Suppose we have n objects that are to be put into boxes, with each box having k objects. (Therefore, we will need n/k boxes.) Then there will be

$$\frac{n!}{(k!)^{n/k}}$$

ways to split the objects up into the boxes.

(This formula assumes that it makes a difference what box each group is put into. If we care only about which objects are grouped together, then we need to divide by $(n/k)!$ For example, in the roommate problem we were concerned only about the number of ways of dividing the people into pairs, without also worrying about the $(n/2)!$ different ways that the pairs could be put in rooms.)

In general, the multinomial formula says that if you are going to put n objects in m groups, with k_1 objects in the first group, k_2 objects in the second group, and so on, up to k_m objects in group m, then there are

$$\frac{n!}{k_1! \, k_2! \, k_3! \cdots k_m!}$$

ways of doing this. (Note that $k_1 + k_2 + k_3 + \cdots + k_m = n$.) If $m = 2$, then the multinomial formula becomes the same as the binomial formula.

EXAMPLE   Consider an artist who is painting a still life that will consist of three apples, five oranges, two bananas, and one plum, arranged in a row. In how many different ways can these fruits be arranged?

Clearly, if each fruit is distinguishable, then there are 11! ways of arranging them. However, if all of the fruits of each type have the same size and shape, then we need to divide by 3! 5! 2! since there are 3! ways of arranging the apples, 5! ways of arranging the oranges, and 2! ways of arranging the bananas. So there are 11!/(3!5!2!) = 27,720 arrangements.

EXERCISES

1. If 24 pieces of sausage are randomly put onto a pizza that is sliced into 8 pieces (with none of the sausages getting cut), what is the probability that your slice will have 3 pieces of sausage? 4 pieces?

2. A hostess has so many guests coming that she needs to use more than one set of plates. She has 22 guests coming, and she has 10 plates in one set and 12 plates in the other set. All of the people will sit at a round table. How many different ways can the plates be set at the table?

3. How many ways can all 32 chess pieces be arranged in a row? (Each color has 8 pawns, 2 rooks, 2 bishops, 2 knights, 1 king, and 1 queen.)

4. Suppose you suddenly find that you have to cook for yourself for one week. You have the following kinds of frozen dinners: 4 beef dinners, 2 chicken dinners, and 1 turkey dinner. How many ways can you arrange your menus for the week?

5. A choreographer is planning a dance routine consisting of four star dancers and an eight-member chorus line. The indifferent choreographer regards the four stars as indistinguishable, and the chorus line members as indistinguishable. The dance will end with all 12 dancers in a row. How many different ways can that row be arranged?

6. How many ways can the 4 aces be located in a deck of 52 cards?

7. Suppose you are getting dressed in a dark room. In your drawer you have four red socks, three blue socks, and two brown socks. If you randomly select two socks, what is the probability that you will get two socks that match?

8. If you have five pennies and four dimes in your pocket, and you reach in and pick two coins, what is the probability that you will get 20 cents?

9. Messrs. Smith, Jones, and Brown go to a garage sale. At the sale there are nine different bicycle horns. If Smith, Jones, and Brown each buy one horn, how many different possible purchases are there?

10. At a meeting, name tags are being made for four people named John, two people named Julie, and two people named Jane. How many different ways can the name tags be distributed?

11. At a party five people have blue jackets, four people have brown jackets, and two people have red jackets. If, at the end of the party, they each randomly select a jacket of the correct color, in how many different ways can the jackets be mixed up?

12. If you have 10 large chairs and 5 small chairs to be arranged at a round table, how many different ways are there to arrange them?

13. If you are picking four cards from a standard deck, what is the probability that you will pick an ace, 2, 3, and 4?

14. At a picnic the three indistinguishable Smith children and the two indistinguishable Jones children are sitting on a bench. In how many distinguishable ways can they be arranged on the bench?

15. If you are going to buy something from a vending machine that costs 55 cents, and you have five nickels and three dimes in your pocket, in how many different ways can you put change in the machine?

16. If you have 20 blue balls and 30 red balls in a box, and you randomly pull out 20 balls, what is the probability that they will all be blue?

17. What is $\binom{n}{0}$? Explain intuitively.

18. What is $\binom{n}{1}$? Explain intuitively.

19. What is $\binom{n}{n}$? Explain intuitively.

20. What is $\binom{n}{n-1}$? Explain intuitively.

21. Compare $\binom{n}{j}$ and $\binom{n}{n-j}$. Explain intuitively.

22. How many different possible five-letter words are there?

23. A combination for a combination lock consists of three numbers from 1 to 30. What is the probability that you could randomly guess the combination?

24. Suppose a monkey spends a long time at a typewriter. What is the probability that it will type the *Encyclopaedia Britannica?* What is the probability that it will type *Statistics the Easy Way?*

25. Have It Your Way Burgers, Inc., likes to give its customers a lot of choices, and it likes to keep all possible combinations on hand. Customers have their choice between these options: cheese/no cheese, onion/no onion, pickle/no pickle, well done/medium, ketchup/no ketchup, and there are six possible sizes: tiny, small, junior, medium, hefty, and jumbo. If any option can be selected with any other option, how many hamburgers will the hamburger place have to keep on hand in order to have every single possibility available?

26. At a Chinese restaurant, you have a choice between five items in column 1, six items in column 2, and four items in column 3. How many possible choices do you have?

27. If you roll three dice, what is the probability of getting at least two numbers the same?

28. Suppose you roll a die six times. What is the probability that no number will occur twice during the six rolls?

29. Suppose you roll a die n times. What is the probability that no number occurs twice during the n rolls?

30. If you roll three dice, what is the probability that they will all turn up the same?

31. If you roll five dice, what is the probability that they will all turn up the same?

32. If you roll a die n times, what is the probability that at least one 1 will turn up?

33. If you draw cards from a well-shuffled deck, what is the probability that you will draw all four kings before drawing the ace of spades?

34. What is the probability that you will draw all four kings before you draw a single ace?

35. Suppose you are playing a card game where you need to get either four in a row of the same suit, or four of a kind. You currently have 5D, 5C, 5H, 6H, and 7H, and you must discard one of these cards. Which card should you discard?

36. Consider an 8-team league, where each team plays the other teams in the league once during the season. How many different ways can the schedule be arranged?

37. If there are n people in a room, what is the probability that at least one was born on February 29? (Assume that leap year occurs every four years.) How large must n be to make this probability larger than 1/2?

❑ 38. Write a program that prints out all of the possible results of rolling three dice.

❑ 39. Write a program that calculates the probability that the sum of four dice will equal x, for each value of x from $x = 4$ to $x = 24$.

❑ 40. Write a program that prints out all of the possible orderings of five objects.

❑ 41. Write a subroutine that calculates $n!$.

❑ 42. Use the subroutine from Exercise 41 in a program that reads in n and j, and then calculates the number of permutations of n things taken j at a time.

❏ **43.** Use the subroutine from Exercise 41 in a program that reads in n and j and then calculates the number of combinations of n things taken j at a time.

❏ **44.** The programs in Exercises 42 and 43 are not very efficient. Write a more efficient program to calculate $n!/(n - j)!$.

❏ **45.** Write a more efficient program to calculate $n!/[(n - j)!j!]$.

46. Consider the example where a committee is to be selected from a group of 20 people, only this time the size of the committee is different from 5. If there are n people on the committee, make a table that shows the probability that both you and your dream lover will be on the committee for values of n from $n = 2$ to $n = 20$.

47. Suppose n people are voting in an election with two candidates. Assume that each voter is equally likely to vote for either of the two candidates. What is the probability that each candidate will get exactly the same number of votes?

❏ **48.** Write a program that reads in the number of voters n and then calculates the probability of a tie in that election. (Use the result from Exercise 47.)

49. Suppose a group of 16 people is being divided into roommates. Half of the people are day people (that is, they like to get up early) and half of the people are night people (that is, they like to stay up late and sleep late). If the selection is made completely at random, what is the probability that every day person will be matched with a night person?

50. In the situation described in the previous exercise, what is the probability that no roommate pairs will contain both a day person and a night person?

❏ **51.** Write a program that prints a table of the number of roommate combinations for $n = 1$ to $n = 20$.

52. Explain intuitively why the probability that one person will draw his or her own name does not go to zero as the number of people in the Secret Santa drawing becomes very large.

☆ **53.** Derive the multinomial formula. Start by asking yourself: How many ways are there to select the k_1 items in the first group. Then, how many ways are there to choose the k_2 items for the next group from the remaining $n - k_1$ items, and keep going like that.

CHAPTER 6

CONDITIONAL PROBABILITY

With random events we're often totally in the dark about what will happen, as we have seen. However, it sometimes happens that we can get some information that sheds light on the issue by telling us whether a particular random event is more or less likely to occur.

For example, suppose we want to know the probability that an 8 will·turn up when we roll two dice. Ordinarily, we know that the probability this will happen is 5/36. However, suppose we roll one of the dice first. Then we'll have a better idea about how likely we are to get an 8. For example, suppose we get a 5 on the first die. Then, to get a total of 8, we need to roll a 3 on the second die, and we know that the probability of that happening is 1/6. Therefore, once we are given the fact that the first die was 5, our chances of rolling an 8 have improved from 5/36 to 1/6.

On the other hand, suppose that the first die came up 1. Then we know that there is no way to roll an 8, no matter what happens with the second die. Therefore, the probability that we will roll an 8 given that we rolled a 1 on the first die is 0.

Or suppose we're interested in the probability of flipping four heads in a row. We know that ordinarily the probability is 1/16. However, suppose that we've already flipped the coin twice and it turned up heads both times. Once that has happened, the probability of getting two more heads is 1/4. On the other hand, if we flip the coin twice and it comes up heads first and then tails, we know that there is no probability of getting four heads in a row.

EXAMPLE Suppose we're interested in the probability of getting a royal flush. Ordinarily this probability is only $4/2{,}598{,}960 = 1.54 \times 10^{-6}$. (See Chapter 5.) However, suppose that we already have drawn the ace of hearts and the king of hearts, and we are going to draw three more cards. Then there are $\binom{50}{3} = 19{,}600$ ways of drawing the remaining three cards, so our probability of getting a royal flush has improved to $1/19,600 = 5.1 \times 10^{-5}$.

EXAMPLE   Suppose we're throwing a dart at the dart board in Figure 6–1.

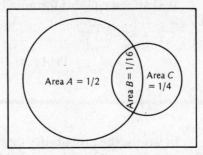

FIGURE 6–1   Area of rectangle = 1

Ordinarily, we know that the probability of hitting area A is 1/2. But suppose we know that the dart hit area C. Then the probability that it also hit area A is 1/4.

Calculating Conditional Probabilities

All of these situations are examples of *conditional probability*. A conditional probability tells us: What is the probability that one particular event will occur, *if* we already know that another specific event has occurred. In particular, suppose we know that event B has occurred and we want to know the probability that event A will occur The conditional probability that event A will occur given that event B has occurred is written like this:

$$\Pr(A \mid B)$$

The vertical line means "given that."

Now we have to figure out how to calculate conditional probabilities. In ordinary circumstances the probability that event A will occur is $N(A)/s$, where s is the total number of outcomes and $N(A)$ is the number of events in A. However, we know that not all of these outcomes are possible. We know that event B has occurred, so only those outcomes in event B need to be considered. So the number of possibilities is $N(B)$. The next question is: How many of these remaining possibilities also have event A occurring? Ordinarily there are $N(A)$ ways for event A to occur, but not all of these are possible now. The outcomes that are in A but not in B cannot occur. Therefore, the number of possible outcomes in which event A can occur is equal to the number of outcomes that are in both event A and event B. But we already gave a name to that event:

$$A \text{ and } B = A \cap B$$

The event in which both A and B occur is called A intersect B. Therefore, the probability that event A will occur given that event B occurs is given by

$$Pr(A \mid B) = \frac{N(A \cap B)}{N(B)}$$

We can rewrite this formula by dividing both the top and bottom by s:

$$Pr(A \mid B) = \frac{N(A \cap B)/s}{N(B)/s}$$

$$= \frac{Pr(A \cap B)}{Pr(B)}$$

In words, the probability that event A will occur, given that event B occurs, is equal to the probability that both A and B will occur, divided by the probability that B will occur. (Note that this definition does not work when $Pr(B) = 0$, because then we would be dividing by 0, which is no help at all.)

We can use this formula on the examples we discussed earlier.

EXAMPLE Let A = event of getting an 8 on a pair of dice.
Let B = event of getting a 5 on first roll; $Pr(B) = 1/6$.
$A \cap B$ = event of getting a 5 on first roll and 8 total.
$A \cap B$ can occur only if we roll 5, 3, so $Pr(A \cap B) = 1/36$. Thus

$$Pr(A \mid B) = \frac{1/36}{1/6} = 6/36 = 1/6$$

EXAMPLE Let A be the event of getting 4 heads in a row.
Let B be the event of getting 2 heads in the first two rolls.

$$Pr(B) = 1/4$$

$$Pr(A \cap B) = 1/16$$

$$Pr(A \mid B) = \frac{1/16}{1/4} = 4/16 = 1/4$$

EXAMPLE Let A be the event of getting a royal flush.
Let B be the event of getting AH, KH on the first two cards.

$$Pr(B) = \frac{\binom{50}{3}}{\binom{52}{5}}$$

$$= \frac{19,600}{2,598,960}$$

$$= 7.54 \times 10^{-3}$$

$A \cap B$ is the event of getting both KH, AH, and a royal flush, so it means getting the hand AH, KH, QH, JH, 10H.

$$\Pr(A \cap B) = 1/2{,}598{,}960$$

Therefore,

$$\Pr(A \mid B) = \frac{1/2{,}598{,}960}{19{,}600/2{,}598{,}960}$$

$$= 1/19{,}600$$

EXAMPLE Let A be the event of getting an 8 on two dice.
Let B be the event of getting a 1 on the first roll.

In this case A and B can't happen together. (We used the term *disjoint* for two events that cannot occur together.) Therefore, $A \cap B = \emptyset$, so $\Pr(A \cap B) = 0$, so $\Pr(A \mid B) = 0$. In general, when $\Pr(A \cap B)$ is zero, $\Pr(A \mid B)$ is zero. This result should be intuitively clear. It is like asking, "What is the probability that you will flip tails, given the fact that you have already done the flip and it came up heads?"

Another situation occurs if event A is a subset of event B. For example, suppose A is the event of rolling a 1 on the dice and B is the event of rolling an odd number. Then A contains the outcome $\{1\}$, and B contains the outcomes $\{1, 3, 5\}$, and $A \cap B$ contains the outcome $\{1\}$. Since $A \cap B = A$, then $\Pr(A \cap B) = \Pr(A)$, so $\Pr(A \mid B) = \Pr(A)/\Pr(B)$.

In general, if A is a subset of B, then

$$\Pr(A \mid B) = \frac{\Pr(A)}{\Pr(B)}$$

For another example, consider throwing a dart at the dart board in Figure 6–2. In this case region A is enclosed by region B. If you know that your dart will hit area B, then the probability that it will hit area A is area A/area B = 1/3.

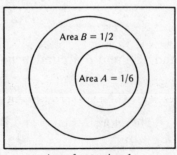

Area $B = 1/2$

Area $A = 1/6$

Area of rectangle = 1

FIGURE 6–2

Independent Events

As we have seen, often knowing whether one event has occurred will help tell you if another event is more likely or less likely. However, there are some cases in which knowing that one event has occurred does not give you a clue about whether another event will occur. For example, suppose you know that a family just had a baby girl. What is the probability that their next baby will be a girl? In this case, knowing about the last baby does not give you any information about the next baby.

Or, suppose that you roll a 3 on the first roll of a die. What is the probability that you will roll a 5 on the next roll? Knowing that the first roll came up 3 does not help you know what will happen on the next roll. In this case, if A is the event of getting a 3 on the first roll and B is the event of getting a 5 on the second roll, then $\Pr(A) = 1/6$, $\Pr(B) = 1/6$, and $\Pr(A \mid B) = 1/6$, since the fact that B has occurred does not affect the probability that A will occur.

We will give a special name to this situation. We will say that these two events are *independent*. That is a logical name, since two events are independent if they don't affect each other. Knowing that one of the events has occurred does not give you any information about whether the other event will occur.

The formal definition of independence is:

Events A and B are independent if $\Pr(A \mid B) = \Pr(A)$

Here are some more examples of independent events:

- The probability that you will draw two pairs in a card game is not affected by the fact that you drew two pairs in a card game yesterday.

- The probability that you will roll a 4 on a die is not affected by the fact that you just flipped a "head" on a coin.

There is an interesting result that we can get from the formula for conditional probability. Note that, in general,

$$\Pr(A \mid B) = \frac{\Pr(A \cap B)}{\Pr(B)}$$

And, if A and B are independent, then

$$\Pr(A \mid B) = \Pr(A)$$

Therefore, when A and B are independent we can write:

$$\Pr(A) = \frac{\Pr(A \cap B)}{\Pr(B)}$$

Therefore:

$$\Pr(A \cap B) = \Pr(A)\,\Pr(B), \quad \text{or} \quad \Pr(A \text{ and } B) = \Pr(A)\,\Pr(B)$$

This result gives us a nice, simple rule to find the probability of $A \cap B$ if A and B are independent.

Bayes' Rule

Suppose that tuna comes in two types of cans: green cans and purple cans. A study has revealed that 5 percent of all the tuna is spoiled when it is sold. Further research shows that 35 percent of the spoiled tuna comes in purple cans, and 60 percent of the good tuna comes in purple cans. If you purchase a particular can of purple tuna, what is the probability that it is spoiled?

To do this problem, we need to know how to reverse a conditional probability. In other words, if we know $\Pr(A \mid B)$, then we need to find $\Pr(B \mid A)$. Let P be the event of getting a purple can of tuna, S be the event of getting a spoiled can of tuna, and G be the event of getting a good can of tuna. Then we know that

$$\Pr(P \mid S) = .35$$

(If a given can of tuna is spoiled, then there is a 35 percent chance that it is purple.)

$$\Pr(S) = .05$$
$$\Pr(G) = \Pr(S^c) = .95$$

To derive $\Pr(S \mid P)$, we need to use a formula called *Bayes's rule*. If A and B are two events, then Bayes's rule states that

$$\Pr(B \mid A) = \frac{\Pr(A \mid B)\,\Pr(B)}{\Pr(A \mid B)\,\Pr(B) + \Pr(A \mid B^c)\,\Pr(B^c)}$$

Remember that the little c means complement. B^c comprises all of the possible outcomes that are not in B.

We can use Bayes's rule as follows for the tuna problem:

$$\Pr(S \mid P) = \frac{\Pr(P \mid S)\,\Pr(S)}{\Pr(P \mid S)\,\Pr(S) + \Pr(P \mid G)\,\Pr(G)}$$

$$= \frac{(.35)(.05)}{(.35)(.05) + (.6)(.95)}$$

$$= 0.030$$

The proof of Bayes's rule is left as Exercise 16.

EXERCISES

1. Suppose you have two nickels in your pocket. You know that one is fair and one is two-headed. If you take one out, toss it, and get a head, what is the probability that it was the fair coin?

2. In blackjack, each player is given two cards to start with, and then tries to get a numerical total of 21 in the following way: 2's through 10's are worth their face value, face cards are worth 10,

and an ace can be worth either 1 or 11, depending on the player's preference. The player can take more cards, trying to get as close to 21 as possible without going over (in which case the game is lost). Suppose you are dealt a 4 and a 9. If the dealer is dealing from a single deck of 52 cards, and the 4 and the 9 are the only cards that have been dealt from that deck that you know the value of, should you take another card? In other words, what is the probability that if you take another card you won't go over 21?

3. In some versions of blackjack, one of the two cards dealt each player is turned up. Suppose you can see that your fellow players have been dealt two aces, a 5, and a king. You again have a 4 and a 9. Should you draw another card?

4. What is the probability that you will get a royal flush in your next four cards if your first card is the ace of hearts? What is the probability if the next two cards you draw are the king of hearts and queen of hearts? What is the probability if the fourth card you draw is the jack of hearts?

5. What is the probability that you will draw a straight if you have already drawn a 2 and a 3?

6. Suppose there is a probability p that your team will beat its opponent in any particular World Series game. What is the probability that your team will win the World Series? (The teams in the World Series keep playing until one of the teams has won four games.)

7. If you flip a fair coin twice, and know that at least one head came up, what is the probability of there being two heads?

8. Suppose you remove all the diamonds from a 52-card deck, put the ace of diamonds back in, shuffle the remaining 40 cards, and pick a card at random. Given that the card you pick is an ace, what is the probability that it is the ace of diamonds?

9. Suppose you roll two dice and pick a card at random from a 52-card deck. Suppose further that the number rolled on the dice is the same as the number on the card. What is the probability that the number is 6?

10. What is the probability that you win a lottery with a three-digit number, given that you have two digits of the winning number?

11. What is the probability of getting four aces in a poker hand given that two of the cards in your hand are the ace and king of spades?

12. What is the probability of drawing a jack from a 52-card deck, given that you've drawn a face card?

13. Suppose you roll three dice. Given that one of the dice shows a 5, what is the probability of rolling a 14?

14. Consider the experiment of tossing two coins. Let A be the event of getting a head on the first toss.

    (a) Can you name an event that is disjoint from but not independent of A?

    (b) Can you name an event that is independent of but not disjoint from A?

    (c) Can you name an event that is both disjoint from and independent of A?

    (d) Can you name an event that is neither disjoint from nor independent of A?

15. Suppose that an election is being conducted with two candidates, Smith and Jones. Of the people in the city 2/3 support Jones, but 5/9 of the people from the country support Smith. Half of the people live in the country and half live in the city. If you randomly start talking with a voter who turns out to be a Jones supporter, what is the probability that that voter lives in the country?

☆ 16. Derive Bayes's rule.

17. Suppose that 5 percent of the people with blood type O are left-handed, 10 percent of those with other blood types are left-handed, and that 40 percent of the people have blood type O. If you randomly select a left-handed person, what is the probability that that person will have blood type O?

18. Suppose that 70 percent of the people with brown eyes have brown hair, 20 percent of the people with green eyes have brown hair, and 5 percent of the people with blue eyes have brown hair. Also, suppose 75 percent of the people have brown eyes, 20 percent have blue eyes, and 5 percent have green eyes. What is the probability that a randomly selected person with brown hair will also have green eyes?

CHAPTER 7

DISCRETE RANDOM VARIABLES

It often happens in probability that the events we're interested in involve counting something or measuring something. For example, we have been interested in the number of heads that appear when we flip a coin or the number that appears on a pair of dice. In these cases it is easier to talk about *random variables* rather than probability spaces and events. If X is the number of heads that appear when you flip a coin three times, then X is a random variable. If Y is the number that appears when you toss one die, then Y is also a random variable. If W represents the number of times that the word "tennis" is used on the 11 o'clock news, then W is a random variable (which can take on values anywhere from zero during the dead of winter to 50 during Wimbledon). We'll use capital letters to stand for random variables, to avoid confusion with the ordinary variables used in algebra.

Suppose we roll a die and then write down the number Y that appears. This process is called *observing* (or *measuring*) the value of Y. If we roll the die ten times, then we have ten observations of the random variable Y.

As we have seen, a random event is something of which we don't know for sure whether or not it will happen, but we can often calculate the probability that it will happen. By analogy, a random variable is a variable such that we're not sure what it will equal, but for which we can often calculate the probability that it will equal a particular value. (Formally, a random variable is a variable that takes on a specified value when a particular random event occurs, so it is a function from sets to numbers.)

Although we usually cannot tell exactly what the value of a random variable will be, we often can determine what its values will *not* be. For example, the tennis variable W cannot be $3\frac{1}{3}$ or π or any other weird number. W must be a whole number. The number on the die (Y) must also be a whole number, but it can have only one of six possible values: 1, 2, 3, 4, 5, or 6. Random variables that can only take on isolated values are called *discrete random variables.* (We'll later talk about *continuous random variables.*)

Discrete random variables don't have to take just whole-number values, though. Suppose we roll two dice, and let T be the average of the two numbers that appear. Then T has the possible values $1, 1\frac{1}{2}, 2, 2\frac{1}{2}, 3, 3\frac{1}{2}, 4, 4\frac{1}{2}, 5, 5\frac{1}{2}$, and 6.

Probability Density Functions

Now let's figure out what we need to know about random variables. With ordinary variables, about all we need to know is their value. However, with random variables it is much more complicated. First, we need to know which values are possible and which are impossible. For example, if a random variable X can never take the value 3/2, we can write

Probability that $X = 3/2$ is 0

We can write that in a shorter fashion:

$$\Pr(X = 3/2) = 0$$

Once we've made a list of all the possible values, the next thing we would like to know is: How likely are these different values? In the case of tossing one die, the situation is very simple: There are only six possible values and they are all equally likely. We can make a list of these:

$$\Pr(Y = 1) = 1/6$$
$$\Pr(Y = 2) = 1/6$$
$$\Pr(Y = 3) = 1/6$$
$$\Pr(Y = 4) = 1/6$$
$$\Pr(Y = 5) = 1/6$$
$$\Pr(Y = 6) = 1/6$$

We can also make a list of the probabilities for the random variable X defined as the number of heads in three tosses:

$$\Pr(X = 0) = 1/8$$
$$\Pr(X = 1) = 3/8$$
$$\Pr(X = 2) = 3/8$$
$$\Pr(X = 3) = 1/8$$

In both of these cases we understand the process that is generating the random variable, so it is easy to calculate the probability of each possible value. In other circumstances, such as the tennis example, we cannot calculate the probabilities because we do not understand the process well enough. (However, later we will discuss ways to estimate the probabilities of these occurrences.)

To make things a little more convenient, we will define a *probability density function* for a random variable. The value of the probability density function for a particular number is just the probability that the random variable will equal that number. We'll use a small letter f to stand for the probability density function. So we can make the definition:

$$f(a) = \Pr(X = a)$$

(The probability density is also sometimes called the *probability mass function*.) When we start talking about more than one random variable at a time, we will write the probability density function as $f_X(a)$ to make it clear that f is the density function for the random variable X.

Here is the density function for the toss of one die:

$$f(1) = 1/6$$
$$f(2) = 1/6$$
$$f(3) = 1/6$$
$$f(4) = 1/6$$
$$f(5) = 1/6$$
$$f(6) = 1/6$$

(This function is graphed in Figure 7–1.)

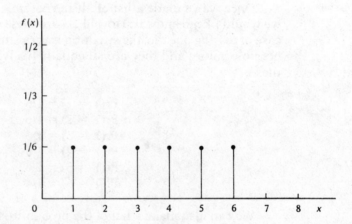

FIGURE 7–1

Here is the density function for flipping a coin three times:

$$f(0) = 1/8$$
$$f(1) = 3/8$$
$$f(2) = 3/8$$
$$f(3) = 1/8$$

Figure 7–2 shows a graph of this function. (In both of these cases $f(a) = 0$ for all values of a except the ones that are listed.)

There is a close connection between the density function of a random variable and the frequency diagram for the numbers in a sample. For example, suppose we roll a die 6,000 times and then make a frequency diagram showing the number of times that each possible

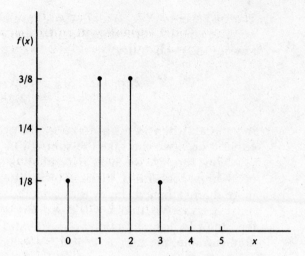

FIGURE 7–2

result appears (Figure 7–3). The frequency diagram has approximately the same shape as the density function.

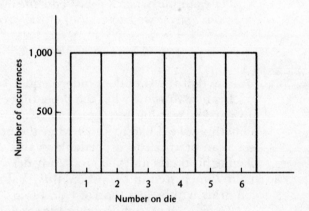

FIGURE 7–3

We can quickly establish two obvious properties that a probability density function must satisfy:

$$f(a) \leq 1 \quad \text{for all possible values of } a$$
$$f(a) \geq 0 \quad \text{for all possible values of } a$$

These two statements just point out that there is no such thing as a probability that is greater than 1 or less than 0.

Suppose we would like to know the probability that a random variable will have either one of two values. For example, what is the probability that X will equal 2 or 3? We can write it like this:

$$\Pr[(X = 2) \text{ or } (X = 3)]$$

We can rewrite that probability as the probability of a union of two events:

$$\Pr[(X = 2) \cup (X = 3)]$$

The two events $(X = 2)$ and $(X = 3)$ are clearly disjoint. (Just try to make X equal both 2 and 3 at the same time!) Therefore, we can rewrite the probability:

$$\Pr[\ (X = 2)\ \text{or}\ (X = 3)\ ] = \Pr(X = 2) + \Pr(X = 3)$$
$$= f(2) + f(3)$$

In general, when we want to know the probability that X will equal either a or b, we can take the sum of $f(a) + f(b)$.

Now, suppose we make a list of all of the possible values and add up their probabilities. If the probabilities add up to less than 1 or more than 1, then we know that something is wrong. The probability must be exactly 1 that X will equal one of its possible values. Therefore, in order for a function f to be a valid density function for a random variable, the sum of its possible values must be 1: If the possible values are $a_1, a_2, a_3, \ldots, a_n$,

$$f(a_1) + f(a_2) + f(a_3) + \cdots + f(a_n) = 1$$

For example, when X represents the number of heads that appear on 3 coin tosses, we can add all of the probabilities:

$$1/8 + 3/8 + 3/8 + 1/8 = 8/8 = 1$$

to show that the sum does indeed equal 1.

It's nice to know what the probability will be that X will take on any particular value, but sometimes we don't need to know all of that. Sometimes we'd like to know what the probability is that X will be less than or equal to a particular value a^*. For example, if you're playing blackjack and you've already drawn a 7 and an 8, then you're mainly interested in the probability that the value of the next card you draw will be less than or equal to 6.

To find the probability that the random variable Y in the case of rolling a die will be less than or equal to 3, we need to add $\Pr(Y = 1) + \Pr(Y = 2) + \Pr(Y = 3) = 1/2$. In general, if $a_1, a_2, a_3, \ldots a^*$ are all of the possible values Z that are less than or equal to a^*, then

$$\Pr(Z \le a^*) = f(a_1) + f(a_2) + fa_3) + \cdots + f(a^*)$$

We will give a special name to the function that tells the probability that Z will be less than or equal to a particular value. We'll call that function the *cumulative distribution function*, and we'll represent it by a capital F:

$$F(a) = \Pr(Z \le a)$$

We can derive some properties that a cumulative distribution function must satisfy:

(1) $F(a)$ must be between 0 and 1 all of the time, since $F(a)$ is itself the probability of an event (the event that $X \le a$).

(2) If we keep letting a become smaller and smaller, eventually we will find $F(a) = 0$. Sooner or later a will become less than the

smallest possible value of X, and there is 0 probability that X can be less than a number if that number is smaller than the smallest possible value of X. Likewise, if we make a big enough, eventually we must have $F(a) = 1$. Formally, we can say that $\lim_{a \to \infty} F(a) = 1$ and $\lim_{a \to -\infty} F(a) = 0$. (In this paragraph we have assumed that X has only a finite number of possible values, but the same property holds even if X has an infinite number of possible values.)

(3) If $a \leq b$, then $F(a) \leq F(b)$. That means that, as you go from left to right along the number line, $F(a)$ must always be either getting bigger or staying the same. (Formally, F is a *monotone increasing* function.)

(4) A graph of a cumulative distribution function looks like an irregular staircase. Figure 7–4 shows the graph of a typical cumulative distribution function. (Formally, this means that $F(a)$ is *piecewise constant*. It will stay flat for a while until it comes to one of the possible values, and then it will increase in a jump.)

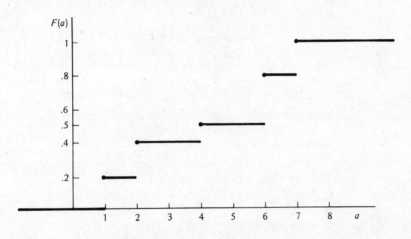

FIGURE 7–4

We can calculate the cumulative distribution function for the number of heads X on three coin tosses:

$$F(a) = \begin{cases} 0 & \text{if } a < 0 \\ 1/8 & \text{if } 0 \leq a < 1 \\ 1/2 & \text{if } 1 \leq a < 2 \\ 7/8 & \text{if } 2 \leq a < 3 \\ 1 & \text{if } 3 \leq a \end{cases}$$

As we can see, this function satisfies the properties that a cumulative distribution function must satisfy.

Expectation Value

Once we know the density function or the cumulative distribution function for a particular random variable, we know just about everything we might possibly need to know about it. However, many times we would like to summarize the information that we have about the random variable. We showed that we can summarize a group of numbers by single number (the average). We will develop a similar concept for a random variable.

Consider the variable X (the number of heads in 3 coin tosses.) Suppose we measure X 8 million times. How many times are we likely to get no head, 1 head, 2 heads, or 3 heads? You can guess that we will likely observe the value $X = 0$ close to 1 million times, the value $X = 1$ close to 3 million times, the value $X = 2$ 3 million times, and the value $X = 3$ 1 million times. In reality, we would probably not get exactly these numbers, but let us assume for a moment that we performed this experiment 8 million times and did get exactly these results. (In general, if you measure a random variable N times, then the number of times that you can expect to get the value a will be equal to $f(a) \times N$.)

Now, we have 8 million numbers written down (one number for each of the 8 million repetitions of our experiment.) Since we don't want to carry around all 8 million numbers, we'd like to summarize all of these values by taking their average:

$$
\begin{aligned}
(\; 0 + 0 + 0 + 0 + \cdots & \qquad \text{(1 million zeros)} \\
+ 1 + 1 + 1 + 1 + \cdots & \qquad \text{(3 million ones)} \\
+ 2 + 2 + 2 + 2 + \cdots & \qquad \text{(3 million twos)} \\
+ 3 + 3 + 3 + 3 + \cdots) \, / \, 8{,}000{,}000 & \qquad \text{(1 million threes)}
\end{aligned}
$$

We can rewrite that in a shorter fashion:

$$
\begin{aligned}
(1{,}000{,}000 \times 0 & \\
+ 3{,}000{,}000 \times 1 & \\
+ 3{,}000{,}000 \times 2 & \\
+ 1{,}000{,}000 \times 3) / 8{,}000{,}000 &
\end{aligned}
$$

It's even shorter to write it like this:

$$
1/8 \times 0 + 3/8 \times 1 + 3/8 \times 2 + 1/8 \times 3 = 1\tfrac{1}{2}
$$

So the average of all the values is $1\tfrac{1}{2}$. We can also write that expression in terms of the density function f:

$$
\text{average} = f(0) \times 0 + f(1) \times 1 + f(2) \times 2 + f(3) \times 3
$$

We will call this quantity the *expectation value of X*, or the *expectation of X*. The expectation value of a random variable tells us the average of all the values we would expect to get if we measured the random variable many times. We'll use the capital letter E to stand for expectation, and write it like this:

$$
E(X) = \text{expectation of } X
$$

The general formula for calculating an expectation is

$$
E(X) = f(a_1) \, a_1 + f(a_2) \, a_2 + f(a_3) \, a_3 + \cdots + f(a_n) \, a_n
$$

$$
= \sum_{i=1}^{n} f(a_i) \, a_i
$$

where $a_1, a_2, \ldots, a_n$ are all of the possible values of the random variable X.

The expectation of X is also called the *mean* of X, or the mean of the distribution of X, and it is usually symbolized by the Greek letter μ (mu). Note that $E(X) = \mu$ is not itself a random variable. It is a regular constant number.

The expectation of a random variable does not itself have to be one of the possible values of the random variable. For example, we found that the expectation value for the number of heads in three tosses is $1\frac{1}{2}$, but we strongly caution you against betting that the number of heads will ever come out to be $1\frac{1}{2}$ (unless you make the bet with us).

The expectation of the number (Y) that shows up on a die is easy to calculate:

$$
\begin{aligned}
E(Y) &= f(1) \times 1 + f(2) \times 2 + f(3) \times 3 \\
&\quad + f(4) \times 4 + f(5) \times 5 + f(6) \times 6 \\
&= 1/6 \times 1 + 1/6 \times 2 + 1/6 \times 3 \\
&\quad + 1/6 \times 4 + 1/6 \times 5 + 1/6 \times 6 \\
&= 3\tfrac{1}{2}
\end{aligned}
$$

There are two important properties of expectations that we can establish. If c is a constant number (in other words, not a random variable), then

$$E(cX) = c\,E(X)$$

For example, if Y_2 equals twice the number that appears on a die, then $E(Y_2) = 2\,E(Y) = 7$.

Suppose we have two random variables X and Y, and we form a new random variable V which is equal to $V = X + Y$. In general, putting two random variables together creates a lot of complications, and we will not talk about these problems much until Chapter 13. However, one property we can establish is

$$E(X + Y) = E(X) + E(Y)$$

There will also be times when we would like to calculate the expectation of a particular function of a random variable. For example, suppose $Z = X^2$, and we want to calculate $E(Z) = E(X^2)$. From the definition, we would have to use the formula:

$$E(Z) = \sum_{i=1}^{n} z_i\, f(z_i)$$

However, this method requires us to calculate the density function for Z, which can sometimes be a real bother. We do already know the density function of X, though, and fortunately we can use this simple formula:

$$E(X^2) = \sum_{i=1}^{n} x_i^2\, f(x_i)$$

For example, when X is the number of heads that appear on three coins, we can calculate $E(X^2)$:

$$E(X^2) = 0 \times 1/8 + 1 \times 3/8 + 4 \times 3/8 + 9 \times 1/8$$
$$= 24/8 = 3$$

Note that it would have been even easier if we could say that $E(X^2) = [E(X)]^2$, but as we can see that formula does not work. In general, though, if $g(x)$ is any function,

$$E[g(X)] = \sum_{i=1}^{n} g(x_i) f(x_i)$$

Variance

Although the expectation value of a random variable tells us a lot about its behavior, it doesn't tell the whole story. For example, let's consider one simple random variable that really isn't a random variable at all. Suppose U represents the number of times that Wile E. Coyote, the cartoon character, will catch the roadrunner. Then we know for sure that $U = 0$, so the density function has the value 1 at $U = 0$ and the value 0 everywhere else. In this case we can easily see that $E(U) = 0$.

Let us consider another random variable, T, which represents the number on the first die you toss minus the number on the second die. Then $f(5) = 1/36$, $f(4) = 2/36$, $f(3) = 3/36$, $f(2) = 4/36$, $f(1) = 5/36$, $f(0) = 6/36$, $f(-1) = 5/36$, $f(-2) = 4/36$, $f(-3) = 3/36$, $f(-4) = 2/36$, $f(-5) = 1/36$. We can easily show that $E(T) = 0$. However, the behavior of the random variable T is much more unpredictable than the behavior of the random variable U. To consider an even more extreme example, suppose that S is a random variable that represents your profit on the following stock market transaction: You pay 1 million dollars for the stock, which has a 50 percent chance of doubling in value and a 50 percent chance of becoming worthless. Then $S = 1$ million with probability $1/2$ and $S = $ minus 1 million with probability $1/2$. $E(S) = 0$, but as we can see, the actual value of S will never be close to $E(S)$. So, in addition to the expectation, we need something that tells us how unpredictable a random variable is—in other words, we would like something that tells us whether or not the random variable is likely to be close to its expectation value.

You might suggest that we look at how far away from the mean each possible value of X is, and then find out what the expected value of the distance from $E(X)$ will be, like this:

(unpredictability measure) $= E[a - E(X)]$
$$= f(a_1) [a_1 - E(X)] + f(a_2)[a_2 - E(X)]$$
$$+ \cdots + f(a_n)[a_n - E(X)]$$

However, the problem with this measure is that some of the possible values of X will be less than $E(X)$ and others will be greater, so we will get a lot of positive and negative numbers that will cancel each other out.

You might think that what we should do is take the *absolute value* of [a_i − E(X)] (that is, if a_i is a negative number, make it into a positive number), and then calculate the average of the absolute values of the distances from each value of X to the expectation of X. This is a reasonable procedure; however, we will adopt a different procedure that will be more convenient later on. We will take the *square* of the distance from each value a to E(X), and then find the expectation of that quantity. The result is called the *variance* of the random variable X.

$$\text{Variance } (X) = f(a_1) [a_1 - E(X)]^2 + f(a_2) [a_2 - E(X)]^2$$
$$+ \cdots + f(a_n) [a_n - E(X)]^2$$
$$= E[(X - E(X))^2]$$

The variance of X is usually written Var(X). The variance is also represented by the symbol σ^2; σ is the Greek lower-case letter sigma. The symbol σ itself stands for the square root of the variance, which is called the *standard deviation*.

$$\text{(standard deviation)} = \sigma = \sqrt{\text{Var}(X)}$$

For computational purposes, it is much easier to derive a shortcut formula for the variance:

$$\text{Var}(X) = E[(X - E(X))^2]$$
$$= E[X^2 - 2 X E(X) + (E(X))^2]$$
$$= E(X^2) - E[2 X E(X)] + E[(E(X))^2]$$
$$= E(X^2) - 2 E(X) E(X) + (E(X))^2$$
$$= E(X^2) - (E(X))^2$$

Now we can calculate the variances of U, T, and S. It is clear that $E(U^2) = 0$, so Var(U) also is 0. In general, if c is any constant, then Var(c) = 0.

We can find $E(T^2)$:

$$E(T^2) = 25 \times 1/36 + 16 \times 2/36 + 9 \times 3/36 + 4 \times 4/36$$
$$+ 1 \times 5/36 + 0 \times 6/36 + 1 \times 5/36 + 4 \times 4/36$$
$$+ 9 \times 3/36 + 16 \times 2/36 + 25 \times 1/36$$
$$= 210/36$$

Since E(T) = 0, it follows that Var(T) = 210/36.

The variance of the stock market variable S is

$$\text{Var}(S) = E(S^2)$$
$$= 1/2 \times 1,000,000^2 + 1/2 \times (-1,000,000)^2$$
$$= 10^{12}$$

Just as we suspected, the variance of S is much greater than the variance of the other two random variables.

We can calculate the variance of X, the number of heads in three coin tosses, since we have already found that $E(X^2) = 3$. Therefore,

$$\text{Var}(X) = 3 - (1\tfrac{1}{2})^2$$
$$= 3/4.$$

The variance of the number that appears on a die turns out to be 35/12 = 2.9167. (See Exercise 12.)

Now we'll do another simple random variable that illustrates all of these concepts. Let us consider a Mad Scientist who repeats a particular experiment each day. There is a probability p that the experiment will succeed on any particular trial; let's suppose that $p = 1/5$. (An experiment like this that can have only two possible results, success or failure, is called a *Bernoulli trial*.) Let Z be the random variable that is equal to the number of successes on a particular day. Then Z has only two possible values: 0 and 1. We can easily calculate the complete density function:

$$f(0) = \Pr(Z = 0) = 1 - p$$
$$f(1) = \Pr(Z = 1) = p$$
$$f(a) = 0 \text{ for all other values of } a$$

Figure 7–5 shows a graph of this density function.

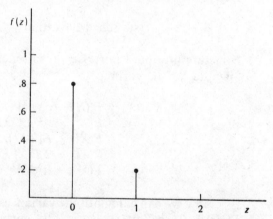

FIGURE 7–5

Next, we can calculate the cumulative distribution function:

$$F(a) = 0 \qquad \text{if } a < 0$$
$$F(a) = 1 - p \qquad \text{if } 0 \le a < 1$$
$$F(a) = 1 \qquad \text{if } a \ge 1$$

Figure 7–6 illustrates this function.

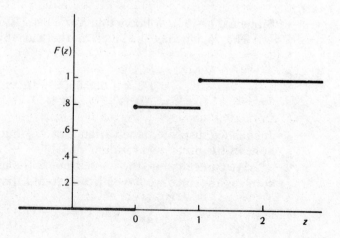

FIGURE 7–6

The expectation can be found from:

$$E(Z) = 0 \times (1 - p) + 1 \times p = p$$

We can calculate the variance two ways. First, we can use the definition:

$$\begin{aligned}
\text{Var}(Z) &= f(0)\,(0 - p)^2 + f(1)\,(1 - p)^2 \\
&= (1 - p)\,p^2 + p\,(1 - p)^2 \\
&= p^2 - p^3 + p - 2p^2 + p^3 \\
&= p - p^2 \\
&= p(1 - p) \\
&= .16 \text{ (when } p = 1/5)
\end{aligned}$$

We can also use the short-cut formula to calculate the variance:

$$\begin{aligned}
\text{Var}(Z) &= E(X^2) - [E(X)]^2 \\
&= 0^2\,(1 - p) + 1^2\,p - p^2 \\
&= p(1 - p)
\end{aligned}$$

Note that if $p = 0$, we know for sure that $Z = 0$; and if $p = 1$, we know for sure that $Z = 1$. In either case, Var(Z) is 0, which we know must be the case.

Variance of a Sum

In this section we will develop two useful properties of variances. First, if c is a constant, we can show that

$$\text{Var}(cX) = c^2\,\text{Var}(X)$$

For example, if Y is the number that appears on a die, and $Z = 2Y$, then Var(Z) = 35/3.

If we have two random variables X and Y added together to form a new random variable $V = X + Y$, then we cannot say in general what is the variance of V. We need to know something about how the two random variables are related to each other. For example, let's say that X is the number on the top of a die when it is tossed, and Y is the number on the bottom of the die. Then Var(X) = Var(Y) = 2.9167. However, $V = X + Y = 7$ all of the time, so Var(V) = 0. So we clearly do not have a simple formula such as Var(X + Y) = Var(X) + Var(Y).

However, suppose that we have two random variables X and Y that are unrelated to each other. Then it turns out that Var(X + Y) does equal Var(X) + Var(Y). (We need to establish what we mean by completely unrelated. Formally, Var(X + Y) = Var(X) + Var(Y) if X and Y are *independent* random variables. We define what we mean by independent in Chapter 13.)

For example, suppose X is the number that is the result of tossing one die, and Y is the number that results from tossing a different die. Then Var(X + Y) = Var(X) + Var(Y) = 2.9167 + 2.9167 = 5.8334. (See Exercise 13.)

**NOTE TO
CHAPTER 7**

It is possible for a discrete random variable to have an infinite number of possible values, just so long as all of the probabilities still add up to 1. For example, suppose the density function for a random variable X looks like this: $f(2) = 1/2$, $f(4) = 1/4$, $f(8) = 1/8$, $f(16) = 1/16$, and so on. Then all the probabilities add up to 1. However, if we try to calculate the expectation of X, the result turns out to be infinity. In cases such as this when the expectation formula leads to a value of infinity, it is said that the expectation does not exist.

EXERCISES

1. List five quantities not yet mentioned in this book that can be represented by a discrete random variable (such as the number of slices cut from a pizza), and give their possible values.

2. In a given city in a given year, let X be the number of days that it rained and Y be the time (measured in seconds) that it rained. Which of these are discrete random variables? (Check the possible values.)

3. Let X be the number rolled by two fair dice. Determine $f_X(k)$, the density function of X.

4. Let X be a discrete random variable. If $\Pr(X < 7) = 1/3$, and $\Pr(X > 7) = 1/5$, then what is $f_X(7)$?

5. X is a discrete random variable. If $\Pr(X < 5) = 5/6$, and $\Pr(X \leq 5) = 11/12$, then what is $f_X(5)$?

6. Suppose X is a discrete random variable, and suppose that at every point the value of the density function for X is either 0 or 1/5. How many possible values are there for X?

7. Flip a fair coin a few times, and let X be the number of heads you get before your first tail. Determine the density function for X.

8. Let X be a random variable with the following density function:

$$\begin{aligned}
f(-1/2) &= 1/2 \\
f(1/2) &= 1/6 \\
f(2) &= 1/3 \\
f(k) &= 0 \text{ otherwise}
\end{aligned}$$

Make a graph of $F_X(a)$.

9. Let X be a discrete random variable such that $F(a)$ is constant for $a \geq 10$. What can you say about $f(k)$ if $k \geq 10$?

10. Show that $E(X + Y) = E(X) + E(Y)$ for any two random variables.

11. Show that Var(c) = 0 if c is a constant number.

12. Calculate Var(Y) when Y represents the number that appears when a single die is thrown.

13. Verify that Var($X + Y$) = Var(X) + Var(Y) if X and Y are the results of tossing two different dice.

14. Suppose you toss a die n times. Let X represent the total of all of the numbers that appear. What is $E(X)$? What is Var(X)?

15. You and a friend play the following game: You flip a fair coin. If it comes up heads, you pay $1. If it comes up tails, your friend rolls a die. If the result is an even number, you are paid $2; if the result is an odd number, then you pay your friend $3. What is your expected payoff—that is, the average amount you will win or lose?

16. You and a friend play the following game: You pay your friend $3 each turn and then flip a fair coin. If it's tails, your friend pays you $($2^n$)$, where n is the number of times you've flipped the coin, and the game ends. If it's heads, you have the choice of stopping or continuing. If you have m dollars to start with, and you play the game either until you win or until you have no money left, what will you win on the average?

17. Let X be a random variable that equals 1 on Sunday, 2 on Monday, and so on, up to 7 on Saturday. Calculate $E(X)$ and Var(X).

18. If X is a discrete random variable with this cumulative distribution:

$$F(a) = \begin{cases} 0 & a < -2 \\ .4 & -2 \le a < 4.5 \\ .85 & 4.5 \le a < 9 \\ 1 & 9 \le a \end{cases}$$

what is the density function for X?

19. Let X be a discrete random variable representing one half of the number of seconds that have elapsed since this book was purchased. What is the set of possible values for X?

20. Let X be a discrete random variable. If $f(0) = .5$, $f(1) = .2$, $f(2) = .1$, $f(3) = c$, and $f(x) = 0$ everywhere else, then what is the value of c?

21. Let X be a discrete random variable representing the average of the numbers rolled on two dice. What is the density function for X?

22. Let X be a discrete random variable representing the number of the television channel that you last watched. What are the possible values for X?

23. Let X be the numerical value of the card you draw from a 52-card deck. Suppose that kings, jacks, and queens are worth 10. Find $E(X)$.

24. What is the variance of a Bernoulli-trial variable when the probability of success is .6 and the probability of failure is .4?

25. Let X and Y be two random variables representing the numbers that come up on two dice. Let $Z = X + Y$. Calculate the density function of Z and then calculate $E(Z)$. Show that $E(Z) = E(X) + E(Y)$.

26. Show that $E(cX) = c\, E(X)$ for any random variable X and any constant c.

27. Show that $\text{Var}(cX) = c^2\, \text{Var}\,(X)$ for any random variable X and any constant c.

28. Show that $E(X + Y + Z) = E(X) + E(Y) + E(Z)$, for any three random variables X, Y, and Z.

29. Derive the density function for the random variable whose cumulative distribution function is illustrated in Figure 7–4.

☆ 30. Prove that any cumulative distribution function F is nondecreasing.

☆ 31. Prove that any cumulative distribution function F is piecewise constant.

☆ 32. Show that $E(X^2) \geq [E(X)]^2$ for any random variable X.

☆ 33. Let X be a discrete random variable with the following density function:

$$f(k) = c\, 2^{-k} \quad \text{if } k \text{ is a positive integer}$$
$$f(k) = 0 \quad\quad\ \text{if } k \text{ is not a positive integer}$$

What is the value of c?

CHAPTER 8

THE BINOMIAL DISTRIBUTION

Several types of random variable are so important and are so frequently used that they have been given special names. In the next two chapters we will discuss some important special types of discrete random variable.

The binomial distribution is a generalization of what we were doing in Chapter 1. Remember when we were flipping coins. We found that it is easy to show that the probability of getting four heads in four flips is $(1/2)^4$, since the probability of getting a head for each toss is $(1/2)$. Since there are four possible ways of getting three heads and one tail (HHHT, HHTH, HTHH, THHH) we said that the probability of this occurring is $4 \times (1/2)^4 = 1/4$. We said that the probability of getting i heads in five tosses is $\binom{5}{i} (1/2)^5$ and, in general, the probability of getting i heads from n tosses is $\binom{n}{i} \left(\frac{1}{2}\right)^n$.

All this works if we have a fair coin. However, what if the coin isn't fair? Let's assume that the probability of getting a head in one toss is p, and the probability of getting a tail is $(1 - p)$ $(0 \leq p \leq 1)$. (We'll also assume that we know for sure what p is.) Then the probability of getting n heads in n tosses is p^n.

The probability of getting first $n - 1$ heads and then one tail in n tosses is $p^{n-1}(1 - p)$, since the probability of getting the $n - 1$ heads in $n - 1$ tosses is p^{n-1}, and the probability of getting that one tail on the last toss is $(1 - p)$. This is also the probability of getting any single combination of $n - 1$ heads and 1 tail. (For example, it is also the probability of getting 1 tail first and then $n - 1$ straight heads.) Now, suppose we want to know the probability of getting $n - 1$ heads and 1 tail, but we don't care about whether the tail occurs first or last or anywhere in between. Since there are n possible places for the tail to appear, that means that the probability of getting 1 tail in n tosses is $n\,p^{n-1}(1 - p)$. We can also write this using the binomial coefficient, since $n = \binom{n}{1}$:

$$P(\text{getting 1 tail in } n \text{ tosses}) = \binom{n}{1}p^{n-1}(1-p).$$

Now, we want to generalize this to calculate the probability of obtaining i heads in n tosses. We can proceed in the same way as we did in the calculations for a fair coin, and the result is

$$P(\text{getting } i \text{ heads in } n \text{ tosses}) = \binom{n}{i}p^i(1-p)^{n-i}$$

This formula also works for the case of a fair coin; if you set $p = 1/2$ you get the same result that we had earlier.

In general, the distribution of a random variable X, representing the number of successes in n independent trials with each trial having a probability p of success, is called a *binomial distribution*. (In the example above, each "trial" consisted of a coin flip, and it was a "success" if the coin came up heads.) In a binomial distribution

$$P(X = i) = \binom{n}{i}p^i(1-p)^{n-i}$$

Figure 8–1 shows a graph of a density function for a sample binomial distribution. We will show later that as n becomes large, the binomial density function can be approximately represented by a bell-shaped curve known as the *normal* curve.

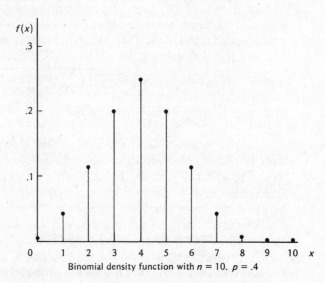

FIGURE 8–1

Binomial density function with $n = 10$. $p = .4$

Some cases where the binomial distribution can be applied are:

- the number of questions you can expect to guess right on a multiple-choice exam

- the number of casualty claims that an insurance company must pay

- the number of free throws that a basketball player will make during a season

The probabilities of the various outcomes must add up to 1 if the binomial distribution is a legitimate probability distribution. To prove that they do we can use a useful theorem called the binomial theorem, which states that

$$(x + y)^n = \sum_{i=0}^{n} \binom{n}{i} x^i y^{n-i}$$

Using this, with $x = p$ and $y = 1 - p$, gives

$$\sum_{i=0}^{n} P(x = i) = \sum_{i=0}^{n} \binom{n}{i} p^i (1 - p)^{n-i}$$
$$= (p + 1 - p)^n$$
$$= 1^n$$
$$= 1$$

Now we have to calculate the expectation value and the variance. Intuitively, we should expect that the expectation will be np. For example, if $p = 1/2$, then the expected number of successes is $n/2$.

We can show this by considering X to be the sum of n independent random variables $X_1, X_2, \cdots, X_n$. We'll say that $X_1 = 1$ if the first trial is a success and $X_1 = 0$ if the first trial is a failure. We'll make the same definitions for X_2, X_3, and so on. Then, $X = X_1 + X_2 + \cdots + X_n$ will be the number of successes in n trials. We have already discussed a random variable that will be 1 with probability p and 0 with probability $1 - p$ (see the end of Chapter 7). We found that the expectation of such a random variable is p and that its variance is $p(1 - p)$. Since X is the sum of n of these random variables, its expectation must be np. Since each X is independent of all of the others, the variance of X must be $np(1 - p)$. We can also show these results using the definitions of expectation and variance.

Here are some examples of applications of the binomial distribution:

EXAMPLE   Suppose you are taking a 20-question multiple choice exam. Each question has four possible answers, so the probability is .25 that you can answer a question correctly by guessing. What is the probability that you can get at least 10 questions right by pure guessing?

To solve this problem, we need to calculate the probabilities for a binomial distribution with $n = 20$ and $p = .25$:

k	$Pr(X = k)$
0	.003
1	.021
2	.066
3	.133
4	.189
5	.202
6	.168
7	.112
8	.060
9	.027
10	.009
11	.003

The remaining probabilities are all less than .001; but if we add them all up we find that your chance of getting at least ten right is .01386. So it would seem in this case that studying is a better strategy than random guessing. (Of course, you can look at the bright side— there is only a 9 percent probability that you will get less than 3 answers correct.)

EXAMPLE   Suppose you have three red sweaters and two blue sweaters in a drawer. Every day you randomly pull out one sweater (and you put it back at the end of the day). If X is the number of red sweaters you select during a week, then X has a binomial distribution with parameters $n = 7$ and $p = .6$. We can calculate the probabilities:

k	$Pr(X = k)$
0	.001
1	.017
2	.077
3	.193
4	.290
5	.261
6	.130
7	.027

EXERCISES

1. Suppose that 1,000 meteorites hit the earth each year. What is the probability that the town of Wethersfield, Connecticut will be struck by two meteorites in 11 years? (See Chapter 4, Exercise 11.)

2. What is the probability of getting three primes in five rolls of a die?

3. In tossing a fair coin, what is the probability of getting at least four heads in five tosses?

4. Pennsylvania has a daily lottery. A three-digit number is chosen every night. What is the probability of getting a number less than 100 more than five times in one week?

5. You're hunting Moby Dick. Each day you send out one small boat with harpooners from your ship. (You never catch Moby Dick, just because Moby Dick *is* Moby Dick.) The probability is 2/3 that the small boat will be sunk on any particular day. You plan to hunt Moby Dick for four days. What is the probability that you will lose three or more small boats?

6. Assume that you've been given a 100-question true/false exam on a subject that you know nothing about. If you guess randomly, what is the probability of getting at least 75 answers correct?

7. How many times must you toss a fair coin for the probability to be greater than 1/2 that you will get two heads?

8. Assume that 10 percent of the population is left-handed. If three people are chosen at random, what is the probability that at least one will be left-handed?

9. What is the probability that two of the next three Presidents of the United States will have been born on a Sunday?

10. Assume that 2/5 of the population have O+ blood type. If you randomly choose six people, what is the probability that four of them are O+?

11. Suppose X_1 has a binomial distribution with parameters n_1 and p, and X_2 has a binomial distribution with parameters n_2 and p. Show that $X_1 + X_2$ has a binomial distribution with parameters $(n_1 + n_2)$ and p.

12. Assume that 45 percent of the Smiths in the world are women. If you randomly run into three Smith siblings, what is the probability that at least two are sisters?

13. Suppose you are running an insurance company. You have N customers. There is a probability $p = .05$ that any particular customer will file a claim in a year, in which case you have to pay $C = \$1,000$. You collect a premium of $50 per year from each customer.

    (a) What is the expected value for your profits each year?

    (b) Suppose you have $N = 20$ customers. What is the probability that your profits will be $2,000? What is the probability they will be $1,000? 0? $-$1,000? $-$2,000? $-$3,000?

    (c) Repeat the above calculations for $N = 50$ and $N = 100$.

14. Consider the total profits of the insurance company in the preceding question over a ten-year period. What is the expected value of total profit? Calculate the probability that the total profit will equal these values: $2,000, $1,000, 0, −$1,000, −$2,000, −$3,000, for three different values of N: $N = 20$, $N = 50$, $N = 100$.

15. Suppose you are running an airline company. You know that there is a probability $p = .07$ that a customer with a reservation will not show up for a particular flight. The plane can hold 200 people. You would like the plane to be full, but you know that if you take only 200 reservations there will probably be some empty seats. So you decide to overbook—that is, take more reservations than you have room for, and then hope that fewer than 201 people will show up. Suppose you accept R reservations. Let X be the number of people who actually show up at the plane. What should R be so that the chance of an overflow crowd is less than 5 percent?

☐ 16. Write a program that reads in n and p, and then prints a table showing the probability that a binomial random variable with parameters n and p will equal i, for values of i from 1 to n.

☐ 17. Write a program similar to the previous exercise except that it prints a table showing the cumulative distribution function for the binomial random variable.

☆ 18. Calculate the mean and the variance of a binomial random variable using the binomial density function.

CHAPTER 9

OTHER DISCRETE DISTRIBUTIONS

There are several other important special types of discrete random-variable distribution.

The Poisson Distribution

Let X be the number of telephone calls that arrive at a particular office in an hour. X is a random variable, and it turns out that its density function often looks like this:

$$f(k) = e^{-\lambda} \frac{\lambda^k}{k!} \qquad (k = 0, 1, 2, 3, \ldots)$$

A random variable with this distribution is called a *Poisson random variable.* (λ is the Greek letter lambda, which is used as the parameter for the Poisson distribution.) As an example, suppose a study has determined that the number of phone calls arriving at the office every hour can be represented by a Poisson random variable with parameter $\lambda = 5$. Then we can calculate the probabilities for X:

k	$\Pr(X = k)$ (probability of getting exactly k phone calls)
0	.006
1	.033
2	.084
3	.140
4	.175
5	.175
6	.146
7	.104
8	.065
9	.036
10	.018
11	.008
12	.003

Figure 9–1 shows a graph of a Poisson density function.

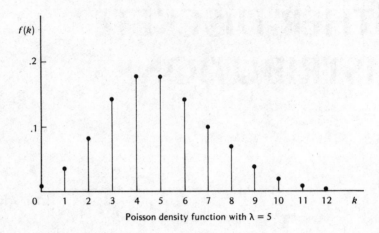

FIGURE 9–1

Poisson density function with $\lambda = 5$

Note that, in theory, there is an infinite number of possible values for X, but the probability that X will equal k becomes very small as k becomes large.

Another important use of the Poisson distribution is as an approximation for the binomial distribution. Suppose that we have a binomial distribution such that n is very large and np is moderate (not too large and not too small.) For example, suppose we have 500 students each of whom has a probability of .00002 of cutting a little finger on his or her test paper during finals. The calculation of the probability of i "successes" using the binomial density function becomes unmanageable. If we let $\lambda = np$, then the binomial density function can be approximated by the Poisson distribution:

$$P(X = i) = e^{-\lambda}\frac{\lambda^i}{i!}$$

We need to show that this distribution really is a good approximation to the binomial distribution as n becomes large, and we also need to prove that it is a legitimate probability distribution with all of the probabilities adding up to 1. (See Exercises 24 and 25.)

In the example given above, $\lambda = np = 500 \times (.00002) = .01$, so the probability of two people getting paper cuts from their finals is

$$e^{-.01}(.01)^2(1/2) = 4.95 \times 10^{-5}$$

Other examples where a Poisson distribution is applicable include:

- the number of novae in our galaxy in a given decade

- the number of movies to gross over 25 million dollars in a year

- the number of Ph.D. students who don't finish their dissertations on time

- the number of people who have bought this book who bought it in New York City

The expectation value of a random variable with a Poisson distribution can be found in this way:

$$E(X) = \sum_{i=0}^{\infty} i e^{-\lambda} \frac{\lambda^i}{i!}$$

$$= \sum_{i=1}^{\infty} e^{-\lambda} i \frac{\lambda^i}{i!}$$

$$= \sum_{i=1}^{\infty} e^{-\lambda} \frac{\lambda^i}{(i-1)!}$$

Let $j = i - 1$. Then

$$E(X) = \sum_{j=0}^{\infty} e^{-\lambda} \frac{\lambda^{j+1}}{j!}$$

$$= \lambda \sum_{j=0}^{\infty} e^{-\lambda} \frac{\lambda^j}{j!}$$

$$= \lambda$$

since the probabilities sum to 1. This agrees with our intuition, if we interpret λ as np. The variance can be found as follows:

$$E(X^2) = \sum_{i=0}^{\infty} i^2 e^{-\lambda} \frac{\lambda^i}{i!}$$

$$= \sum_{i=0}^{\infty} (i^2 - i) e^{-\lambda} \frac{\lambda^i}{i!} + \sum_{i=0}^{\infty} i e^{-\lambda} \frac{\lambda^i}{i!}$$

The second sum equals λ, as we have just shown above. Now:

$$\sum_{i=0}^{\infty} (i^2 - i) e^{-\lambda} \frac{\lambda^i}{i!} = \sum_{i=2}^{\infty} i(i-1) e^{-\lambda} \frac{\lambda^i}{i!}$$

$$= \sum_{i=2}^{\infty} e^{-\lambda} \frac{\lambda^i}{(i-2)!}$$

Let $j = i - 2$. Then

$$\sum_{i=2}^{\infty} e^{-\lambda} \frac{\lambda^i}{(i-2)!} = \sum_{j=0}^{\infty} e^{-\lambda} \frac{\lambda^{j+2}}{j!}$$

$$= \lambda^2$$

again since the probabilities sum to 1. Thus

$$E(X^2) = \lambda^2 + \lambda$$

$$\text{Var}(X) = (\lambda^2 + \lambda) - \lambda^2 = \lambda$$

Therefore, the variance is λ. The Poisson distribution has the very peculiar property that its expectation is equal to its variance.

The Geometric and Negative Binomial Distributions

Suppose that we still have the same unfair coin we had when we discussed the binomial distribution. In that case, we fixed the number of tosses and counted the number of heads that resulted. This time we're going to fix the number of heads that we want and then we're going to count the number of tosses until we get that number of heads. More precisely, we want to know what the probability is that it will take n tosses to get i heads (assuming again that the probability of getting a head on one toss is p).

First, note that the last toss must be a head. Otherwise, we would have had i heads already so we wouldn't have had to make that last toss. Then there must be $i - 1$ heads in the first $n - 1$ tosses, in any combination. The probability of this happening can be found from the binomial distribution formula

$$\binom{n-1}{i-1} p^{i-1} (1-p)^{n-i}$$

The probability of getting i heads in the n tosses is exactly p times this last expression (since that is the probability that toss number n will be a head). Therefore, this probability is

$$\binom{n-1}{i-1} p^{i} (1-p)^{n-i}$$

If $i = 1$, this expression reduces to

$$p(1-p)^{n-1}$$

In general, a random variable X representing the number of independent trials necessary to obtain i successes, where each trial has a probability p $(p > 0)$ of success, is said to have a *negative binomial distribution*. The corresponding probability is

$$P(X = n) = \binom{n-1}{i-1} p^{i}(1-p)^{n-i}$$

If $i = 1$, the distribution is called a *geometric distribution*. The proof that the sum of the probabilities for a geometric distribution is 1 is very simple. Since

$$\sum_{i=0}^{\infty} x^i = \frac{1}{1-x} \qquad \text{for } |x| < 1,$$

$$\sum_{n=1}^{\infty} p(1-p)^{n-1} = p \sum_{n=1}^{\infty} (1-p)^{n-1}$$

$$= p \left(\frac{1}{1-(1-p)} \right)$$

$$= \frac{p}{p}$$

$$= 1$$

The expectation of a negative binomial random variable is i/p. For example, if the probability of success is 1/3, then you can expect to make 30 attempts before attaining 10 successes. The variance of a negative binomial random variable is $i(1-p)/p^2$. For the geometric distribution, the mean is $1/p$ and the variance is $(1-p)/p^2$.

The Hypergeometric Distribution

Suppose you are given a box containing 10 pieces of candy, all of which look alike on the outside. Suppose further that you know that 8 of the pieces are marshmallow-filled (which you love) and 2 contain almonds (which you despise). If you take 5 pieces out of the box, what is the probability that you will get exactly 3 marshmallow-filled pieces?

This is a case of the probability being the number of "successes" divided by the number of possible outcomes. First, we need to know the total number of ways of picking the 5 pieces from the box of 10. We can use the usual formula for this:

$$\binom{10}{5} = \frac{10!}{5!\,5!} = 252$$

Now we need to calculate how many of these possibilities have exactly 3 marshmallow-filled pieces. Since there are 8 possible marshmallow-filled candies to choose from, there are $\binom{8}{3}$ ways of picking the 3 marshmallow candies. We need to multiply this by the number of possible ways of picking the two almond-flavored candies from the two almond candies in the box, and this will be just $\binom{2}{2}$ (which is, of course, equal to 1).

Therefore, the probability of picking exactly 3 marshmallow candies is

$$\frac{\binom{8}{3}\binom{2}{2}}{\binom{10}{5}} = \frac{56}{252} = \frac{2}{9}$$

Let's generalize. The 10 pieces of candy become N objects. The 8 marshmallow candies become the M objects in the desired state, with the almond candies becoming the $N - M$ objects in the undesired state. (Note that $M < N$). The 5 pieces that you take become n trials (selections without replacement from the N objects.) The 3 pieces of marshmallow candy become the i desired objects selected. (Note that $i < M$, the total number of desired objects, and that $i < n$, the total number of objects selected.) Letting X be the random variable standing for the number of desired objects selected, we have

$$\Pr(X = i) = \frac{\binom{M}{i}\binom{N-M}{n-i}}{\binom{N}{n}}$$

(for $0 \le i \le n$, and $i \le M$; $\Pr(X = i) = 0$ otherwise). X is said to have the *hypergeometric distribution* with parameters n, N, and M.

Examples of hypergeometric distributions include:

- the number of defective merchandise items in a random sample of a large shipment

- the number of persons you will meet in your lifetime with the name Fred

- the number of pennies drawn out of a jar filled with M pennies and $(N - M)$ nickels. If only one draw is made, then $n = 1$, and the probability of getting a penny is M/N, as is to be expected.

Another important application comes when you are conducting an opinion poll, such as the Gallup survey. The people who are asked questions during the poll are analogous to the candies that are chosen from the box, and the entire population of people is analogous to the whole box of candies. When we conduct an opinion poll we need to know how likely it is that the proportion of people with a particular opinion in the sample is the same as the proportion of people with that opinion in the population. We will discuss this question in Chapter 18.

Since the probability of picking the kind of object you want in any one pick is M/N, it follows that in n picks you would expect to get nM/N of the right kind of object. The expectation of a hypergeometric random variable does turn out to be nM/N, which agrees with our intuition. The variance of a hypergeometric random variable is

$$n\left(\frac{M}{N}\right)\left(1 - \frac{M}{N}\right)\left(\frac{N-n}{N-1}\right)$$

Note that $(N - n)/(N - 1)$ can be written $(1 - n/N)/(1 - 1/N)$. This expression becomes about equal to 1 when N becomes very large compared to n. That means that the variance of the hypergeometric random variable becomes

$$n\left(\frac{M}{N}\right)\left(1 - \frac{M}{N}\right)$$

This formula should look a bit familiar. Suppose we draw n candies from the box, only this time we put each candy back after we draw it. We'll call it a success if we draw the kind of candy we want. The probability of success is therefore M/N. If X is the number of successes in the n draws, we know that X has a binomial distribution with parameters N and M/N, and we know that its variance is $n\,(M/N)\,(1 - M/N)$. That is the same as the variance of the hypergeometric distribution when N is very large. This fact illustrates the difference between the two distributions. With the binomial distribution, each draw is independent of the others, because you always put the candy you draw back in the box. With the hypergeometric distribution, you're not putting the candy back, so each draw is not independent of the others. The probability of success of each draw depends on how many of each type of candy are left in the box, which depends in turn on what candies you removed in the preceding draws. However, if the number of candies in the box is very, very large, then removing a few candies is not going to change the probabilities for future draws very much. In that case it doesn't make too much difference whether you draw the candies with replacement (and use the binomial distribution) or draw the candies without replacement (and use the hypergeometric distribution).

EXERCISES

1. Calculate the mean and variance of a hypergeometric random variable with parameters $N = 1,000$, $M = 300$, and $n = 25$.

2. Calculate the mean and variance of a negative binomial random variable with parameters $p = 1/3$ and $i = 25$.

3. Calculate the mean and variance of a negative binomial random variable with parameters $p = 1/4$, $i = 16$.

4. Suppose that you pull 15 balls out of a jar containing 30 white balls and 15 black balls. How many white balls would you expect to pull out on the average?

5. Let X be a random variable representing the number of times that you have to roll two dice until you get ten 11's. Calculate the mean and variance of X.

6. Let X be a random variable representing the number of times the word "platypus" is said on a given day. Assume X has a Poisson distribution with parameter $\lambda = 1/2$. What is $\Pr(X > 1)$?

7. What is the maximum value for $\Pr(X = n)$ if X is a Poisson random variable with parameter $\lambda > 0$?

8. If X is a Poisson random variable with parameter $\lambda = 10$, what is $\Pr(1 \le X \le 3)$?

9. If X is a geometric random variable with parameter $p = 1/3$, what is $\Pr(X \leq 4)$?

10. If X is the same as in the preceding problem, what is the smallest n such that $\Pr(X \leq n) \geq 1/2$?

11. Fastburgers, Inc. starts to give away free soft drinks in the following fashion. With each purchase it gives you a card containing an X or an O (under ink that has to be rubbed off, so that the card's contents aren't visible), and it gives a small soft drink for five cards containing X's. If the probability of getting an X on a given card is 1/3, what is the probability of getting your fifth X on your tenth card?

12. Your cruel building superintendent refuses to turn on the heat in your building until it has snowed three times this winter. If the probability that it will snow on a given winter day is 1/5, what is the probability that your building superintendent won't turn the heat on until the 13th day of winter?

13. Given that 20 books in a shipment of 200 books (for a bookstore) contain misprints, and you buy three of them, what is the probability that one of your books will contain a misprint?

14. You're dressing in the dark because of a power failure. You have two black socks and six red socks in a drawer. You pull out three. What is the probability that two are black?

15. Let X be a Poisson random variable with parameter $\lambda = 3$, representing the number of people who use a given dictionary in a given library on a given day. If $F(a)$ is the cumulative distribution function, what is $F(4)$?

16. Suppose that the probability is 1/3 that it will rain on a given day in your neighborhood. What is the probability that it will be four days before it rains next?

17. Suppose that you want to collect eight toy boats (all the same kind) which are included in one out of every three Sweet-Tooth cereal boxes. What is the probability that you'll find the last one in your 20th cereal box?

18. A dictionary has 300 pages. What is the probability that if you look up five words at random, two of them will be on pages with page numbers ending in zero? (Assume that the two words you look up are on different pages.)

19. In the Gobbler, a new video game, an alien monster roams the screen intending to eat your character. You're armed with a laser pistol. If you have a one out of twelve chance of hitting the monster if you fire randomly, what is the probability that it will take you 20 shots to hit the monster?

☐ **20.** Write a computer program that prints a table of the Poisson density function and cumulative distribution function.

☐ **21.** Write a computer program that reads in values of N, M, and n, and then prints a table of hypergeometric probabilities. Use a subroutine to calculate the binomial coefficients, and then call that subroutine three times.

☐ **22.** Write a new program to perform hypergeometric calculations that requires fewer calculations than the program in the preceding exercise.

☐ **23.** Write an even more efficient program to calculate a hypergeometric table by finding an expression for $f(k + 1)/f(k)$, when f is the hypergeometric density function.

☆ **24.** Show that all of the probabilities for the Poisson distribution add up to 1.

☆ **25.** Show that the binomial density function becomes approximately the same as the Poisson distribution with $\lambda = np$ as n becomes very large.

☆ **26.** Derive the formula for the mean of a hypergeometric random variable.

☆ **27.** Derive the formulas for the mean and variance of a negative binomial random variable.

CHAPTER 10

CONTINUOUS RANDOM VARIABLES

Let us suppose that we randomly select a name from the phone book and then measure the height of the person selected. If H is the height in feet of the person, we can regard H as a random variable. However, it is different from the other random variables that we have done up to now. Suppose we try to list all of the possible values for H. There are clearly some values that are not possible. For example, H can never be less than 1/4 or greater than 9. However, we'll find that we can't list all of the possible values. The height might be 5 feet, or it might be 5.1 feet, or 5.00001 feet, or 5.000000001 feet. In fact, assuming that we can measure the height with perfect accuracy (oh, well, this is theory—not the real world) there is an infinite number of possible values for the height. A discrete random variable cannot be used in a case like this where the result can be any number in a particular range. Instead, we need to use a *continuous random variable.*

Examples of continuous random variables include:

- the height above the floor at the point where a dart hits a dart board

- the length of time until a light bulb burns out

- the length of time until a radioactive atom decays

- the length of the life of a person

Discrete random variables are easier to understand intuitively. However, continuous random variables are usually easier to handle mathematically. If a discrete distribution has many possible values that are close together, then it can usually be approximated by a continuous distribution.

Continuous Cumulative Distribution Functions

Now we have to figure out how to describe the behavior of continuous random variables. There are many similarities between discrete random variables and continuous random variables, but there are some important differences. We can estimate the probability that the person we select will have height less than 6 feet. Or we could calculate the probability that the person will have a height greater than 50 feet (which is, of course, zero). Therefore we can define a cumulative distribution function for a continuous random variable, just the same as we did for a discrete random variable. We'll use a capital letter, such as F, to stand for a cumulative distribution function, so we can make the definition:

$$F(a) = \Pr(X \le a)$$

where X is the random variable we are discussing.

A continuous cumulative distribution function satisfies the same requirements that we found for a discrete cumulative distribution function:

(1) $F(a)$ is always between 0 and 1.
(2) As a becomes very large, $F(a)$ approaches 1.
(3) As a becomes very small (approaches minus infinity), $F(a)$ approaches 0.
(4) $F(a)$ is never decreasing.

Two important practical properties are:

If we want to find the probability that X will be greater than a particular value a, we can use the formula

$$\Pr(X > a) = 1 - \Pr(X < a) = 1 - F(a)$$

If we want to find the probability that X will be between two particular values b and c, we can use the formula

$$\Pr(b < X < c) = F(c) - F(b)$$

Figure 10–1 shows a cumulative distribution function for the heights of a group of people.

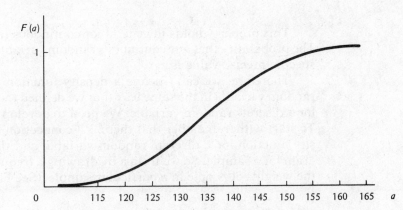

FIGURE 10–1

One example of a continuous random variable is a uniform random variable. That is a random variable that is equally likely to take on any value within a particular interval. For example, let's consider the random variable Y that has an equal chance of taking any value between 0 and 3. Then the probability that Y will be less than 1 is 1/3, the probability that Y will be between 1 and $1\frac{1}{2}$ is 1/6, and so on. If we make a graph of the cumulative distribution function for Y, it looks like the function shown in Figure 10–2.

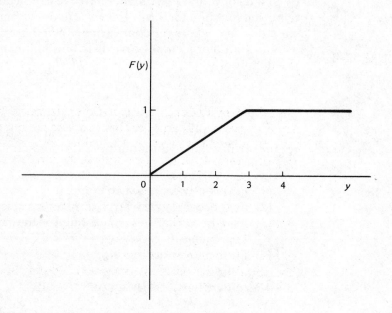

FIGURE 10–2

Continuous Probability Density Functions

Now, let's find out the probability that Y will be exactly equal to 2. Any number from 0 to 3 has an equal chance of being selected, so if we let N be the number of numbers from 0 to 3, then $\Pr(Y = 2) = 1/N$. However, there is an infinite number of numbers between 0 and 3 (for example, 0.01, 0.011, 0.0111, 0.01111, and so on). This means that

$$\Pr(Y = 2) = \frac{1}{\infty} = 0$$

This property holds in general for continuous random variables: The probability that *any* continuous random variable will take on *any* specific precise value is zero!

Therefore, we can't define a density function for a continuous random variable in the same way that we defined the density function for a discrete random variable. We need to develop a new approach. To start with, remember that there is a connection between the density function for a discrete random variable and the frequency diagram for a sample. So we'll start by drawing a frequency diagram for the weights of people in a particular sample. (See Figure 10–3.) Note

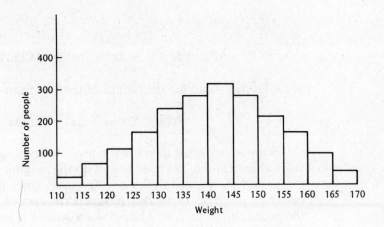

FIGURE 10–3

that the height of each bar is not the number of people whose weight equals a particular amount. Instead, it is the number of people whose weight is between two specified values. For example, the height of the bar between 140 and 145 pounds is the number of people in the sample whose weights are between 140 and 145. We'll call the width of each bar Δx. (In this case, $\Delta x = 5$.)

We can, by analogy, draw an approximate density function such that the height of the function in any given interval is equal to the probability that the random variable will have a value within that interval. It turns out to be more convenient to make the height of each bar equal to the probability of being in that interval divided by Δx, the width of the bar. (See Figure 10–4.)

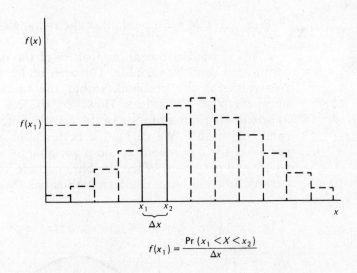

$$f(x_1) = \frac{\Pr(x_1 < X < x_2)}{\Delta x}$$

FIGURE 10–4

Then:

$$(\text{height of a bar between } a \text{ and } a + \Delta x) = \frac{\Pr(a < X < a + \Delta x)}{\Delta x}$$

And therefore,

$$\Pr(a < X < a + \Delta x) = (\text{height of bar}) \times \Delta x$$

We'll let $f(a)$ stand for the height of the bar from a to $a + \Delta x$, so

$$\Pr(a < X < a + \Delta x) = f(a)\,\Delta x$$

Suppose we need to know the probability that X will be between two values a and b. We need to add up the heights of all the bars from a to b and then multiply by Δx. However, since $f(x)$ is the height of each bar and Δx is the width, $f(x)\,\Delta x$ is the area of the bar. Therefore, the probability that X will be between a and b is just equal to the area of all of the bars between a and b. (See Figure 10–5.)

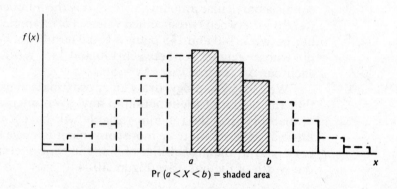

FIGURE 10–5

Pr $(a < X < b)$ = shaded area

$$\Pr(a < X < b) = (\text{area of all of the rectangles between } a \text{ and } b)$$

This is the basic defining feature of the density function for a continuous random variable: The area under the function between two values is the probability that the random variable will be between those two values. However, the bar diagram is only an approximate representation of the density function for a continuous random variable. We can get a better approximation of the true nature of the continuous random variable by making the bars narrower and narrower. When the bars become very, very narrow, the density function looks like a smooth curve. (See Figure 10–6.)

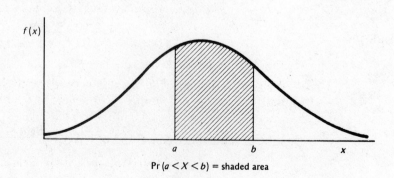

FIGURE 10–6

Pr $(a < X < b)$ = shaded area

We will make this definition: The function $f(x)$ is a density function for the random variable X if it satisfies the property that the area under the curve $y = f(x)$, to the left of the line $x = b$, to the right of the line $x = a$, and above the x axis, is equal to $\Pr(a < X < b)$. (Remember that capital letters represent random variables and small letters represent ordinary variables.)

It would help to be able to write this area expression in a shorter fashion, so we will just write

$$\text{Area } f(x) \text{ from } a \text{ to } b$$

to mean "the area under the curve $f(x)$ between a and b."

We know that if $F(x)$ is the cumulative distribution function, then

$$\text{Area } f(x) \text{ from } a \text{ to } b = \Pr(a < X < b) = F(b) - F(a)$$

Now, suppose we look at the interval from minus infinity to plus infinity. We know that $F(+\infty) - F(-\infty) = \Pr(-\infty < X < \infty) = 1$, since the value of X must be somewhere between $-\infty$ and $+\infty$. (It doesn't have any other choice.) This means that

$$\text{Area } f(x) \text{ from } -\infty \text{ to } +\infty = 1$$

In other words, the total area under the function $f(x)$ must be equal to 1. If $f(x)$ doesn't have this property, then it can't be a legitimate probability density function. We can show that this condition is met for the density function of the uniform variable Y. (See Figure 10–7.)

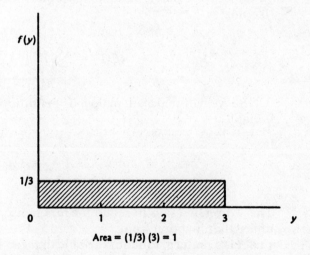

FIGURE 10–7

Area = (1/3) (3) = 1

We would like an even shorter way to write the area under the function $f(x)$ between a and b. We'll symbolize area with a squiggle, like this:

$$\text{Area } f(x) \text{ from } a \text{ to } b = \int_a^b f(x)\, dx$$

In this notation, the function whose area is to be found [in this case $f(x)$] is placed in the middle, surrounded by the squiggle on the left and the dx on the right. The left-hand limit of the area is written at the bottom of the squiggle, and the right-hand limit is written at the top of the squiggle.

Therefore, by definition, these four quantities are all equal:

area $f(x)$ from a to b

$$\int_a^b f(x)\, dx$$

$$F(b) - F(a)$$

$$\Pr(a < X < b)$$

Of course, if you know calculus, you will realize that $\int$ is the symbol for an *integral*, and you will know how to calculate explicit values for the area if you are given a specific form for the function $f(x)$. However, many of the density functions that we use in probability (such as the normal density function) cannot be integrated by any easy method, so in that respect the people who know calculus don't have much of an unfair advantage over the people who don't. They have to look up the values in the tables just like everybody else.

Expectation and Variance

We would like to be able to calculate the expectation and variance for a continuous random variable, just as we did for a discrete random variable. For discrete random variables, we defined the expectation like this:

$$E(Y) = \sum_{i=1}^{n} Y_i\, f(y_i)$$

So we will make an analogous definition for continuous random variables:

$$E(X) = \int_{-\infty}^{\infty} x\, f(x)\, dx$$

This expression says to set up the function $x \times f(x)$, then find the area under that function from $x = -\infty$ to $x = +\infty$. For example, let's say that X is a uniform random variable that can have any value from 0 to 5. Then $f(x) = 1/5$ if $0 < x < 5$ and $f(x) = 0$ everywhere else. So we need to find the area under the function $x\, f(x) = x/5$ from $x = 0$ to $x = 5$. If we make a graph of that function, we can see that it is just a triangle. (See Figure 10–8).

The area of the triangle is $(1/2)(5)(1) = 2\frac{1}{2}$, so $E(X) = 2\frac{1}{2}$. Of course, you could have figured that out on your own. In general, the expec-

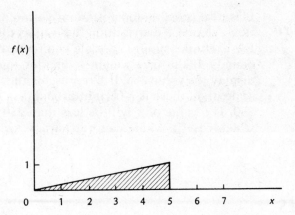

FIGURE 10–8

tation of any uniform random variable will be the point halfway between the two boundaries.

You'll note that the function $x\,f(x)$ is negative whenever x is negative. So how do you calculate the area? What you do is just subtract the total area enclosed by the curve below the horizontal axis from its total area above the axis. For example, suppose T is a uniform continuous random variable with possible values between -1 and 5. Then the value of $f(t)$ is 1/6 if t is between -1 and 5, and 0 otherwise. The function $t\,f(t)$ is shown in Figure 10–9. The total positive area is

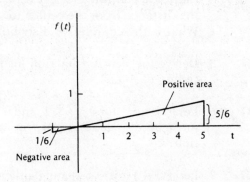

FIGURE 10–9

25/12 and the total negative area is 1/12. If you subtract, you can see that $E(T) = 24/12 = 2$.

If you know calculus, then you're used to calculating these types of integrals. If not, and you trust us, then you can just take our word when we tell you what the expectation of a continuous random variable is.

The variance of a continuous random variable is defined in exactly the same way as is the variance of a discrete random variable:

$$\text{Var}(X) = E\{[X - E(X)]^2\} = E(X^2) - [E(X)]^2$$

For example, the variance of the uniform random variable which can be between 0 and 3 is 9/12.

NOTE TO CHAPTER 10

It is also possible for a random variable to have a mixed distribution—that is, a distribution that is part discrete and part continuous. For example, suppose a scale can represent only weights up to 250 pounds. If the true weight is greater than 250, then the scale will display the value 250. If X represents the weight as measured by this scale, then there is a certain probability p that X will exactly equal 250. The value of X will be less than 250 with probability $1 - p$, in which case its value can be characterized by a continuous density function.

EXERCISES

1. Given a person chosen at random, which of the following data constitute continuous random variables: height, social security number, weight, temperature?

2. Under what circumstances can the cumulative distribution function of a continuous random variable have a maximum? a minimum?

3. $f(x) = 1/2$ when $-1 \leq x \leq 1$ and 0 otherwise. Draw a graph of $F(a)$.

4. Suppose that you are throwing a dart at a circular dart board of radius 30 centimeters. Let R be a random variable representing the distance from the center to the point where the dart strikes. What is the cumulative distribution function for R?

☆ 5. Derive the density function for the random variable in the preceding problem.

☆ 6. Let $f(x) = c x^n$ for $0 < x < 1$, and 0 otherwise. (Assume $n > 0$.) What must be the value of c if f is to be a probability density function?

☆ 7. Let $f(x) = 1/x$ if $x \geq 1$, and 0 otherwise. What is $F(a)$ for $a = 0$, $a = 1/2$, and $a = 10$?

☆ 8. If $F(a) = 1 - e^{-a}$ if $a \geq 0$, and 0 otherwise, and $f(0) = 0$, what is $f(x)$?

☆ 9. Why can't the function

$$
\begin{aligned}
g(a) &= 0 && \text{if } a \leq 0 \\
&= a && \text{if } 0 \leq a \leq 2 \\
&= 4 - a && \text{if } 2 \leq a \leq 3 \\
&= 1 && \text{if } a \geq 3
\end{aligned}
$$

be a cumulative distribution function?

☆ **10.** If $f(x) = (1/\pi)[1/(1 + x^2)]$, what is $\Pr(-1 \le X \le 1)$?

☆ **11.** Let $f(x) = |\sin x|$ if $-\pi/3 \le X \le \pi/3$, and 0 otherwise. What is $F(a)$?

☆ **12.** If $f(x) = (3/4)(1 - x^2)$ if $-1 \le x \le 1$, and 0 otherwise, what is $F(x)$?

☆ **13.** Calculate the variance of the random variable Y which is a uniform random variable between 0 and 3.

☆ **14.** Calculate the variance of the random variable that has a uniform distribution between two fixed numbers a and b.

☆ **15.** If $f(x)$ is the density function for X, and if $f(c - x) = f(c + x)$ for all values of x, then X is said to be *symmetric* about the point $x = c$. Show that $E(X) = c$.

☆ **16.** If $F(x)$ is the cumulative distribution function of X, and if X is symmetric about c, then show that $F(c - x) = 1 - F(c + x)$.

☆ **17.** Let X be a continual random variable with density function $f(x) = 2e^{-x}$ if $x \ge a$. What is a?

☆ **18.** Let X be a continuous random variable with density function $f(x) = x^{-2}$ if $x > 1$. What is $\Pr(5 < X < 6)$?

☆ **19.** Let X be a continuous random variable with density function $f(x) = 0$ if $x < 0$, $f(x) = x$ if $0 < x < 1$, and $f(x) = x^{-3}$ if $x \ge 1$. What is the cumulative distribution function?

☆ **20.** Let X be a continuous random variable with cumulative distribution function $F(a) = 0$ if $a \le -1$, $F(a) = 1/2 (a + 1)(a + 2)$ if $-1 < a \le 0$, and $F(a) = 1$ if $a > 0$. What is the density function?

☆ **21.** Let X be a continuous random variable with cumulative distribution function $F(a) = 0$ if $a \le 0$, $F(a) = a$ if $0 < a \le 1$, and $F(a) = 1$ if $1 \le a$. Where is $f(x)$ nonzero?

22. Suppose that a certain train always pulls into a certain station between 1 P.M. and 1:05 P.M. Let X be a random variable representing the number of minutes after 1 P.M. that the train arrives. Suppose that the density function of X is equal to c times the number of seconds after noon that the train would arrive if $X = x$. What is the value of c? What is the cumulative distribution function for X?

CHAPTER 11

THE NORMAL DISTRIBUTION

The Normal Density Function

Suppose you make a graph of the probabilities of the numbers of heads you will expect to see if you repeatedly flip a coin 15 times. (See Figure 11-1.) Or suppose you select 1,000 people off the street and make a frequency diagram of their heights. (Figure 11-2.)

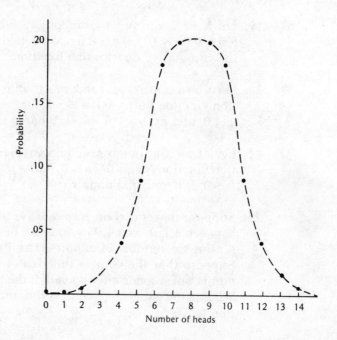

FIGURE 11–1

These graphs look similar. Their bell-shaped curve is the most important density function in probability and statistics. A random variable whose density function looks like this is called a *normal* ran-

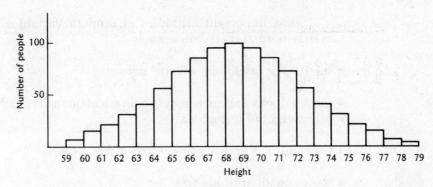

FIGURE 11–2

dom variable. Let's see if we can make up a mathematical function that has this kind of shape. The function $f(x) = e^{-(1/2)x^2}$ looks right. (See Figure 11-3.) We could use any positive number as the base of this

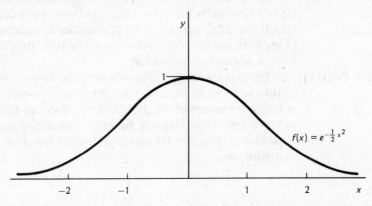

$$f(x) = e^{-\frac{1}{2}x^2}$$

FIGURE 11–3

function, but it is most convenient to use the special number symbolized by the letter e. The value of e is about 2.71828. This function is very close to the normal probability curve, but we need to make a couple of adjustments. First, we want to be able to adjust the peak and shape of the distribution, so we need to put in two parameters (called μ and σ):

$$f(x) = e^{-1/2\left(\frac{x-\mu}{\sigma}\right)^2}$$

This function can be a true probability function only if the area under it is 1. The area under the function turns out to be $\sqrt{2\pi}\ \sigma$ (see Exercise 28). Pi (π) is a Greek letter used to stand for a special number about equal to 3.14159. So we need to divide by $\sqrt{2\pi}\ \sigma$ to make the area equal to 1. Therefore, the density function for a normal random variable is defined as follows:

$$f(x) = \frac{1}{\sqrt{2\pi}\ \sigma}\ e^{-1/2\left(\frac{x-\mu}{\sigma}\right)^2}$$

Note that it is a continuous, rather than a discrete, distribution. The normal distribution is important both because we'll be interested in a lot of random variables that have normal distributions and because the normal distribution can be used as an approximation for many other distributions, such as the binomial distribution.

Some important examples of random variables with approximately normal distributions are:

- the IQ of a randomly selected person

- the result of a measurement of a physical quantity, such as the molecular weight of a chemical

- the total that appears if you toss many dice

- scores on an aptitude test

- the velocities of molecules in a gas

The normal density function often applies to quantities in situations where extreme values are less likely to occur. Also, we will show that if you add together a large number of independent random variables with identical distributions, the resulting random variable will have a normal distribution.

The parameter μ defines where the center, or peak, of the distribution will be. In fact, as you've probably guessed, μ turns out to be equal to the mean of the distribution. You can tell that just by looking at the form of the density function, since the function is symmetric about $x = \mu$. Figure 11-4 shows a density function for a typical normal distribution.

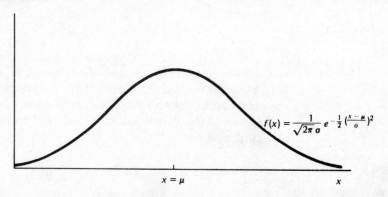

$$f(x) = \frac{1}{\sqrt{2\pi}\,\sigma} e^{-\frac{1}{2}\left(\frac{x-\mu}{\sigma}\right)^2}$$

$x = \mu$

x

FIGURE 11–4

It turns out that σ^2 is the variance. (See Exercise 27.) By adjusting the value of σ^2, you can determine whether the distribution will be very spread out or whether most of the probability will be concentrated near the peak. Figure 11-5 shows four different normal density functions that have different values of σ^2.

An important property of a normal random variable is the addition property. If X is a normal random variable with mean μ and variance σ^2, and $Y = aX + b$, where a and b are two constants, then Y has a normal distribution with mean $a\mu + b$ and variance $a^2\sigma^2$.

Also, suppose X and Y are two independent random variables with normal distributions. (Two random variables are independent if they don't affect each other. We'll define exactly what independence means in Chapter 13.) Suppose that

$$E(X) = \mu_x, \qquad \text{Var}(X) = \sigma_x^2, \qquad E(Y) = \mu_y, \qquad \text{and} \qquad \text{Var}(Y) = \sigma_y^2.$$

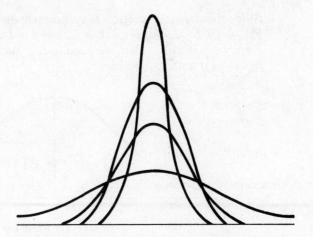

FIGURE 11–5

If we form a new random variable by adding these two together, $V = X + Y$, then V will also have a normal distribution. (We already know that $E(V) = \mu_x + \mu_y$ and $\mathrm{Var}(V) = \sigma_x^2 + \sigma_y^2$.)

For example, suppose you decide to enter the hamburger business by opening restaurants at two different locations. The number of hamburgers that you sell each day at the downtown location is given by a normal random variable with mean 200 and variance 1,600. The number of hamburgers sold at the suburban location has a normal distribution with mean 100 and variance 400. Then the total number of hamburgers that you will sell at both restaurants has a normal distribution with mean 300 and variance 2,000.

The Standard Normal Density Function

The normal random variable with $\mu = 0$ and $\sigma = 1$ is referred to as a *standard normal* random variable. Its density function is

$$f(x) = \frac{1}{\sqrt{2\pi}}\, e^{-(1/2)x^2}$$

Suppose that Z is a random variable with a standard normal density function. Figure 11-6 shows a graph of the density function for Z.

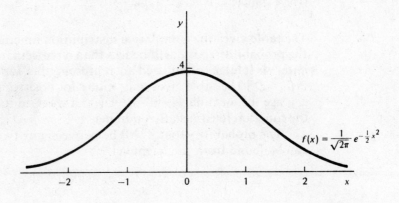

FIGURE 11–6

Since the density function is symmetric about $\mu = 0$, we can see that $\Pr(Z > 0) = 1/2$. Suppose that we need to know the probability that Z is between 0 and 1. Then we need to calculate the area under the curve between 0 and 1. (See Figure 11-7.)

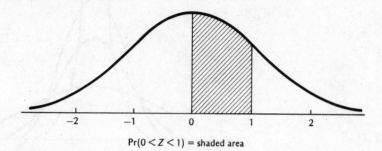

FIGURE 11–7

$\Pr(0 < Z < 1)$ = shaded area

Unfortunately, there is no simple formula that tells us what this area is. We have to look up the results in a table such as Table 11-1 or Table A3-1 at the back of the book.

TABLE 11-1: Standard Normal Random Variable Table

z	$\Pr(Z < z) = \Phi(z)$
0	.5000
.2	.5793
.4	.6554
.6	.7257
.8	.7881
1.0	.8413
1.2	.8849
1.4	.9192
1.6	.9452
1.8	.9641
2.0	.9773
2.2	.9861
2.4	.9918
2.6	.9953
2.8	.9974
3.0	.9987
3.5	.9998

(For a complete table, see Table A3-1).

The table gives the cumulative distribution function, which tells you the probability that Z will be less than a particular value. [The Greek letter Φ (phi) is often used to represent this function. $\Phi(z)$ equals $\Pr(Z < z)$.] The table gives only values for positive values of z, but we can use the formula $\Phi(-z) = 1 - \Phi(z)$ if we need to know the value of the function for a negative number.

The probability that Z will be between any two numbers a and b can be found from the formula

$$\Pr(a < Z < b) = \Phi(b) - \Phi(a)$$

We have already figured out that $\Phi(0) = .5$. We can see from the table that $\Phi(1) = .8413$. Therefore, the probability that Z will be between 0 and 1 is $.8413 - .5000 = .3413$.

Because of the symmetry of the density function, we can see that there is also a .3413 probability that Z will be between -1 and 0. (See Figure 11-8.) We can add these two probabilities together:

$$\Pr(-1 < Z < 0) + \Pr(0 < Z < 1) = .3413 + .3413$$

$$\Pr(-1 < Z < 1) = .6826$$

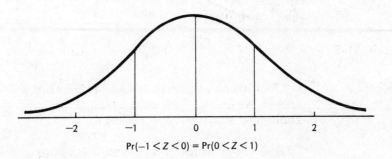

FIGURE 11-8

$\Pr(-1 < Z < 0) = \Pr(0 < Z < 1)$

Therefore, there is a 68 percent chance that a standard normal random variable will be between -1 and 1. Putting it another way, there is a 68 percent chance that the value of a standard normal random variable will be within one standard deviation of its mean. (In this case the mean is 0 and the standard deviation is 1.)

This particular property also holds for *any* normal random variable, regardless of its mean and standard deviation: There is a 68 percent chance that any normal random variable will be within one standard deviation of its mean. For example, if X is a normal random variable with mean 200 and standard deviation 30, then there is a 68 percent chance that X will be between 170 and 230.

We can also use the table to show that there is a 95 percent chance that Z will be between -1.96 and 1.96. In general, we can say that any normal random variable has a 95 percent chance of being less than about 2 standard deviations away from its mean.

It will often be helpful to know the probability that a standard normal random variable will be between a and $-a$, where a is a particular number. So, to make things more convenient, Table A3-2 at the back of the book lists these values. For example, the table shows that there is a .3830 probability that Z will be between -0.5 and 0.5.

The value of the standard normal random variable could conceivably be anything, since the density function never quite touches the axis. There is no number k such that $\Pr(Z > k) = 0$. However, you can see from the table that there is only a .0002 probability that Z will be greater than 3.5. Larger values are even less likely, so we don't have to worry too much about the likelihood that Z might take on extreme values.

It wouldn't be possible to produce a different table for every single possible value of μ and every single possible value of σ. However, we can use the standard normal tables to find the probabilities for any normal random variable by using the following trick. Suppose Y has a normal distribution with mean 6 and variance 9, and we need to know the probability that Y will be between 5 and 8. We can create the random variable Z:

$$Z = \frac{Y - 6}{3}$$

which will have a normal distribution with mean 0 and variance 1 because of the addition property. It should be clear that if Y is between 5 and 8, Z will be between $-1/3$ and $2/3$. Now we can look up the probability in the tables:

$$
\begin{aligned}
P(5 < Y < 8) &= P(-1/3 < Z < 2/3) \\
&= \Phi(.6667) - \Phi(-.3333) \\
&= .7486 - (1 - .6293) \\
&= .7486 - .3707 \\
&= .3779
\end{aligned}
$$

In general, if X is a normal random variable with mean μ and variance σ^2, then $(X - \mu)/\sigma$ is a standard normal random variable. For example, suppose we would like to know the probability that you will sell more than 230 hamburgers at your downtown hamburger store. Let X_1 represent the number of hamburgers. In this case $\mu = 200$, $\sigma^2 = 1,600$, and $\sigma = 40$. Let's create the standard normal random variable Z_1:

$$Z_1 = \frac{X_1 - 200}{40}$$

If X_1 is greater than 230, then Z_1 is greater than 3/4. Table A3-1 tells us that the probability of this occurring is $1 - Pr(Z_1 < .75) = 1 - .7734 = .2266$.

Now, suppose we would like to know the probability that you will sell a total of more than 330 hamburgers at the two locations. Let X be the total number of hamburgers. Then $\mu = 300$, $\sigma^2 = 2,000$, and $\sigma = 44.72$. Set up the standard normal random variable:

$$Z = \frac{X - 300}{44.72}$$

If $X > 330$, then $Z > .671$, and the probability of this happening is .2514.

EXERCISES

1. Suppose the annual rainfall in a city has a normal distribution with mean 40 and standard deviation 5. What is the probability that the city will get less than 33 inches of rain next year? What is the probability that the city will get more than 38 inches of rain?

2. Suppose that the score that a student will get on an entrance exam is a random variable selected from a normal distribution with mean 550 and variance 900. If you need a score of 575 to get into a certain college, what is the probability that you will get in? If instead you need a score of 540, what is the probability that you will get in?

3. You're coach of a football team that faces a third-down situation with four yards needed for a first down. If you select a play involving a runoff tackle, the number of yards you will gain on the play is given by a normal random variable with mean 2.5 and standard deviation 1. What is the probability that you will make the first down if you run this play?

4. Consider the same situation as in Exercise 3. Another play you might run is a tricky end-around double reverse. The results of that play are given by a normal random variable with mean 3 and variance 6. What is the probability that you will make the first down if you run that play?

5. Suppose you are measuring the speed of light. The result of your measurement is given by a normal random variable whose mean is the true value and whose standard deviation is 5×10^9 centimeters per second. What is the probability that your measurement will be within 2×10^9 centimeters per second of the true value?

6. Suppose you are running a lemonade stand. The number of glasses of lemonade that you sell each day is given by a normal random variable with mean 15 and standard deviation 10. What is the probability that you will sell at least 120 glasses of lemonade in a week (seven days)? What is the probability that you will sell at least 100 glasses? Is it all right to represent a variable such as the number of glasses of lemonade as a normal random variable?

7. List four other quantities that you think have approximately normal distributions.

In the following exercises, let X be a normal random variable with parameters μ and σ^2, density function $f_X(x)$, and cumulative distribution function $F_x(a)$. Use Table A3-1 to calculate $\Phi(x)$.

8. If $\mu = 0$ and $\sigma^2 = 100$, what is $\Pr(5 < X < 10)$?

9. If $\mu = -3$ and $\sigma^2 = 9$, and $F_X(a) = .6$, what is a?

10. If $\mu = 0$ and $F_X(5) = .8$, what is σ^2?

11. If $\mu = 3$, why can't $F_X(4) = .4$?

12. If $\mu = 73$ and $\sigma^2 = 81$, what is $\Pr(|X| > 100)$?

13. If $\mu = 25$ and $\sigma^2 = 100$, what is $\Pr(X = 25)$?

14. If $\mu = 1$ and $\sigma^2 = 64$, for what values of a is $.1 < F_x(a) < .3$?

15. If $f_X(X)$ takes a maximum value of 5 at $x = 10$, what are μ and σ^2?

16. On the same graph, plot $f_X(X)$ for $\mu = 0$ and a) $\sigma^2 = 1$, b) $\sigma^2 = 4$, and c) $\sigma^2 = 9$.

17. If X is a normal random variable with mean μ_1 and standard deviation σ_1, and Y is a normal random variable with mean μ_2 and standard deviation σ_2, what is $\Pr(Y > X)$?

18. Suppose you have your choice between two jobs. Your annual earnings from an industrial job will have a normal distribution with mean \$15,000 and standard deviation \$2,000. Your annual earnings from a traveling sales job will have a normal distribution with mean \$12,000 and standard deviation \$10,000. What is the probability that you would earn more from the traveling sales job?

19. Show that $(X - \mu)/\sigma$ is a standard normal random variable.

20. Show that, for any normal random variable, there is a probability of .68 that the value of the random variable will be within one standard deviation of the mean.

21. Show that $\Phi(-x) = 1 - \Phi(x)$.

22. The median of a continuous random variable is the number x^* such that $\Pr(X < x^*) = 1/2$. What is the median of a random variable with a normal distribution?

23. The mode of a continuous random variable is the point where the density function reaches its maximum value. What is the mode for a random variable with a normal distribution?

24. Show that, if three normal random variables are added together, the resulting random variable has a normal distribution.

25. Write a program that prints a table of the standard normal cumulative distribution function $\Phi(x)$ for values of x starting at 0.00, 0.01, 0.02, and so on, up to $x = 3$. You will have to find the area under the standard normal density function. You can't find the area exactly, but you can approximate it by a series of rectangles,

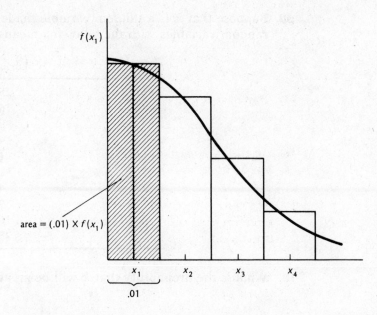

FIGURE 11–9

as shown in Figure 11-9. Each rectangle has width 0.01, and height $f(x_i)$. If you add together the area of all of the rectangles, then you can find a good approximation to the area under the curve between two points. (This procedure is called *numerical integration*.)

☆ **26.** Show that μ is the mean for a random variable with a normal distribution by calculating the integral.

☆ **27.** Show that σ^2 is the variance for a normal random variable.

☆ **28.** Calculate the area under the standard normal density function by evaluating the integral $\displaystyle\int_{-\infty}^{\infty} e^{-(1/2)x^2}\, dx$ (HINT: Multiply by $\displaystyle\int_{-\infty}^{\infty} e^{-(1/2)y^2}\, dy$ and then convert the result to polar coordinates.)

29. Suppose that the grade that a student receives in an individual course is not very accurate, since there are many random factors that could cause the grade to be higher or lower than the student's true abilities would indicate. Suppose that the grade is given by a random variable with a normal distribution with mean 3.5 and variance 1/16. What is the probability that the student's grade for an individual course will be between 3.4 and 3.6? Now, suppose a student takes 36 courses, whose grades all have the same normal distribution. What is the probability that the average grade for all of the courses will be between 3.4 and 3.6?

30. Suppose that X is a random variable made up of the sum of 10 random variables with the following means and variances:

Mean	Variance
−5	25
−4	16
−3	9
−2	4
−1	1
1	1
2	4
3	9
4	16
5	25

What is the probability that X will be greater than 1?

Moment Generating Functions

 WARNING: You are now entering a difficult mathematical area. We will need these results for some important theoretical proofs later on, but you are free to skip this section if you'd like.

Often you will want to know the value of $E(X)$, $E(X^2)$, $E(X^3)$, etc. (Take our word for it—you will.) These are called the *moments* of X. Specifically, $E(X^n)$ is called the *n th moment of X*. These can be calculated from a function $\psi(t)$ that is called the *moment generating function*. (ψ is the Greek letter *psi*.) The definition of the moment generating function (mgf for short) is

$$\psi(t) = E(e^{tX})$$

X is the random variable whose moment generating function we are calculating, and t is an ordinary variable that the mgf is a function of.

We can find the moments in the following way:

$$\psi'(t) = \frac{d}{dt} E(e^{tX})$$

$$= E\left(\frac{d}{dt} e^{tX}\right)$$

$$= E(X e^{tX})$$

Notice that we have assumed that you can take the *d/dt* inside the parentheses (which you can for nice distributions, and certainly all of the ones used in this book are nice).

In general:

$$\psi^{(n)}(t) = \left(\frac{d}{dt}\right)^n E(e^{tX})$$

$$= E(X^n e^{tX})$$

Then, if we calculate the value of the mgf when $t = 0$, we get

$$\psi^{(n)}(0) = E(X^n)$$

Therefore, if you know the moment generating function for a distribution, you can easily calculate all of the moments. To find the nth moment, just take the nth derivative and evaluate it at the point where $t = 0$.

Here are some examples. Suppose X has a binomial distribution with parameters n and p. Then

$$\psi(t) = \sum_{i=0}^{n} e^{it} \binom{n}{i} p^i (1 - p)^{n-i}$$

$$= \sum_{i=0}^{n} \binom{n}{i} (pe^t)^i (1 - p)^{n-i}$$

$$= (pe^t + 1 - p)^n$$

(by the binomial theorem).

If we take the derivative $\psi'(t)$, we get

$$\psi'(t) = npe^t(pe^t + 1 - p)^{n-1}$$

$$\psi'(0) = E(X)$$

$$= np \text{ (which is what we found earlier)}$$

Now, suppose X has a normal distribution with mean μ and variance σ^2. Then

$$\psi(t) = E(e^{tx})$$

$$= \frac{1}{\sigma\sqrt{2\pi}} \int_{-\infty}^{\infty} e^{tx} e^{-(x-\mu)^2/2\sigma^2} dx$$

$$e^{tx} e^{-(x-\mu)^2/2\sigma^2} = \exp\left[\frac{2\sigma^2 tx - (x - \mu)^2}{2\sigma^2}\right]$$

$$= \exp\left[\frac{-x^2 + 2(\sigma^2 t + x) - \mu^2}{2\sigma^2}\right]$$

$$= \exp\left[\frac{((\sigma^2 t + \mu)^2 - \mu^2) - (x - (\sigma^2 t + \mu))^2}{2\sigma^2}\right]$$

$$= \exp\left[\frac{((\sigma^2 t + \mu)^2 - \mu^2)}{2\sigma^2}\right] \exp\left[\frac{-(x - (\sigma^2 t + \mu))^2}{2\sigma^2}\right]$$

$$= \exp\left[\frac{\sigma^2 t^2}{2} + t\mu\right] \exp\left[\frac{-(x - (\sigma^2 t + \mu))^2}{2\sigma^2}\right]$$

$$\psi(t) = \exp\left[\frac{\sigma^2 t^2/2}{\sigma\sqrt{2\pi}} + t\mu\right] \int_{-\infty}^{\infty} \exp\left[\frac{-(x - (\sigma^2 t + \mu))^2}{2\sigma^2}\right] dx$$

(To save us from having to write complicated expressions as exponents, we write exp [*expression*] to mean $e^{(expression)}$.)

If we let $v = \sigma^2 t + \mu$, then that second integral becomes equal to:

$$\frac{1}{\sigma\sqrt{2\pi}} \int_{-\infty}^{\infty} \exp\left[\frac{-(x - v)^2}{2\sigma^2}\right] dx$$

which is equal to 1, since it is just the total area under the density function for a normal random variable. Therefore

$$\psi(t) = \exp\left[\frac{\sigma^2 t^2}{2} + t\mu\right]$$

If we calculate the derivative $\psi'(t)$, we get

$$\psi'(t) = (\sigma^2 t + \mu) \exp\left[\frac{\sigma^2 t^2}{2} + t\mu\right]$$

We can see that $\psi'(0) = \mu$.

If X is a standard normal random variable, the moment generating function is even simpler:

$$\psi(t) = \exp\left(\frac{t^2}{2}\right)$$

The moment generating function contains a great deal of information about its random variable. (In fact, each random variable has its own unique mgf.) Moment generating functions will be very useful in showing some important properties of random variables, and they will be used in the proof of the central limit theorem.

EXERCISES

☆ **31.** Let X and Y be two independent random variables, and let $Z = X + Y$. Show that $\psi_Z(t) = \psi_X(t)\,\psi_Y(t)$.

☆ **32.** Use the binomial mgf to calculate $E(X^2)$ when X has a binomial distribution.

☆ **33.** Calculate the moment generating functions of the following random variables, and use the moment generating function to calculate the mean and the variance:
Poisson variable with parameter $\lambda > 0$.
Geometric random variable with parameter p, $0 < p \leq 1$.

☆ **34.** If X has a normal distribution, show that $Y = aX + b$ also has a normal distribution, when a and b are constants. Use moment generating functions.

☆ **35.** If X and Y are independent random variables with normal distributions, show that $Z = X + Y$ has a normal distribution. Use moment generating functions.

CHAPTER 12

OTHER CONTINUOUS DISTRIBUTIONS

In this chapter we will discuss some probability distributions that seem rather esoteric at first, but turn out to be essential tools in statistics.

The Chi-square Distribution

Suppose Z is a standard normal random variable (that is, it has mean 0 and variance 1). Then suppose that $Y = Z^2$. This means that Y will also be a continuous random variable. We'd like to know what its probability density function will be. It's obvious that Y can't be less than 0, so its density function will look different from the standard normal density function. We'll give a name to this type of random variable: We'll say that it is a *chi-square* random variable. Since χ is the Greek letter chi, this distribution is usually symbolized by χ^2. You're probably wondering where the name chi-square comes from. (If you find out, let us know.)

To give you an idea what the density function looks like, Figure 12-1 shows the frequency diagram for the squares of a group of numbers chosen from a standard normal distribution.

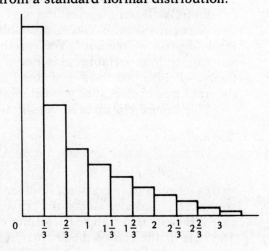

FIGURE 12–1

Some mathematical gymnastics show that the density function for the random variable $Y = Z^2$ is

$$f(y) = (2\pi)^{-1/2}y^{-1/2}e^{-y/2} \qquad \text{for } y \geq 0; f(y) = 0 \text{ if } y < 0$$

This function is drawn in Figure 12-2.

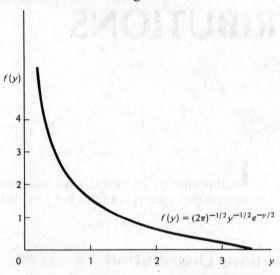

FIGURE 12–2

The mean of this random variable is easy to calculate. Since Z has a standard normal distribution, by definition $E(Z) = 0$ and $\text{Var}(Z) = 1$. Since $\text{Var}(Z) = E(Z^2) - E(Z)^2 = E(Z^2)$, it follows that $E(Z^2) = E(Y) = 1$. The variance of Y turns out to be 2.

There actually are several different types of chi-square random variables. The variable Y is strictly speaking called a chi-square variable with one *degree of freedom*. Suppose we square a lot of independent normal random variables and then take their sum, calling the result Y_n:

$$Y_n = Z_1^2 + Z_2^2 + \cdots + Z_n^2$$

Then Y_n is said to have the chi-square distribution with n degrees of freedom. (We'll write χ_n^2 to stand for "chi-square distribution with n degrees of freedom.") You're probably wondering why we use the term "degrees of freedom." You can think of it this way. Each of the normal random variables acts like a number that you can choose freely, so since you have n of these numbers, it's as if you have n different free choices that you can make.

The general chi-squared density function is

$$f(y) = \frac{1}{c}\, y^{n/2-1}e^{-y/2}$$

In this formula c is a constant number that has the appropriate value so that the total area under the curve is 1 (as we know must be the case if the function is to be a legitimate probability density function). The note at the end of the chapter tells how to calculate the value of c.

We can easily calculate the expectation and variance of a χ^2 random variable with n degrees of freedom. Since Y_n is the sum of n random variables, each with expectation 1, $E(Y_n) = n$. Each χ^2 random variable is independent, so the variance is just the sum of all of the individual variances, and therefore

$$Var(Y_n) = 2n$$

Figure 12-3 shows several different chi-squared distributions with different degrees of freedom.

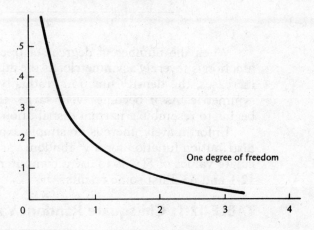

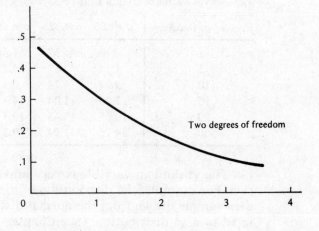

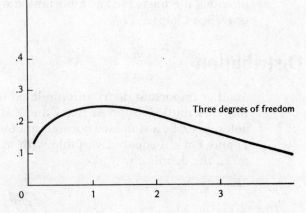

FIGURE 12–3

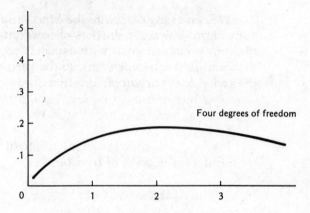

FIGURE 12–3

When the number of degrees of freedom is small, the density function is severely asymmetric. As the number of degrees of freedom increases, the density function gradually becomes more and more symmetric. As n becomes very large, the chi-square distribution begins to resemble a normal distribution.

Unfortunately, there is no simple expression for the cumulative distribution function for a χ^2 random variable. The only way to calculate values of $F(y)$ is to use a computer. (See Exercise 10.) Tables 12-1 and A3-3 list some results.

TABLE 12-1: Chi-square Random Variable

Table gives value of x such that $\Pr(X < x) = p$

Degrees of freedom	$p = .05$	$p = .25$	$p = .50$	$p = .75$	$p = .90$	$p = .95$
2	.10	.57	1.38	2.77	4.60	5.99
5	1.14	2.67	4.35	6.62	9.23	11.07
10	3.94	6.74	9.3	12.5	15.9	18.3
15	7.26	11.04	14.3	18.2	22.3	25.0
20	10.85	15.45	19.3	23.8	28.4	31.4
50	34.76	42.94	49.3	56.3	63.2	67.5

The χ^2 random variable is very important in statistical estimation. For example, the distribution of the sample variance of a random sample drawn from the normal distribution will be closely related to a χ^2 distribution. (See Chapter 16.) Also, this distribution provides the basis for an important statistical test known as the χ^2 test. (See Chapter 17.)

The t Distribution

Another important distribution related to the normal distribution is the t distribution. Suppose that Z and Y are independent random variables. Let Z be a standard normal random variable (mean 0, variance 1) and Y a chi-squared variable with m degrees of freedom. Let us make the definition

$$T = \frac{Z}{\sqrt{Y/m}}$$

Then it is said that the variable *T* has the *t distribution* with *m* degrees of freedom. (The *t* distribution is sometimes called *Student's distribution*.) This definition looks somewhat mystifying and pointless at first, but the *t* distribution does have important uses in statistics. The derivation of the density function is a very arduous, complicated process. (The function itself is complicated enough.) The resulting density function looks like this:

$$g(x) = c\left(1 + \frac{x^2}{m}\right)^{-(n + 1)/2}$$

Once again, *c* is an appropriate constant whose nature is described in the note at the end of the chapter.

Looking at the form of the density function provides some clues about the nature of the *t* distribution. Since $g(x) = g(-x)$, it follows that the density function is symmetric about $x = 0$. You can also see that the maximum value of $g(x)$ occurs when $x = 0$. Figure 12-4 shows a sample *t* density function.

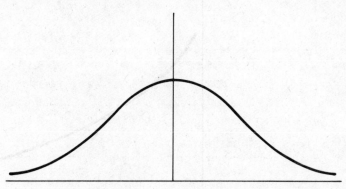

FIGURE 12–4

The density function has a bell shape that is roughly similar to the standard normal distribution. In general, though, the *t* distribution has thicker tails than the normal distribution does. In other words, a *t* random variable has a higher chance of being far from 0 than does a standard normal random variable. However, as the number of degrees of freedom (*m*) increases the *t* distribution approaches very close to the standard normal distribution.

If $m = 1$ the mean of the *t* distribution doesn't exist. (The *t* distribution with $m = 1$ is also called the *Cauchy distribution*.) If $m > 1$, then the mean does exist, and it is equal to 0 because the distribution is symmetric about zero. The variance of the *t* distribution does not exist if $m = 1$ or $m = 2$, but if $m > 2$ the variance is $m/(m - 2)$.

Now we will mention one other distribution related to the chi-square distribution that has important uses in statistics. If *X* and *Y* are independent chi-square random variables with degrees of freedom *m* and *n*, respectively, then the random variable

$$F = \frac{X/m}{Y/n}$$

is said to have the *F distribution with m and n degrees of freedom*. Note that the order of *m* and *n* makes a big difference. Table A3-6 lists some values for the cumulative distribution function.

The Exponential Distribution

Light bulbs have a tendency to burn out unpredictably, so the length of time that a light bulb burns before it burns out is a good example of a continuous random variable. The type of distribution that is often appropriate in this situation is that of the *exponential random variable*. The density function for an exponential random variable is

$$f(x) = \lambda e^{-\lambda x} \qquad \text{if } x \geq 0$$
$$f(x) = 0 \qquad \text{if } x < 0$$

The Greek letter lambda (λ) is used as a parameter of the distribution. An exponential distribution is completely determined once you know the value of λ. Figure 12–5 illustrates a sample exponential density function.

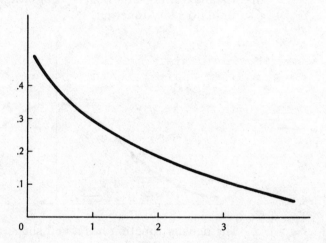

FIGURE 12–5

We can use calculus to derive the cumulative distribution function:

$$F(a) = \Pr(X < a) = 1 - e^{-\lambda x}$$

and therefore

$$\Pr(X > a) = e^{-\lambda x}$$

The exponential distribution has an interesting and unique property. Suppose we are interested in the probability that the light bulb will survive a particular day. If time is measured in hours, then the probability that the light bulb will survive the first day that we install it is $\Pr(X > 24) = e^{-24\lambda}$. Suppose that the light bulb does indeed survive the first day, and in fact it survives the first week. Then we want to know the probability that it will survive the next day. That means we want to know $\Pr(X > 168 + 24) = \Pr(X > 192)$. However, we know that the light bulb has already survived 168 hours (there are 168 hours in one week), so we are really interested in the conditional probability that X will be greater than 192, given that we know that it is already greater than 168. We can use the formula for conditional probability:

$$\Pr(X > 192 \mid X > 168) = \frac{\Pr[(X > 192) \text{ and } (X > 168)]}{\Pr(X > 168)}$$

$$= \frac{\Pr(X > 192)}{\Pr(X > 168)}$$

$$= \frac{e^{-192\lambda}}{e^{-168\lambda}}$$

$$= e^{-24\lambda}$$

Therefore, the probability that the bulb will survive the eighth day, given the fact that it has survived the first seven days, is exactly the same as the probability that it will survive the first day. In general, for an exponential distribution,

$$\Pr[[X > (t + s)] \mid (X > t)] = \Pr(X > s)$$

This property is called the *lack of memory property*. (Actually, real light bulbs probably do not satisfy the lack of memory property exactly, since the chances that a particular light bulb will burn out on a given day probably do go up with time.)

The expectation of the exponential random variable is $1/\lambda$, and the variance is $1/\lambda^2$. (See Exercise 12.)

NOTE TO CHAPTER 12   The constant factors in the chi-square density function and the t density function can be defined by using an unusual function called the *gamma function*, symbolized by Γ. The Γ function has these properties:

$$\Gamma(0) = 1$$

$$\Gamma(1/2) = \sqrt{\pi}$$

$$\Gamma(n) = (n - 1)\,\Gamma(n - 1)$$

Therefore, if n is an integer,

$$\Gamma(n) = (n - 1)!$$

The chi-squared density function can be written

$$f(x) = \frac{1}{2^{n/2}\Gamma(n/2)}\, x^{n/2 - 1} e^{-x/2}$$

The t density function can be written:

$$g(x) = \frac{\Gamma[(m + 1)/2]}{\sqrt{m\pi}\,\Gamma(m/2)} \left(1 + \frac{x^2}{m}\right)^{-(m + 1)/2}$$

The gamma function can be defined by the integral

$$\Gamma(n) = \int_0^\infty x^{n-1} e^{-x}\, dx$$

It also is used in the definition of the *gamma distribution* with parameters a and b:

$$f(x) = \frac{b^a}{\Gamma(a)} x^{a-1} e^{-bx} \qquad (\text{if } x > 0)$$

There are two other quantities (in addition to the mean and the variance) that we can calculate to learn about the shape of the distribution of a random variable. The *skewness* of a distribution measures whether or not the distribution is symmetric. The skewness is defined to be

$$\frac{E[(X - \mu)^3]}{\sigma^3}$$

If a distribution is symmetric, then its skewness is 0. If it has a long tail in the positive direction, then it has positive skewness; if it has a long tail in the negative direction then it has negative skewness.

The *kurtosis* of a distribution measures the thickness of the tails of a distribution. It is defined to be

$$\frac{E[(X - \mu)^4]}{\sigma^4}$$

EXERCISES

1. What is the probability that a chi-square random variable with three degrees of freedom will be greater than 4?

2. What is the probability that a chi-square random variable with five degrees of freedom will be less than 2?

3. What is the probability that a random variable with a t distribution with five degrees of freedom will be between 0 and 1?

4. What is the probability that a random variable with a t distribution with 10 degrees of freedom will be between -2 and -1?

5. Suppose someone tells you that he observed the value 16 as the result of a chi-square random variable with 12 degrees of freedom. Do you believe him?

6. If someone tells you that he observed the value 5 for a chi-square random variable with 16 degrees of freedom, do you believe him?

7. If someone tells you that he observed the value -2.3 for a random variable that was selected from a t distribution with 3 degrees of freedom, do you believe him?

8. If someone tells you that he observed the value 0.7 for a random variable selected from a t distribution with 12 degrees of freedom, do you believe him?

9. Suppose X has a t distribution with n degrees of freedom. How can you characterize the distribution of X^2?

☐ **10.** Write a program that prints a table of the chi-squared cumulative distribution function for $n = 1$ to $n = 30$. Use the method of rectangles described in Chapter 11, Exercise 25. Decide for yourself which values you should include in the table.

☐ **11.** Write a program that prints a table of the t cumulative distribution function for $m = 1$ to $m = 30$. The cumulative distribution function for a t distribution with one degree of freedom can be found from the formula

$$\Pr(t < x) = \frac{1}{\pi} \arctan x + \frac{1}{2}$$

For the other cases, you will need to use the rectangle method.

☆ **12.** Calculate the expectation and variance for an exponential random variable with parameter λ.

☆ **13.** Derive the cumulative distribution function for an exponential random variable.

☆ **14.** Calculate the moment generating function for an exponential random variable.

☆ **15.** If X has an exponential distribution, show that

$$\Pr[X > (a + b)] = \Pr(X > a) \Pr(X > b).$$

☆ **16.** Derive the density function for a chi-square random variable with one degree of freedom.

☆ **17.** Calculate the mean and variance for a chi-square random variable with one degree of freedom.

☆ **18.** Calculate the moment generating function for a chi-square random variable with n degrees of freedom.

☆ **19.** Suppose Y_1 has a chi-square distribution with n_1 degrees of freedom, and Y_2 has a chi-square distribution with n_2 degrees of freedom. Show that $Y_1 + Y_2$ has a chi-square distribution with $n_1 + n_2$ degrees of freedom. (Use moment generating functions.)

☆ **20.** Show that the t distribution approaches the normal distribution as the number of degrees of freedom becomes very large. (To make things easier, assume that the value of the constant c approaches $1/\sqrt{2\pi}$ as m becomes large.)

☆ **21.** Calculate the skewness and kurtosis for the normal, chi-square, and t distributions. Compare the results as the number of degrees of freedom for the chi-square and t distributions increases.

CHAPTER 13

DISTRIBUTIONS WITH TWO RANDOM VARIABLES

Joint Density Functions

Suppose we have two discrete random variables X and Y, and we are interested in the probabilities that they will take on particular values. Just as in the case of one random variable, we can define a probability density function and a cumulative distribution function. Let's say that X has six possible values: X_1, X_2, X_3, X_4, X_5, and X_6. Also, we'll say that Y has six possible values: $Y_1, Y_2, Y_3, Y_4, Y_5, Y_6$. Now, let's conduct a random experiment in which we observe values for X and Y. The result of the experiment consists of two numbers: the observed value of X and the observed value of Y. Then there are 36 possible outcomes for the experiment. (In general, if there are m possible values for X and n possible values for Y, there will be mn possible results.) To characterize the experiment completely, we need to calculate the probability for each one of the 36 possible results. We can arrange our results in a table.

For example, suppose that X is the number that shows up on the top of a die when it is rolled and Y is the number on the bottom of the die. Then the probability table is:

Y	$X = 1$	$X = 2$	$X = 3$	$X = 4$	$X = 5$	$X = 6$
1	0	0	0	0	0	1/6
2	0	0	0	0	1/6	0
3	0	0	0	1/6	0	0
4	0	0	1/6	0	0	0
5	0	1/6	0	0	0	0
6	1/6	0	0	0	0	0

(The table looks like this because dice are marked so that the numbers on any two opposite faces add up to 7.)

For another example, suppose that X and Z are the numbers that appear on two different dice. Then the probability table looks like this:

Z	X = 1	X = 2	X = 3	X = 4	X = 5	X = 6
1	1/36	1/36	1/36	1/36	1/36	1/36
2	1/36	1/36	1/36	1/36	1/36	1/36
3	1/36	1/36	1/36	1/36	1/36	1/36
4	1/36	1/36	1/36	1/36	1/36	1/36
5	1/36	1/36	1/36	1/36	1/36	1/36
6	1/36	1/36	1/36	1/36	1/36	1/36

(In this case, obviously, each of the 36 outcomes is equally likely.)

When there are many possible values for either X or Y it will be too cumbersome to make a table. In general, though, we can define a *joint probability density function* $f(x,y)$ like this:

$$f(x,y) = \Pr[(X = x) \text{ and } (Y = y)]$$
$$= \Pr[(X = x) \cap (Y = y)]$$

In this case f is a function of two variables. (Note that an ordinary probability density function is a function of only one variable.) Note that $f(x,y) = 0$ if (x,y) is not a possible result for X and Y. The sum of all of the possible values of the function $f(x,y)$ must be 1.

We can also define the *joint cumulative distribution function:*

$$F(x,y) = \Pr[(X \leq x) \text{ and } (Y \leq y)]$$
$$= \Pr[(X \leq x) \cap (Y \leq y)]$$

The joint cumulative distribution function for two continuous random variables can be defined in the same way. The joint density function for two continuous random variables can be pictured as follows. Imagine a little hill spread out across a flat plane with an x axis and a y axis marked on it. The total volume under the hill must be 1. Then the probability that the values of X and Y will be within any specified rectangle of the plane is equal to the volume of the hill above that rectangle.

Marginal Density Functions for Individual Random Variables

Suppose that we are interested in the value of X but don't care about the value of Y. (For example, most people don't really care what number shows up on the bottom of a die they have just tossed.) In that case, the joint probability density function gives us far more information than we want. What we'd like to do is to figure out some way to derive the regular density function for X alone. (We will write $f_X(x)$ to stand for the density function of X.) Let's look at the joint density function for X and Y shown above. We should be able to use this information to find the probability that X will equal 1. As you can see from the table, there are six possible outcomes of the experiment that have X equal to 1:

$$(X = 1, Y = 1); (X = 1, Y = 2); (X = 1, Y = 3);$$
$$(X = 1, Y = 4); (X = 1, Y = 5); (X = 1, Y = 6)$$

To get the probability that X will equal 1, we need to add all these probabilities. We get $0 + 0 + 0 + 0 + 0 + 1/6 = 1/6$.

Now, look at the table that gives us the joint density function for X and Z. Once again we can get the probability that X will equal 1 by adding all of the terms in the first column: $1/36 + 1/36 + 1/36 + 1/36 + 1/36 + 1/36 = 1/6$. Likewise, by adding up each of the other columns in the tables we can find $Pr(X = 2)$, $Pr(X = 3)$, and so on.

In general, if there are n possible values for Y, then

$$Pr(X = x) = Pr[(X = x) \text{ and } (Y = y_1)]$$
$$+ Pr[(X = x) \text{ and } (Y = y_2)] + \cdots$$
$$+ Pr[(X = x) \text{ and } (Y = y_n)].$$

We can write this relation in terms of the joint density function:

$$f_X(x) = f(x,y_1) + f(x,y_2) + \cdots + f(x,y_n)$$

$$f_X(x) = \sum_{i=1}^{n} f(x,y_i)$$

An individual density function derived from a joint density function in this way is sometimes called a *marginal density function*.

We can also find the marginal density function for y:

$$f_Y(y) = f(x_1,y) + f(x_2,y) + \cdots + f(x_m,y)$$

If $f(x,y)$ is a continuous joint density function for X and Y, then the marginal density function of X can be found from the formula

$$f_X(x) = \int_{-\infty}^{\infty} f(x,y)\, dy$$

That formula will not mean anything to you unless you know something about calculus. If you don't, then you're free to ignore that formula.

Conditional Density Functions

There will often be times when we know the value of one of two random variables and would like to know the value of the other. Sometimes knowing the value of one random variable will help us a lot when we try to guess the value of the other one. For example, if we know that the variable Y discussed above has the value 4, then we know for sure that X has the value 3. However, knowing that Z (the number on another die) is 4 does not tell us anything about the value of X.

The *conditional density function* for X tells us what the density function for X is, given that Y has a specified value. Note that this concept is very much like the conditional probabilities that we discussed in Chapter 6. We will write "the conditional probability of X given that Y has the value y^*" like this:

$$f[x \mid (Y = y^*)] \qquad \text{or} \qquad f(x \mid y^*)$$

(Remember that the vertical line $\mid$ means "given that.") Then we can use the definition of conditional probability to find

$$f(x \mid Y = y^*) = \frac{\Pr[(X = x) \text{ and } (Y = y^*)]}{\Pr(Y = y^*)}$$

$$= \frac{f(x, y^*)}{f_Y(y^*)}$$

In other words, the conditional density function is equal to the joint density function $f(x, y^*)$ divided by the marginal density function of y. For example, suppose $Y = 3$. Then $f_Y(3) = 1/6$, so

$$f(x \mid Y = 3) = \begin{cases} \dfrac{0}{1/6} & \text{when } x = 1 \\[2mm] \dfrac{0}{1/6} & \text{when } x = 2 \\[2mm] \dfrac{0}{1/6} & \text{when } x = 3 \\[2mm] \dfrac{1/6}{1/6} & \text{when } x = 4 \\[2mm] \dfrac{0}{1/6} & \text{when } x = 5 \\[2mm] \dfrac{0}{1/6} & \text{when } x = 6 \end{cases}$$

Independent Random Variables

It would be nice if we could tell whether two random variables affect each other. We will say that two random variables X and Y are *independent* if knowing the value of Y does not tell you anything about the value of X, and vice versa. That means that the conditional density for X given Y is equal to the regular marginal density for X (since knowing the value of Y does not change any of the probabilities for X.) Therefore, if X and Y are independent,

$$f(x \mid y) = f_X(x)$$

We know from the definition of conditional probability that

$$f(x \mid y) = \frac{f(x,y)}{f_Y(y)}$$

Therefore, when X and Y are independent,

$$f_X(x) = \frac{f(x,y)}{f_Y(y)}$$

$$f(x,y) = f_X(x)\, f_Y(y)$$

When the two variables are independent, the joint density function can be found simply by multiplying together the two marginal density functions. This means that independent random variables are much easier to deal with. In general, it is very difficult to reconstruct the joint density function for two individual random variables if you are given their marginal density functions. (In fact, it is impossible unless you have some additional information about how the two random variables are related.)

In the examples above, X, Y, and Z all have identical marginal density functions. However, the joint density function for X and Y is much different from the joint density function for X and Z, since X and Z are independent but X and Y are not.

Here is an example of the joint density function for two independent random variables U and V:

V	$U = 1$	$U = 2$	$U = 3$	$U = 4$		$f(v)$
1	.02	.04	.06	.08		.2
2	.02	.04	.06	.08		.2
3	.06	.12	.18	.24		.6
$f(u)$	.1	.2	.3	.4		1

The marginal density function for U can be found by adding each column, and the marginal density function for V can be found by adding each row. You can see that for each entry in the table $f(u,v)$ is equal to $f(u)\, f(v)$, so the two random variables are independent.

Here is another useful result that works if two random variables are independent. If U and V are independent, then

$$E(UV) = E(U)\, E(V)$$

In other words, the expectation of their product is just equal to the product of their individual expectations. That is another reason why life is much simpler when we have independent random variables.

Covariance and Correlation

Suppose X and Y are two random variables that are not independent. We still would like to be able to measure how closely they are related. If X and Y are very closely related, learning the value of X tells you a lot about the value of Y. If they are only slightly related, then knowing the value of X helps you a little bit, but not much, when you try to guess the value of Y.

The quantity that measures the degree of dependence between two random variables is called the *covariance*. The covariance of X and Y [written Cov(X,Y)] is defined as follows:

$$\text{Cov}(X,Y) = E[[X - E(X)][Y - E(Y)]]$$

Suppose that, when X is larger than $E(X)$, you know that Y is also larger than $E(Y)$. In that case, $E[[X - E(X)][Y - E(Y)]]$ will be positive. In general, when two random variables tend to move together, their covariance is positive. And if two random variables tend to move in the opposite direction (for example, if X tends to be big at the same time Y is small, and vice versa) then their covariance is negative.

There is a short-cut formula for calculating covariances that is much easier to use than the defining formula.

$$E[[X - E(X)][Y - E(Y)]]$$
$$= E[XY - Y\,E(X) - X\,E(Y) + E(X)\,E(Y)]$$
$$= E(XY) - E[Y\,E(X)] - E[X\,E(Y)] + E(X)\,E(Y)$$
$$= E(XY) - E(X)\,E(Y) - E(X)\,E(Y) + E(X)\,E(Y)$$
$$\text{Cov}(X,Y) = E(XY) - E(X)\,E(Y)$$

For example, when X and Y are the numbers on the top and bottom of a die, respectively, we can find that

$$E(XY) = 1/6 \times 6 + 1/6 \times 10 + 1/6 \times 12$$
$$+ 1/6 \times 12 + 1/6 \times 10 + 1/6 \times 6$$
$$= 9.333$$

Therefore,

$$\text{Cov}(X,Y) = 9.333 - 3.5 \times 3.5 = -2.917$$

The covariance is negative, because larger values of X are associated with smaller values of Y.

Here is another example. Suppose that the joint density function for S and T is

T	$S = 1$	$S = 2$	$S = 4$
0	0	.1	.3
1	.6	0	0

Then we can find that $E(TS) = .6$, $E(S) = 2$, and $E(T) = .6$. The covariance is $E(ST) - E(S) E(T) = .6 - 2 \times .6 = -.6$.

From the short-cut formula you can see immediately that $Cov(X,Y) = 0$ if X and Y are independent. (Use the result $E(XY) = E(X) E(Y)$ if X and Y are independent.) Therefore $Cov(X,Z) = 0$ when X and Z are the numbers on two different dice. (However, it unfortunately works out that just showing that $Cov(X,Y) = 0$ is not enough to ensure that X and Y are independent.)

If $Cov(X,Y)$ is nonzero, then we know that X and Y are not independent. However, the size of $Cov(X,Y)$ does not tell us much, because it depends mostly on the size of X and Y. We define a new quantity, called the *correlation*, that we can use directly to tell how strong the relation between X and Y is. We will write the correlation between X and Y as $r(X,Y)$. (The Greek letter rho (ρ) is also often used to stand for correlation, as in $\rho(X,Y)$). The definition of the correlation coefficient is

$$r(X,Y) = \frac{Cov(X,Y)}{\sqrt{var(X)\, var(Y)}} = \frac{Cov(X,Y)}{\sigma_x \sigma_y}$$

The most important property of the correlation coefficient is that its value is always between -1 and 1. If X and Y are independent, then clearly their correlation is zero. If the correlation coefficient is positive, you know that when X is big, Y is also likely to be big. They are then said to be *positively correlated*. X and Y are more closely related the closer the correlation coefficient is to 1. On the other hand, if the correlation is negative, then Y is more likely to be small when X is big. They are *negatively correlated*, and the negative relationship is stronger if the correlation coefficient is closer to -1.

In the preceding example we found that $Cov(S,T) = -.6$. We can also find that $\sigma_S = 1.34$, and $\sigma_T = .49$. Therefore, the correlation between S and T is

$$r(S,T) = \frac{-.6}{(1.39)(.49)} = -.881$$

EXAMPLE   Suppose you flip three pennies and three nickels. Let U be the total number of heads, and let V be the number of heads on the pennies. Then the joint probability table looks like this:

V	$U = 0$	$U = 1$	$U = 2$	$U = 3$	$U = 4$	$U = 5$	$U = 6$	$f(v)$
0	1/64	3/64	3/64	1/64	0	0	0	1/8
1	0	3/64	9/64	9/64	3/64	0	0	3/8
2	0	0	3/64	9/64	9/64	3/64	0	3/8
3	0	0	0	1/64	3/64	3/64	1/64	1/8
$f(u)$	1/64	6/64	15/64	20/64	15/64	6/64	1/64	1

We can calculate that $E(UV) = 5.25$. We already know that $E(U) = 3$ and $E(V) = 3/2$. Therefore, $Cov(U,V) = 5.25 - 3 \times 3/2 = .75$. We also have found that $\sigma_U = 1.225$, and $\sigma_V = .8660$. That means that $r(U,V) = .75/(1.225 \times .8660) = .7070$. The correlation is positive, because larger values of U are associated with larger values of V.

Two random variables are *perfectly correlated* when there is a relationship between them of the form

$$Y = aX + b$$

where a and b are two constants, and a is greater than 0. For example, suppose the joint density function for X and Y is:

Y	X = 0	X = 1	X = 2	X = 3	X = 4	X = 5	X = 6	
0	1/7	0	0	0	0	0	0	1/7
4	0	1/7	0	0	0	0	0	1/7
8	0	0	1/7	0	0	0	0	1/7
12	0	0	0	1/7	0	0	0	1/7
16	0	0	0	0	1/7	0	0	1/7
20	0	0	0	0	0	1/7	0	1/7
24	0	0	0	0	0	0	1/7	1/7
	1/7	1/7	1/7	1/7	1/7	1/7	1/7	1

In this case it is clear that Y is always equal to $4X$. We can calculate that $E(X) = 3$, $\sigma_X = 2$, $E(Y) = 12$, $\sigma_Y = 8$, and $E(XY) = 52$. Therefore $\text{Cov}(X,Y) = 52 - 3 \times 12 = 16$, and the correlation is $16/(2 \times 8) = 1$, which confirms what we suspected.

Variance of a Sum

We can now derive a general formula for $\text{Var}(X + Y)$.

$$\begin{aligned}
\text{Var}(X + Y) &= E[(X + Y)^2] - [E(X + Y)]^2 \\
&= E[X^2 + 2XY + Y^2] - [E(X) + E(Y)]^2 \\
&= E(X^2) + 2\,E(XY) + E(Y^2) \\
&\quad - (E(X))^2 - 2\,E(X)\,E(Y) - (E(Y))^2 \\
&= E(X^2) - (E(X))^2 + E(Y^2) - (E(Y))^2 + 2\,[E(XY) - E(X)\,E(Y)] \\
&= \text{Var}(X) + \text{Var}(Y) + 2\,\text{Cov}(X,Y)
\end{aligned}$$

For example, suppose you own stock in Worldwide Fastburgers, Inc. Your profit from the stock is a random variable (W) with mean 1,000 and variance 400. You would like to buy some more stock, and you are trying to decide between Have It Your Way Burgers, Inc., and Fun and Good Times Pizza, Inc. Both stocks also have profits which are random variables with mean 1,000 and variance 400. Which one should you choose? (Let H represent your profit if you choose Have It Your Way Burgers, and let F represent your profit if you choose Fun and Good Times Pizza.)

The expected value of your profit will be the same regardless of which one you choose. However, you would also like the variance of your profit to be as small as possible. A smaller variance means that your stock holding is less risky. In order to calculate the total variance of your portfolio, you need to look at the covariance between Worldwide Burgers and the other two companies. Suppose that $Cov(W,H) = 380$. The covariance is positive, meaning that both firms will prosper if the hamburger market is strong, but both firms will suffer if the hamburger market is weak. Suppose also that $Cov(W,F) = -200$. The negative covariance means that the pizza market is booming when the hamburger market is in a slump, and vice versa.

If you buy the Have It Your Way Burger stock, then the total variance of your profit will be

$$Var(W + H) = Var(W) + Var(H) + 2\,Cov(W,H)$$
$$= \quad 400 \quad + \quad 400 \quad + \quad 2 \times 380$$
$$= 1{,}560$$

If you buy the pizza stock, then the variance is

$$Var(W + F) = Var(W) + Var(F) + 2\,Cov(W,F)$$
$$= \quad 400 \quad + \quad 400 \quad + 2 \times (-200)$$
$$= 400$$

Clearly, it is much less risky to buy the pizza stock. In general, you can lower the risk of your stock holdings by diversifying and buying stocks that have negative covariances with each other. Or, to put it another way, don't put all your eggs in one basket.

The Multinomial Distribution

It is possible to have a distribution for more than two random variables. An important example is called the *multinomial distribution*.

The multinomial distribution is a generalization of the binomial distribution. With the binomial distribution we had two outcomes which we called successes and failures. (In the example of the tossed coin there were heads and tails.) We now assume that there are m different outcomes for each trial. Let $X_1, X_2, \cdots X_m$ be the random variables representing the number of times each outcome occurs. For each of the m outcomes let p_i be the probability that outcome number i will be the result of any one trial. (So we must have $p_1 + p_2 + p_3 + \cdots + p_m = 1$.) Then the joint probability density function is

$$Pr(X_1 = n_1, X_2 = n_2, \cdots, X_m = n_m)$$

$$= \frac{n!}{n_1!\,n_2! \cdots n_m!}\, p_1{}^{n_1} \times p_2{}^{n_2} \times p_3{}^{n_3} \times \cdots \times p_m{}^{n_m}$$

where $n_1 + n_2 + n_3 + \cdots + n_m = n$.

This formula follows by the same reasoning as the binomial distribution, since the probability of any single combination of n_1 occurrences of outcome number 1, n_2 occurrences of outcome number 2, etc., is $p_1{}^{n_1} \times p_2{}^{n_2} \times \cdots \times p_m{}^{n_m}$, and there are

$$\frac{n!}{n_1!\,n_2! \cdots n_m!}$$

such outcomes.

As an example, what is the probability of rolling 3 ones, 4 twos, and 1 three out of 10 rolls of a die? Let X_1 equal the number of ones rolled, X_2 equal the number of twos rolled, X_3 equal the number of threes rolled, and X_4 equal the number of rolls that are not one, two, or three. Then $p_1 = p_2 = p_3 = 1/6$, and $p_4 = 3/6 = 1/2$. Also, $n_1 = 3, n_2 = 4, n_3 = 1, n_4 = 10 - 3 - 4 - 1 = 2$. So we have

$$\Pr(X_1 = n_1, X_2 = n_2, X_3 = n_3, X_4 = n_4)$$

$$= \frac{10!}{3!\, 4!\, 1!\, 2!} \left(\frac{1}{6}\right)^3 \left(\frac{1}{6}\right)^4 \left(\frac{1}{6}\right)^1 \left(\frac{1}{2}\right)^2$$

$$= 1.875 \times 10^{-3}$$

EXERCISES

1. Roll three dice (one red, one blue, and one green.) Let X equal the sum of the numbers on the red and blue dice and let Y equal the sum of the numbers on the blue and green dice. Find the joint distribution of X and Y.

2. Roll two dice (one red and one blue). Let X be the sum of the numbers on two dice and let Y be the number on the red die. Find the joint distribution of X and Y.

3. Let X, Y be discrete random variables with $p_{X,Y}(x,y)$ their joint density function and $p_X(x)$ the density function of X. For a given x, which is larger: $p_X(x)$ or $p_{X,Y}(x,y)$?

4. Let X and Y be discrete random variables such that their joint density function $p_{X,Y}(x,y) = 1/15$ or 0. Suppose that X has only five possible values. What is the least number of possible values that Y can have?

   For the next four exercises, calculate the marginal density functions for X and Y, the covariance between X and Y, and the correlation between X and Y. In each case the table gives the joint density function.

5.

X	$Y = 0$	$Y = 2$	$Y = 4$	$Y = 6$
-2	.1	0	.1	.2
4	0	.1	0	.1
5	.1	0	.1	.2

6.

X	$Y = 3$	$Y = 5$	$Y = 9$
-2	.15	.05	0
-1	.05	0	.2
0	0	.1	0
1	.15	0	.2
2	0	.1	0

7.

X	Y = 1	Y = 4	Y = 5	Y = 6	Y = 9
0	.1	0	.1	0	0
5	0	.1	0	0	.15
9	0	.05	0	0	0
11	0	.3	0	.05	0
13	.15	0	0	0	0

8.

X	Y = -9	Y = -4	Y = -3	Y = -1	Y = 0
-3	0	.1	0	.05	.1
2	.05	0	0	0	0
4	0	0	.1	0	.05
5	0	0	0	.05	0
7	0	.25	.05	0	.2

9. Suppose the joint density function for X and Y is given by the following table. Find $f_X(x)$ and $f_Y(y)$.

X	Y = 1	Y = 2	Y = 3	Y = 4
1	.2	.1	.1	0
2	0	0	0	0
3	0	.1	.1	.2
4	0	0	.1	.1

10. Roll two dice. Let X represent the sum of the numbers on the top of the dice, and let Y represent the sum of the numbers on the bottom of the dice. Determine the joint density function.

11. Let X be the number of the month (January is 1, February is 2, etc.), and let Y be the day of the month for a randomly selected day in a regular (non-leap) year. Determine the joint density function for X and Y.

12. Give an example of two random variables X and Y such that $f_{X,Y}(x,y) = f_X(x)f_Y(y)$. Give another example such that
$$f_{X,Y}(x,y) \neq f_X(x)f_Y(y).$$

13. If $f_{X,Y}(x_1,y_1) > 0$, then we call (x_1,y_1) a *possible combined value* for X and Y. If $f_{X,Y}(x,y) \geq .13$ for all possible combined values (x,y), what is the largest number of possible combined values?

14. In a lottery based on a randomly selected three-digit number, let X be the first two digits and Y be the last two. Describe $f_{X,Y}(x,y)$.

15. Suppose the following table gives the joint density function for two random variables X and Y.

X	$Y = 7$	$Y = 10$	$Y = 13$	$Y = 14$
1	.1	0	.1	0
2	0	0	0	.15
5	0	.25	0	.1
9	.1	.1	.1	0

Find the joint cumulative distribution function.

16. Why can't

$$g(x,y) = \begin{cases} .1 & x = 2, \quad y = 3/2 \\ .3 & x = 1/2, y = 4 \\ .5 & x = 2, \quad y = 1 \\ .2 & x = 4, \quad y = 1 \\ 0 & \text{everywhere else} \end{cases}$$

be a joint density function?

17. Calculate the covariance and correlation between X and Y when X represents the number on the top of a die and Y represents the number on the bottom of the die.

18. Calculate the covariance and correlation between X and Z when they represent the numbers that appear when two separate dice are tossed.

The next four exercises refer to the random variables U *and* V *whose joint density function is given in Chapter 13.*

19. Calculate the covariance and correlation for U and V.

20. Calculate the marginal density functions for U and V.

21. Find the conditional density function for U given that $V = 2$.

22. Find the conditional density function for V given that $U = 3$.

☆ 23. Show that $E(XY) = E(X) E(Y)$ if X and Y are independent.

☆ 24. Show that $[Cov(X,Y)]^2 \leq Var(X) Var(Y)$ for any two random variables X and Y.

25. Show that the correlation coefficient between any two random variables is always between -1 and 1. Use the result of the preceding exercise.

26. Let $Y = aX + b$, where X and Y are two random variables and a and b are two constants (with $a > 0$). Show that the correlation coefficient for X and Y is 1.

CHAPTER 14

LAW OF LARGE NUMBERS AND CENTRAL LIMIT THEOREM

$\blacksquare$ n this chapter we are going to derive the most important results in probability theory. We've already indicated that if you measure a random variable many times, then the average of all those observations will be close to the expectation value. Now we will prove that proposition. Also, we'll show some amazing features of the normal distribution.

Markov's Inequality

We'll start by stating a proposition called *Markov's inequality*. Let's suppose that X is a random variable that you are absolutely sure will always have a positive value. (In other words, $F(0) = \Pr(X \leq 0) = 0$.) Then Markov's inequality states that if $a > 0$

$$\Pr(X \geq a) \leq \frac{E(X)}{a}$$

(For the proof, see answer to Exercise 13.)

This result is true for *any* positive value of a, and it is true regardless of the nature of the distribution of X. Notice that, as a becomes very large $E(X)/a$ becomes small, so the probablity that X will be greater than a becomes small. Markov's inequality is valuable because it applies to any random variable, even if you know nothing about its distribution (other than that the random variable is always positive). However, the inequality doesn't always give you very much useful information. For example, suppose $a < E(X)$. Then $E(X)/a > 1$, so all that Markov's inequality tells you is that $\Pr(X \geq a)$ is less than some number greater than one. However, you already knew *that*, since any probability is always less than one.

Here is an example of the use of Markov's inequality. Let's say that Y is a chi-squared random variable with two degrees of freedom. Y will always be positive, so we can use Markov's inequality. We know $E(Y) = 2$. Let's calculate the probability that Y will be greater than 5. From Markov's inequality:

$$\Pr(Y \geq 5) \leq \frac{E(Y)}{5}$$

$$\Pr(Y \geq 5) \leq \frac{2}{5}$$

In this case we know from a chi-square table that the true value is about .1.

Here is an example where the limit set by Markov's inequality is closer to the actual value. Suppose X is a random variable with the following density function:

$$\Pr(X = 2) = .308$$

$$\Pr(X = 3) = .308$$

$$\Pr(X = 4) = .308$$

$$\Pr(X = 50) = .076$$

Then $E(X) = 6.572$. Markov's inequality says that $\Pr(X \geq 49) \leq 6.572/49$, or $\Pr(X \geq 49) \leq .134$.

Chebyshev's Inequality

Markov's inequality can be used to prove another important proposition known as *Chebyshev's inequality*. Chebyshev's inequality works for *all* random variables, not just positive ones as does Markov's inequality. Chebyshev's inequality tells us the answer to an important question: How likely is it that the value of a particular random variable will be very far away from its mean?

We'll say that X is a random variable with mean μ and variance σ^2. Chebyshev's inequality states:

$$\Pr(|X - \mu| \geq k) \leq \frac{\sigma^2}{k^2}$$

To prove this, let's define the random variable Y like this:

$$Y = (X - \mu)^2$$

Since Y is the square of a number, it will always be positive, so it must obey Markov's inequality. So we can write

$$\Pr(Y \geq k^2) \leq \frac{E(Y)}{k^2}$$

Y will be greater than k^2 only if $|X - \mu| \geq k$. Therefore,

$$\Pr(|X - \mu| \geq k) \leq \frac{E(Y)}{k^2}$$

$$\Pr(|X - \mu| \geq k) \leq \frac{E[(X - \mu)^2]}{k^2}$$

The expression $E[(X - \mu)^2]$ is a familiar old friend (or nemesis); it's just the definition of the variance of X (or σ^2). So

$$\Pr(|X - \mu| \geq k) \leq \frac{\sigma^2}{k^2}$$

Therefore, what Chebyshev's inequality does is put an upper limit to the likelihood that any random variable will be very far from its mean. Notice that if σ^2 is smaller, then σ^2/k^2 is smaller, so there is less chance that X will be very far from its mean. As k becomes bigger, σ^2/k^2 becomes smaller, which means that as you go farther and farther away from the mean there is a smaller and smaller chance that you will find the value of X there.

EXAMPLES   Let X be a random variable with a binomial distribution, with parameters p and n. Then we know that $E(X) = np$, and $\mathrm{Var}(X) = np(1 - p)$. Since X will always be positive, we can use Markov's inequality:

$$\Pr(X \geq a) \leq \frac{np}{a}$$

From Chebyshev's inequality we have

$$\Pr(|X - np| \geq k) \leq \frac{np(1 - p)}{k^2}$$

Suppose $p = .4$ and $n = 10$. Then Markov's inequality tells us that $\Pr(X \geq a) \leq 4/a$. For example, if $a = 9$, Markov's inequality states that $\Pr(X \geq 9) \leq 4/9$. In reality, the probability that $X \geq 9$ is .001.
Chebyshev's inequality tells us that

$$\Pr[(X \geq 4 + k) \text{ or } (X \leq 4 - k)] \leq \frac{2.4}{k^2}$$

For example, if $k = 3$, then Chebyshev's inequality says that there is less than a 27 percent chance that X will be less than 1 or greater than 7. The exact value of the probability is .071.
Let X be the uniform random variable on the interval from 0 to 10. Then $\mu = 5$, $\sigma^2 = 100/12 = 25/3$, and $f(x) = 1/10$ if $0 < x < 10$, and

$$\Pr(X \geq a) = 1 \qquad \text{if } a \leq 0$$

$$= 1 - \frac{a}{10} \qquad \text{if } 0 < a < 10$$

$$= 0 \qquad \text{if } a \geq 10$$

Markov's inequality states that, if $a > 0$, then

$$\Pr(X \geq a) \leq \frac{E(x)}{a} = \frac{5}{a}$$

From Chebyshev's inequality:

$$\Pr(|X - \mu| \geq k) \leq \frac{25}{3k^2}$$

Law of Large Numbers

Now we can prove a very important result in probability theory. We have already said that if we flip a coin a large number of times the number of heads that appear will be close to $n/2$. If we toss a die many times and take the average of all of the results, we expect that the average will be near $3\frac{1}{2}$. Both of these situations are examples of a more general law called the *law of large numbers*. (Strictly speaking, we're going to talk about the weak law of large numbers first, and then we'll talk about the strong law of large numbers later.)

Let us start with a random variable X. As is traditional, we will say $E(X) = \mu$ and $\text{Var}(X) = \sigma^2$. We'll observe X many, many times, and we'll call the observations X_1, X_2, X_3, and so on, up to X_n. We'll assume that all of these random variables are independent of each other. Take the average of all the X's (call it $\bar{x}$):

$$\bar{x} = \frac{X_1 + X_2 + \cdots + X_n}{n}$$

As you've probably guessed by now, $\bar{x}$ will be close to μ if n is very large. You might be skeptical and say, "But there still must be a very small probability that $\bar{x}$ might be a little way away from μ." The law of large numbers says that, as n becomes very, very large (that is, as n approaches infinity) the probability that $\bar{x}$ will not equal μ approaches zero.

To prove this law, we will use Chebyshev's inequality. First, note that $\bar{x}$ depends on the values of a bunch of random variables, so $\bar{x}$ is itself a random variable. We can calculate the mean and variance of $\bar{x}$:

$$E(\bar{x}) = E\left[\frac{X_1 + X_2 + \cdots + X_n}{n}\right]$$

$$= \frac{1}{n} E[X_1 + X_2 + \cdots + X_n]$$

$$= \frac{1}{n} [E(X_1) + E(X_2) + \cdots + E(X_n)]$$

$$= \frac{1}{n} (\mu + \mu + \cdots + \mu)$$

$$= \frac{1}{n} n\mu$$

$$= \mu .$$

We can use the properties of variances to calculate $\text{Var}(\bar{x})$:

$$\text{Var}(\bar{x}) = \text{Var}\left[\left(\frac{1}{n}\right)(X_1 + X_2 + \cdots + X_n)\right]$$

$$= \frac{1}{n^2}[\text{Var}(X_1 + X_2 + \cdots X_n)]$$

$$= \frac{1}{n^2}[\text{Var}(X_1) + \text{Var}(X_2) + \cdots + \text{Var}(X_n)]$$

(The last step works only because all of the X's are independent.)

$$\text{Var}(x) = \frac{1}{n^2}(\sigma^2 + \sigma^2 + \cdots + \sigma^2)$$

$$= \frac{1}{n^2}(n\sigma^2)$$

$$= \frac{\sigma^2}{n}$$

This equation establishes an important result: The variance of the sample average is *less* than the variance of each random variable taken individually. And as you increase the number of items in the sample, the variance of $\bar{x}$ becomes less and less.

Now we can use Chebyshev's inequality, which says:

$$\Pr(|\bar{x} - \mu| \geq \epsilon) \leq \frac{\text{Var}(\bar{x})}{\epsilon^2} \qquad (\epsilon \text{ can be any small positive number.})$$

Since $\text{Var}(\bar{x}) = \sigma^2/n$, we can substitute:

$$\Pr(|\bar{x} - \mu| \geq \epsilon) \leq \frac{\sigma^2}{n\epsilon^2}$$

As n goes towards infinity, we can see that $\sigma^2/n\epsilon^2$ goes to zero. Therefore, as n goes to infinity, the distance from $\bar{x}$ to μ must go to zero.

One other feature of the law of large numbers is important to remember. Suppose that you measure the random variable many times and there is a stretch during which you see many values that are less than the average. That does not mean that in the future you are more likely to get values greater than the average in order to cancel out the earlier values. Each measurement is still independent.

Central Limit Theorem

Now comes something you've undoubtedly been waiting for: a reason to study the normal distribution. From the definition alone, it does seem a pretty weird thing to study so thoroughly. However, it turns out that if you add together a lot of independent identically distributed random variables, the resulting sum will have a normal distribution. That's one of the reasons why the normal distribution pops up everywhere. This is the kind of theorem we will present now. It is called the *central limit theorem*.

Formally, the theorem states: Let $X_1, X_2, \cdots$ be an infinite sequence of independent random variables with identical distributions. (Each X has mean μ and variance σ^2.) Then let $\bar{x} = [X_1 + X_2 + \cdots X_n]/n$. We already know that $E(\bar{x}) = \mu$ and $\text{Var}(x) = \sigma^2/n$. The central limit theorem says that, in the limit as n goes to infinity, $\bar{x}$ has a normal distribution.

EXAMPLE Suppose that you assign a number to each person alive today. Let X_i be the volume of air in the ith person's lungs at a given second. Since n is roughly 4×10^9 and the X's have identical distributions and are independent, $(X_1 + X_2 + \cdots + X_n)/n$ has a distribution very close to the normal distribution.

There are two very simple corollaries we can establish. If we just add all of the x's together, then the result will also have a normal distribution, this time with mean $n\mu$ and variance $n\sigma^2$. Or, if we calculate the random variable

$$Z = \frac{\sqrt{n}(\bar{x} - \mu)}{\sigma}$$

then Z will have a standard normal distribution.

Since the binomial distribution can be thought of as the sum of a group of independent two-valued random variables, the central limit theorem says that the binomial density function begins to look like the normal distribution as n becomes large. Note that this works even though the binomial distribution is a discrete distribution and the normal distribution is a continuous distribution. Table 14-1 illustrates what happens as n increases, and the binomial density function is illustrated in Figure 14-1.

TABLE 14-1: Comparison of Normal and Binomial Probability Density Functions

$\Pr(X = k)$ $p = 0.5$

k	$n = 6$ Binomial	$n = 6$ Normal	$n = 10$ Binomial	$n = 10$ Normal	$n = 20$ Binomial	$n = 20$ Normal	$n = 30$ Binomial	$n = 30$ Normal
1	.0938	.0859	.0098	.0103	$\cdots$	.0001	$\cdots$	$\cdots$
2	.2344	.2334	.0439	.0417	.0002	.0003	$\cdots$	$\cdots$
3	.3125	.3257	.1172	.1134	.0011	.0013	$\cdots$	$\cdots$
4	.2344	.2334	.2051	.2066	.0046	.0049	$\cdots$	$\cdots$
5	.0938	.0859	.2461	.2523	.0148	.0146	.0001	.0002
6			.2051	.2066	.0370	.0360	.0006	.0007
7			.1172	.1134	.0739	.0725	.0019	.0020
8			.0439	.0417	.1201	.1196	.0055	.0056
9			.0098	.0103	.1602	.1614	.0133	.0132
10					.1762	.1784	.0280	.0275
11					.1602	.1614	.0509	.0501
12					.1201	.1196	.0806	.0799
13					.0739	.0725	.1115	.1116
14					.0370	.0360	.1354	.1363
15					.0148	.0146	.1445	.1457

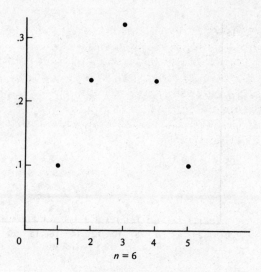

$n = 6$

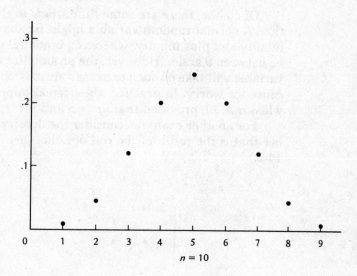

$n = 10$

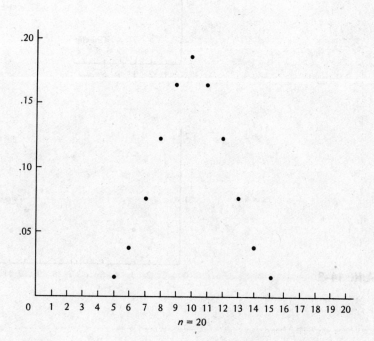

FIGURE 14–1

$n = 20$

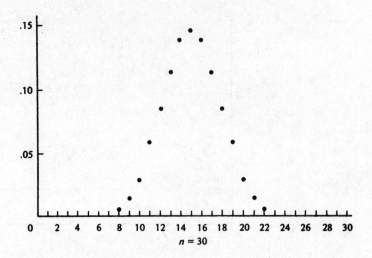

FIGURE 14–1

Of course, there are some limitations to the normal approximation. A normal random variable might be anywhere between minus infinity and plus infinity, whereas a binomial random variable must be between 0 and n. However, the probability that a normal random variable will take on such extreme values is very small, so there is no cause for worry. In practice, the normal approximation is all right when $n > 30$, provided that $np > 5$ and $n(1 - p) > 5$.

For another example, consider the density function for the number that is the result of the roll of a die. (See Table 14-2 and Figure 14-2.)

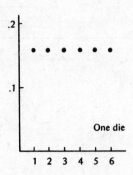

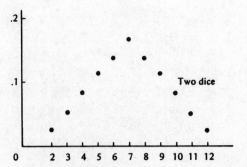

FIGURE 14–2

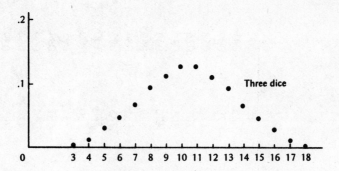

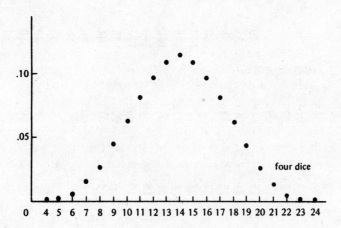

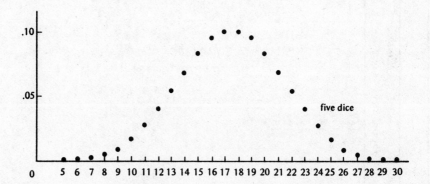

FIGURE 14–2

This density function doesn't look at all like the normal distribution. However, if you roll two dice, then the density function for the result looks a bit more like the normal distribution, and if you increase the number of rolls then the density function looks more and more like the normal density function.

TABLE 14-2

Number on dice	Number of dice: 1		2		3		4		5	
	Number of ways	Probability	Number of ways	Probability	Number of ways	Probability	Number of ways	Probability	Number of ways	Probability
1	1	.167								
2	1	.167	1	.028						
3	1	.167	2	.056	1	.005				
4	1	.167	3	.083	3	.014	1	.001		
5	1	.167	4	.111	6	.028	4	.003	1	..
6	1	.167	5	.139	10	.046	10	.008	5	.001
7			6	.167	15	.069	20	.015	15	.002
8			5	.139	21	.097	35	.027	35	.005
9			4	.111	25	.116	56	.043	70	.009
10			3	.083	27	.125	80	.062	126	.016
11			2	.056	27	.125	104	.080	205	.026
12			1	.028	25	.116	125	.096	305	.039
13					21	.097	140	.108	420	.054
14					15	.069	146	.113	540	.069
15					10	.046	140	.108	651	.084
16					6	.028	125	.096	735	.095
17					3	.014	104	.080	780	.100
18					1	.005	80	.062	780	.100
19							56	.043	735	.095
20							35	.027	651	.084
21							20	.015	540	.069
22							10	.008	420	.054
23							4	.003	305	.039
24							1	.001	205	.026
25									126	.016
26									70	.009
27									35	.005
28									15	.002
29									5	.001
30									1	..

The Proof of the Central Limit Theorem

 WARNING: We are now entering very difficult mathematical terrain. If you don't intend to lose any sleep over the question "How do you prove the central limit theorem?", then you can skip this section.

Now to prove the central limit theorem. We will need to use moment generating functions (described at the end of Chapter 11). First, we will prove a lemma concerning expectations.

Lemma: If X and Y are independent random variables, and g and h are functions, then $E[g(X)h(Y)] = E[g(X)]E[h(Y)]$ (This is a generalization of the result $E(XY) = E(X)E(Y)$ proved earlier.)

Proof: If X and Y are continuous random variables and $f_{X,Y}(x,y) = f_X(x) f_Y(y)$ is their joint density function, then

$$E[g(X)h(Y)] = \int_{-\infty}^{\infty} \int_{-\infty}^{\infty} g(x)h(y)f_{X,Y}(x,y) \, dx \, dy$$

$$= \int_{-\infty}^{\infty} g(x)f_X(x) \, dx \int_{-\infty}^{\infty} h(y)f_Y(y) \, dy$$

$$= E[g(X)]E[h(Y)]$$

(The proof is similar in the discrete random variable case.)

To prove the central limit theorem, we will have to use another lemma which we shall not prove but which should agree with your intuition.

Lemma: Let $X_1, X_2, \cdots$ be an infinite sequence of random variables. Let F_i be the cumulative distribution function and ψ_i be the moment generating function of X_i. Let X be a random variable with cumulative distribution F_X and moment generating function ψ_X. Then, if $\lim_{n \to \infty} \psi_n(t) = \psi_X(t)$ for all t, then $\lim_{n \to \infty} F_n(t) = F_X(t)$ for all t where F_X is continuous. In other words, what this theorem says is that if the sequence of moment generating functions converges to a particular limit, then the corresponding cumulative distribution functions must converge to the corresponding limit.

Assume that this lemma is true. Then we need to show that if

$$Y_n = \frac{X_1 + X_2 + \cdots + X_n - n\mu}{\sigma\sqrt{n}}$$

then

$$\lim_{n \to \infty} \psi_{Y_n}(t) = e^{t^2/2}$$

(Remember that $e^{t^2/2}$ is the moment generating function for the standard normal distribution.)

First assume that $\mu = 0$ and $\sigma^2 = 1$. Then

$$Y_n = \frac{X_1 + X_2 + \cdots + X_n}{\sqrt{n}}$$

Since the X_i's all have identical distributions, we can let $\psi_X(t)$ be their common moment generating function. Then

$$\psi_{X_i/\sqrt{n}}(t) = E(e^{tX_i/\sqrt{n}})$$

$$= \psi_X\left(\frac{t}{\sqrt{n}}\right)$$

and:

$$\psi_{Y_n}(t) = E[e^{tX_1/\sqrt{n}} e^{tX_2/\sqrt{n}} \cdots e^{tX_n/\sqrt{n}}]$$

$$= E[e^{tX_1/\sqrt{n}}] E[e^{tX_2/\sqrt{n}}] \cdots E[e^{tX_n/\sqrt{n}}] \quad \text{(because of the lemma above)}$$

$$= \left[\psi_X\left(\frac{t}{\sqrt{n}}\right)\right]^n$$

Now we expand $\psi_X(t)$ as a Taylor series. (If you haven't heard of Taylor series, you probably won't have made it into this section anyway.)

$$\psi_X(t) = \psi_X(0) + \psi_X'(0)t + \psi_X''(0)\frac{t^2}{2} + R_3(t)$$

$R_3(t)$ is the third-order remainder term, and $\lim_{\to 0} R_3(t)/t^2 = 0$.
Then, since $\psi_X(0) = E[e^{0 X_i}] = 1$, we have :

$$\psi_X(t) = 1 + tE(X) + \frac{t^2}{2}E(X^2) + R_3(t)$$

$$= 1 + t\mu + \frac{t^2}{2}(\sigma^2 + \mu^2) + R_3(t)$$

$$= 1 + \frac{t^2}{2} + R_3(t)$$

$$\psi_X\left(\frac{t}{\sqrt{n}}\right) = 1 + \frac{t^2}{2n} + R_3\left(\frac{t}{\sqrt{n}}\right)$$

$$\psi_{Y_n}(t) = \left[1 + \frac{t^2}{2n} + R_3\left(\frac{t}{\sqrt{n}}\right)\right]^n$$

Let $f(x) = \log(1 + x) - x$.

$$\lim_{x \to 0} \frac{\log(1 + x) - x}{x} = \lim_{x \to 0} \frac{f(x)}{x}$$

$$= \lim_{x \to 0} \frac{1/(1+x) - 1}{1}$$

$$= 0$$

(by l'Hôpital's rule)

Then

$$\log\left[\left(1 + \frac{t^2}{2n} + R_3\left(\frac{t}{\sqrt{n}}\right)\right)^n\right]$$

$$= n\left[\log\left(1 + \frac{t^2}{2n} + R_3\left(\frac{t}{\sqrt{n}}\right)\right)\right]$$

$$= n\left[\frac{t^2}{2n} + R_3\left(\frac{t}{\sqrt{n}}\right) + f\left(\frac{t^2}{2n} + R_3\left(\frac{t}{\sqrt{n}}\right)\right)\right]$$

Let $g(x) = f[x^2/2 + R_3(x)]$.

$$\lim_{x\to 0}\frac{g(x)}{x^2} = \lim_{x\to 0}\frac{f[x^2/2 + R_3(x)]}{x^2}$$

$$= \lim_{x\to 0}\left[\frac{f(x^2/2 + R_3(x))}{x^2/2 + R_3(x)}\right]\left[\frac{x^2/2 + R_3(x)}{x^2}\right]$$

$$= 0 \times \frac{1}{2}$$

$$= 0$$

$$\log\left[\left(1 + \frac{t^2}{2n} + R_3\left(\frac{t}{\sqrt{n}}\right)\right)^n\right] = n\left[\frac{t^2}{2n} + R_3\left(\frac{t}{\sqrt{n}}\right) + g\left(\frac{t}{\sqrt{n}}\right)\right]$$

$$= \frac{t^2}{2} + nR_3\left(\frac{t}{\sqrt{n}}\right) + ng\left(\frac{t}{\sqrt{n}}\right)$$

$$\lim_{n\to\infty} nR_3\left(\frac{t}{\sqrt{n}}\right) = \lim_{n\to\infty}\frac{t^2[R_3(t/\sqrt{n})]}{(t/\sqrt{n})^2}$$

$$= 0$$

$$\lim_{n\to\infty} ng\left(\frac{t}{\sqrt{n}}\right) = \lim_{n\to\infty} t^2\left[\frac{g(t/\sqrt{n})}{(t/\sqrt{n})^2}\right]$$

$$= 0$$

and

$$\lim_{n\to\infty}\log\left[\left(1 + \frac{t^2}{2n} + R_3\left(\frac{t}{\sqrt{n}}\right)\right)^n\right] = \lim_{n\to\infty}\log\left[\left(\psi_X\left(\frac{t}{\sqrt{n}}\right)\right)^n\right]$$

$$= \frac{t^2}{2}$$

$$\lim_{n\to\infty}\left[\psi_X\left(\frac{t}{\sqrt{n}}\right)\right]^n = \lim_{n\to\infty}\psi_{Y_n}(t)$$

$$= e^{t^2/2}$$

which is the moment generating function for the standard normal distribution. Voila! We did it.

If each X doesn't have $\mu = 0$, $\sigma^2 = 1$, set $\overline{X}_i = X_i - \mu/\sigma$; then

$$\frac{\overline{X}_1 + \overline{X}_2 + \cdots + \overline{X}_n}{\sqrt{n}} = \frac{X_1 + X_2 + \cdots + X - n\mu}{\sigma \sqrt{n}}$$

Strong Law of Large Numbers

There is an even stronger theorem (called, coincidentally enough, the *strong law of large numbers*) which says that the average of a large number of independent, identically distributed random variables is their common mean. In other words, if $X_1, X_2, \ldots$ are independent identically distributed random variables with mean μ, then

$$\Pr\left[\lim_{n \to \infty} \frac{X_1 + X_2 + \cdots X_n}{n} = \mu\right] = 1$$

This theorem is even stronger than the weak law of large numbers. The weak law says that for large n $\overline{X}$ will probably stay close to μ, but for any $\epsilon > 0$ there may be an infinite number of times that $|\overline{X} - \mu| > \epsilon$. The strong law says that, with probability 1, this occurrence can happen only a finite number of times, which is more like the intuitive concept of limit.

The proof of this theorem is beyond the scope of this book.

EXERCISES

1. If you flip a coin 400 times, what is the probability that you will get more than 250 heads?

2. If you flip a coin 400 times, what is the probability you will get between 190 and 210 heads?

3. If you roll a die 50 times, what is the probability that the resulting sum will be greater than 200?

4. If you roll a die 50 times, what is the probability that the resulting number will be between 170 and 180?

5. The probability of getting a royal flush when you deal out a five-card hand is 1.54×10^{-6}. Suppose you deal out 8×10^6 hands. What is the probability that you will get 0 royal flush? Make a list of the probabilities that you will get n royal flushes, for $n = 1$ to $n = 10$.

6. Suppose that there is only a 1/10,000,000 probability that a person will get struck by lightning. Out of 200 million people in the country, what is the probability that there are fewer than 15 people who are struck by lightning?

7. Suppose you roll a die 5,000 times. Use Chebyshev's inequality to estimate the probability that the average of the numbers that result will be between 3.4 and 3.6.

8. What is the maximum probability that a random variable might be 2 standard deviations from its mean?

9. What is the maximum probability that a random variable might be 4 standard deviations from its mean?

10. Let $X_1, \cdots, X_{25}$ be binomial random variables with identical parameters $n = 100$ and $p = .3$. Use the central limit theorem to calculate the probability that the sum of all of the X's will be less than 1,000.

11. Let $X_1, \cdots, X_{20}$ be geometric random variables with identical parameters $p = .7$. Use the central limit theorem to approximate the probability that the sum of the X's will be less than 10.

12. Suppose the density function for a random variable looks like the function shown in Figure 14–3.

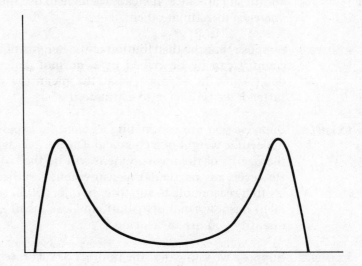

FIGURE 14–3

If you add up 100 random variables that all have this same density function, what will the density function for the sum look like?

☆ 13. Prove Markov's inequality.

☆ 14. Prove $E[g(X)\, h(Y)] = E[g(X)]\, E[h(Y)]$ when X and Y are independent discrete random variables.

CHAPTER 15

STATISTICAL ESTIMATION

U p to now, in most of the problems we have done we have known in advance what all of the probabilities were. For example, when we draw cards or toss coins, we can calculate all of the probabilities explicitly. However, in most real problems we don't know the probabilities in advance. Instead, we have to use the methods of *statistical inference* to estimate them.

EXAMPLE   Suppose that the distribution of the heights of all of the people in the country can be described by a normal distribution. However, we don't know in advance what the mean (μ) of the distribution is. Instead, we will have to estimate it.

EXAMPLE   Suppose you are conducting a scientific experiment to measure the molecular weight of a chemical. On the average, you can expect that the results of the measurement will be the true value of the weight. However, any particular measurement is subject to random errors. It is often reasonable to suppose that the actual result of each measurement has a normal distribution whose mean is the true value of the quantity you are measuring.

EXAMPLE   Suppose we know that the number of successes of an experiment can be characterized by a binomial distribution, but that we don't know in advance the value of the probability-of-success parameter (p). We wish to use our observations of the results of the experiment to estimate the value of p.

EXAMPLE   Suppose we know that a person's scores on two different kinds of tests are given by random variables with unknown correlation. We will try to estimate the correlations.

Estimating the Mean

We will consider the general problem of trying to estimate the mean (μ) of a random variable X that has a normal distribution. Let's say that we have n observations of the value of the random variable, which we can call $X_1, X_2, X_3, \cdots, X_n$. We need to make one more important assumption: We need to assume that each value of X is independent of all of the other values. (This process of drawing numbers is called taking a *random sample* of size n from this particular distribution.)

Intuitively, it is clear what our estimate for the mean should be:

$$\text{(estimate of mean)} = \bar{x} = \frac{X_1 + X_2 + X_3 + \cdots + X_n}{n}$$

This quantity is just the average value of all of the X's, which we called $\bar{x}$, or the sample average; $\bar{x}$ is an example of a *statistic*. A *statistic* is a particular function of the items in a random sample. When a statistic is used to estimate the value of some unknown quantity, it's called an *estimator*. In this case, $\bar{x}$ is used as an estimator for the quantity μ. Often a small hat sign ($\hat{\mu}$) is placed over a quantity to indicate that it is an estimator for a parameter. The statement "$\hat{\mu} = \bar{x}$" means, "We are using the sample average $\bar{x}$ as an estimator for the mean μ." An *estimate* is the value of an estimator in a particular circumstance. If the sample we observe consists of the numbers 5, 7, 4, 10, 12, and 4, then $\bar{x} = \hat{\mu} = 7$ is an estimate for the population mean.

What we'll do now is show that the sample average $\bar{x}$ has some appealing properties when it is used to estimate the mean.

Maximum Likelihood Estimators

Suppose that the true value of μ was 10,000, but the sample average turned out to be 7 for a particular sample. This occurrence is not likely to happen. On the other hand, if $\mu = 7$, then we are much more likely to get a value of 7 for the sample average. In fact, for every possible value of μ we can calculate the probability of getting a particular value $\bar{x}$ for the sample average. Intuitively, we would not estimate that μ has one of the values for which the probability of getting the observed sample average is very low. We would much rather choose our guess for μ to be a value such that the probability of getting the observed sample average is high. In general, the value of μ that gives the highest probability of getting the actual observed value of $\bar{x}$ is called the *maximum likelihood* estimate of μ.

We certainly expect that the sample average $\bar{x}$ will be the maximum likelihood estimator for the mean μ, and we will in fact show this in the mathematical section at the end of the chapter.

The method of maximum likelihood can also be used for many other types of problems. In general, suppose that a is an unknown parameter in a particular probability distribution. Then in many cases we can calculate the maximum likelihood estimator for a. For example, we can show that the maximum likelihood estimator of the variance ($\hat{\sigma}^2$) from a normal distribution is

$$\hat{\sigma}^2 = \frac{(x_1 - \bar{x})^2 + (x_2 - \bar{x})^2 + \cdots + (x_n - \bar{x})^2}{n}$$

(We called this statistic s_1^2, the sample variance.) However, this estimator for the variance does not satisfy all of the criteria for a good estimator. In the next chapter we will discuss another estimate of the variance, s_2^2, which is equal to $s_1^2 \times n/(n - 1)$.

If we are trying to estimate the probability of success p for a random variable with a binomial distribution, then the maximum likelihood estimator is also the obvious one:

$$\frac{\text{(number of successes)}}{\text{(number of attempts)}}$$

Suppose that X and Y are two random variables whose correlation we don't know. We would like to figure out the maximum likelihood estimator for the correlation. Suppose we have n observations each for X and Y:

$$(X_1, Y_1), (X_2, Y_2), (X_3, Y_3), \ldots, (X_n, Y_n)$$

Calculate $\bar{x}$, $\bar{y}$, $\overline{xy}$, $s_x = \sqrt{\overline{x^2} - \bar{x}^2}$, and $s_y = \sqrt{\overline{y^2} - \bar{y}^2}$. Then the maximum likelihood estimator for the correlation is

$$\frac{\overline{xy} - \bar{x}\,\bar{y}}{s_x\, s_y}$$

We call this quantity the *sample correlation coefficient*. For example, suppose we have these observations for X and Y:

$$X: \quad 10 \quad 4 \quad 9 \quad 7 \quad 3 \quad 0 \quad 19$$
$$Y: \quad 12 \quad 6 \quad 18 \quad 10 \quad 6 \quad 0 \quad 29$$

Then $\bar{x} = 7.43$; $\overline{x^2} = 88.0$; $s_x = 5.729$; $\bar{y} = 11.57$; $\overline{y^2} = 211.6$; $s_y = 8.813$; and $\overline{xy} = 135$. The sample correlation coefficient is

$$\frac{135 - 7.43 \times 11.57}{5.729 \times 8.813} = .971$$

Another important property of maximum likelihood estimators is called the *invariance property*. Suppose that $\hat{a}$ is the maximum likelihood estimator for a parameter a, but we really want to know the maximum likelihood estimator of $\sqrt{a}$. If we were forced to make a guess, we would probably estimate that $\sqrt{a}$ is equal to $\sqrt{\hat{a}}$, and fortunately we would be right. For example, the maximum likelihood estimator of the standard deviation ($\hat{\sigma}$) is just the square root of the sample variance. In general, if $h(a)$ is any function of a parameter a, then the maximum likelihood estimator of $h(a)$ is just $h(\hat{a})$.

Consistent Estimators

Another important property that we would like our estimators to have is the consistency property. You've undoubtedly been confused by inconsistent people, and you can be just as confused by inconsistent estimators. Here is what we mean by the consistency property for estimators. Suppose we are able to increase our sample size by a lot and therefore acquire a lot more observations of the random variable X. In that case, do we know that the new value of $\bar{x}$ will be closer to the mean μ or is there a chance that it might be farther away? A consistent estimator is an estimator such that the probability is very high that the value of the estimator will move closer to the true value as you increase the number of elements in the sample.

Fortunately, $\bar{x}$ does satisfy the property of being a consistent estimator of the population mean.

Unbiased Estimators

Another important question we might ask about an estimator is: Do we expect that the result of this estimator will be the true value? An estimator is said to be *unbiased* if the expectation value of the estimator is equal to the true value of the parameter we are trying to estimate.

For example, we have already found that $E(\bar{x}) = \mu$, so the sample average is an unbiased estimator of the population mean μ.

Derivation of the Maximum Likelihood Estimator for the Mean

WARNING: mathematical area

We can show that $\bar{x}$ is the maximum likelihood estimator of μ. First, we show the density function of X_1, since X_1 is selected from a normal distribution:

$$f_{X_1}(x_1) = \frac{1}{\sqrt{2\pi}\,\sigma}\,e^{-\frac{1}{2}\left[\frac{x_1-\mu}{\sigma}\right]^2}$$

Now we can calculate the joint density function of X_1 and X_2. Since X_1 and X_2 are independent, we can get the joint density function by multiplying the two individual density functions together:

$$f(x_1, x_2) = f_{X_1}(x_1)\,f_{X_2}(x_2) = \frac{1}{2\pi\sigma^2}\,e^{-\frac{1}{2}\left[\frac{x_1-\mu}{\sigma}\right]^2}\,e^{-\frac{1}{2}\left[\frac{x_2-\mu}{\sigma}\right]^2}$$

Exponents have the useful property that $e^a e^b = e^{a+b}$, so we can rewrite the joint density function as follows:

$$f(x_1, x_2) = \frac{1}{2\pi\sigma^2}\,e^{-\frac{1}{2\sigma^2}[(x_1-\mu)^2 + (x_2-\mu)^2]}$$

We can follow this same procedure to get the joint density function of all n of the observations of X:

$$f(x_1, x_2, \cdots, x_n) = f_{X_1}(x_1)\,f_{X_2}(x_2)\,f_{X_3}(x_3)\,\cdots\,f_{X_n}(x_n)$$

$$= \frac{1}{(2\pi\sigma^2)^{n/2}}\,e^{-\frac{1}{2\sigma^2}[(x_1-\mu)^2 + (x_2-\mu)^2 + \cdots + (x_n-\mu)^2]}$$

Now, to find the maximum likelihood estimator of μ, we need to find the value of μ that makes this function as large as possible. (When a density function for a group of observations is expressed as a function of an unknown parameter like this, it is called a *likelihood function*.)

To make f as large as possible, we need to make

$$-\frac{1}{2\sigma^2}[(x_1 - \mu)^2 + (x_2 - \mu)^2 + \cdots + (x_n - \mu)^2]$$

as large as possible, which is the same as making

$$(x_1 - \mu)^2 + (x_2 - \mu)^2 + \cdots + (x_n - \mu)^2$$

as small as possible. We can rewrite the last expression as

$$x_1^2 - 2x_1\mu + \mu^2 + x_2^2 - 2x_2\mu + \mu^2 + \cdots + x_n^2 - 2x_n\mu + \mu^2$$
$$= (x_1^2 + x_2^2 + \cdots + x_n^2) - 2\mu(x_1 + x_2 + \cdots + x_n) + n\mu^2$$
$$= (x_1^2 + x_2^2 + \cdots + x_n^2) - 2\mu n\bar{x} + n\mu^2$$

We need to use a little calculus to show that the optimum value of μ (call it $\hat{\mu}$) will satisfy this equation:

$$-2n\bar{x} + 2n\hat{\mu} = 0$$
$$\hat{\mu} = \bar{x}$$

Therefore, just as we suspected all along, $\bar{x}$ is the maximum likelihood for μ.

EXERCISES

1. Suppose you are taking samples from a normal distribution with mean 7 and variance 9. If you observe 10 values, what is the probability that $\bar{x}$ will be between 6 and 8? What is the probability that $\bar{x}$ will be between 8 and 9? What is the probability that $\bar{x}$ will be between 9 and 10?

Estimate the mean and variance for these sets of numbers:

2. 20, 21, 12, 16, 24, 24, 23, 15, 20, 19, 25, 21, 19, 20, 14.

3. 10, 9, 10, 14, 8, 15, 6, 10, 7, 10, 11, 15, 8, 12, 10.

4. 15, 9, 18, 10, 14, 23, 14, 11, 15, 11, 18, 14, 18, 15, 13.

5. Assume that the score that your team makes in each game is selected from a normal distribution. Estimate the mean and variance.

6. For a particular game of your favorite football team, estimate the mean and variance for the yardage it gains on running plays and compare it with the mean and variance of the yardage it gains on passing plays.

7. Show that (successes)/(trials) is an unbiased estimator for the probability of success p for a random variable with a binomial distribution.

8. Show that s_1^2 is the maximum likelihood estimator for the variance when a random sample is taken from a normal distribution.

CHAPTER 16

ACCURACY OF ESTIMATES

In Chapter 15 we discussed how to use observations of a random variable to get information about an unknown parameter for the distribution that generates that variable. However, we still have to face one important question: Are these estimates likely to be very close to the true value?

For example, suppose you are trying to estimate the fraction of days that it rains in Florida. You naturally would use the estimator

$$\frac{\text{(number of days you've been in Florida when it rained)}}{\text{(number of days you've been in Florida)}}$$

However, if you've only been in Florida one day and it rained that day, your estimate that it rains in Florida every day is not likely to be very accurate. If you've spent ten years in Florida you'll be able to estimate the fraction of rainy days much more accurately.

The value of a statistic that is used as an estimator depends on the values of a group of random variables, so that means that the estimator is itself a random variable. It would help if we could figure out what the distribution of the estimator looks like. For example, let's suppose we are using the sample average $\bar{x}$ to estimate the value of the mean of a normal random variable.

$$\bar{x} = \frac{X_1 + X_2 + \cdots + X_n}{n}$$

Each of these X's has a normal distribution, so because of the addition property for normal random variables $\bar{x}$ must also have a normal distribution. ($\bar{x}$ is found by adding up a bunch of normal random variables.) We have already found that $E(\bar{x}) = \mu$ and $\text{Var}(\bar{x}) = \sigma^2/n$.

Confidence Intervals

Now that we know the distribution of $\bar{x}$, we can be more precise about how good our estimate is. We know that the true value of μ is likely to

160

be close to $\bar{x}$, but how close is close? Is $\bar{x}$ likely to be 1 unit away from μ? Or is it likely to be 50 units away? We'd like to know the probability that the distance from $\bar{x}$ to μ will be less than some specific value c. In other words, we want to know the probability that the true value of μ is between $(\bar{x} - c)$ and $(\bar{x} + c)$. Obviously, the probability depends a lot on the value of c that we choose. (See Figure 16-1.)

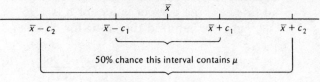

$$\bar{x}$$

| $\bar{x} - c_2$ | $\bar{x} - c_1$ | $\bar{x} + c_1$ | $\bar{x} + c_2$ |

50% chance this interval contains μ

FIGURE 16–1   95% chance this interval contains μ

If we choose a very large value of c, then we can be almost certain that the true value of μ will be in the interval. For example, we could set c to be infinity. Then the probability that μ will be in the interval is 100 percent, since obviously μ must be between $(\bar{x} - \text{infinity})$ and $(\bar{x} + \text{infinity})$. However, an interval that wide is not very useful. If we make the interval narrower by choosing a smaller value for c, then we can be more precise about the true value of μ. However, when we make the interval narrower there is a greater chance that μ won't even be contained in the interval.

The normal procedure in statistics works like this. First, we choose the probability that we want—in other words, we set in advance the probability that μ will be in the interval. Often this probability is set at 95 percent. Then we calculate how wide the interval must be so that there is a 95 percent chance that it contains the true value. This type of interval is called a *confidence interval*, and .95 is the *confidence level*.

Now we need to calculate the value of c that satisfies the equation

$$Pr(\bar{x} - c < \mu < \bar{x} + c) = .95$$
$$Pr(-c < \bar{x} - \mu < c) = .95$$

Once we know the value of c, we know how wide the confidence interval must be. That means that our job is to calculate the value of c. Let's create a new random variable called Z:

$$Z = \frac{\bar{x} - \mu}{\sqrt{\sigma^2/n}}$$

$$= \sqrt{n}\,\frac{\bar{x} - \mu}{\sigma}$$

Using the properties we established for normal random variables, we know that Z has a standard normal distribution (mean 0 and variance 1; see Chapter 11). We can rewrite the equation:

$$Pr\left(\frac{-c\sqrt{n}}{\sigma} < \sqrt{n}\,\frac{(\bar{x} - \mu)}{\sigma} < \frac{c\sqrt{n}}{\sigma}\right) = .95$$

$$Pr\left(\frac{-c\sqrt{n}}{\sigma} < Z < \frac{c\sqrt{n}}{\sigma}\right) = .95$$

This problem calls for the standard normal probability table. Let's define a to be: $a = c\sqrt{n}/\sigma$. Then

$$\Pr(-a < Z < a) = .95$$

Now we need to look in Table A3-2 until we find a value of a that satisfies this equation. Scanning down the columns, we can see that in this case the correct value for a is 1.96.

Now we can find the value for c:

$$c = \frac{1.96\sigma}{\sqrt{n}}$$

Thus we know how wide the confidence interval should be. There is a 95 percent chance that the true value of μ will be between $x - 1.96\sigma/\sqrt{n}$ and $x + 1.96\sigma/\sqrt{n}$.

There are two features of this result that are appealing to common sense. The confidence interval is wider (that is, more uncertain) if σ is bigger. If the variance of each individual observation is bigger, then it will be harder for us to pin down the true value of μ. On the other hand, the confidence interval is smaller if n is bigger. That means that as we take more and more observations we will be able to predict the true value of μ more accurately.

We can be even more cautious if we want to. Suppose that we want to be 99 percent sure that our confidence interval contains the true value of μ. Then we will have to settle for a wider, less precise interval. Or, if we wanted to be less careful, we could have calculated a smaller confidence interval that had a lower probability of containing the true value.

Here is the general procedure for calculating confidence intervals.

1. Decide on the confidence interval you want. If you are more cautious, pick a higher level. (.95 is one of the most common levels.)
2. Look up the value of a in Table 16-1.
3. Calculate $\bar{x}$.
4. The confidence interval is from $\bar{x} - a\sigma/\sqrt{n}$ to $\bar{x} + a\sigma/\sqrt{n}$.

TABLE 16-1

Confidence level	a
.80	1.28
.85	1.44
.90	1.65
.95	1.96
.99	2.58

EXAMPLE   Here is a set of numbers that were drawn from an approximately normal distribution with $\sigma = 4.1835$:

21, 12, 22, 22, 22, 10, 13, 10, 17, 14, 15, 19,
21, 19, 11, 19, 18, 18, 19, 18, 20, 20, 14, 24,
15, 19, 19, 24, 14, 12, 16, 26, 14, 25, 9, 18,
14, 18, 12, 17, 20, 18, 12, 16, 19, 19, 13, 20,
19, 11, 18, 23, 19, 23, 17, 12, 23, 22, 14, 20,
13, 16, 17, 18, 13, 21, 14, 11, 15, 21, 18, 25,
18, 21, 20, 15, 23, 20, 20, 12, 15, 18, 19, 18,
18, 20, 13, 18, 20, 16, 15, 15, 18, 13, 28, 17,
25, 10, 15, 17, 17, 18, 15, 19, 15, 15, 24, 15,
14, 18, 16, 20, 21, 15, 12, 19, 19, 22, 19, 18,
16, 20, 21, 16, 15, 11, 11, 11.

First we need to calculate the sample average: $\bar{x} = 17.3$. There are 128 numbers in the sample, so the value of c for a 95 percent confidence interval is $c = 1.96 \times 4.1835/\sqrt{128} = .7248$. Therefore, the confidence interval is from 16.58 to 18.02.

Calculating Confidence Intervals by Using the *t* Distribution

There is one major difficulty with calculating confidence intervals this way. Often we don't know the true value of σ^2. Our first guess might be that we could use the sample variance to estimate the value of σ^2. It turns out that if the sample size (n) is large enough (for example, if $n > 30$), we can use the same confidence interval formula as in the previous section, with the sample variance s_1^2 used in place of σ^2. However, for small samples we need to develop a new method. First, we need to calculate the distribution of the sample variance s_1^2:

$$s_1^2 = \frac{(X_1 - \bar{x})^2 + (X_2 - \bar{x})^2 + \cdots + (X_n - \bar{x})^2}{n}$$

Anybody have any guesses as to what the distribution of s_1^2 will look like? It turns out that the distribution of s_1^2 is almost the same as the chi-square (χ^2) distribution. In particular, if we create a new random variable

$$Y_1^2 = \frac{n}{\sigma^2} s_1^2$$

then Y_1^2 will have a chi-square distribution with $n - 1$ degrees of freedom. (If you want to see this result for yourself, look at the mathematical section at the end of this chapter.)

We can now find the expectation of s_1^2. Since

$$E\left(\frac{n s_1^2}{\sigma^2}\right) = n - 1$$

(because that's the way chi-square random variables work), it follows that

$$\frac{n}{\sigma^2} E(s_1^2) = n - 1$$

$$E(s_1^2) = \frac{(n-1)}{n} \sigma^2$$

Note that $E(s_1^2)$ does not equal σ^2. This means that s_1^2 is *not* an unbiased estimator of the variance σ^2. However, we can define a new estimator (we'll call it s_2^2), like this:

$$s_2^2 = \frac{n}{n-1} s_1^2$$

The estimator s_2^2, which is an unbiased estimator of σ^2, can be found from the formula

$$s_2^2 = \frac{(X_1 - \bar{x})^2 + (X_2 - \bar{x})^2 + \cdots + (X_n - \bar{x})^2}{n-1}$$

In other words, you find s_2^2 in the same way as you find the original estimate s_1^2, except that the sum of the squared deviations is divided by $n - 1$ instead of by n. We'll call s_1^2 the sample variance, version 1, and s_2^2 the sample variance, version 2. For some purposes it is best to use s_2^2 as the estimator for the variance. As you can see, if n becomes large the values of s_1^2 and s_2^2 will become very close to each other, so in that case it doesn't make too much difference which one you choose.

Now we turn to the problem of calculating a confidence interval for the mean μ when we don't know the value of the variance σ^2. Our original confidence interval calculation was based on the fact that

$$\frac{\sqrt{n}(\bar{x} - \mu)}{\sigma}$$

was a standard normal random variable. So, since we don't know σ, let's try this statistic (we'll call it T):

$$T = \frac{\sqrt{n}(\bar{x} - \mu)}{s_2}$$

We can guess that the distribution of T will look almost like the standard normal distribution. That is what we will proceed to demonstrate. We need to make some changes in the way we write T:

$$T = \frac{\sigma}{s_2} \frac{\sqrt{n}\,(\bar{x} - \mu)}{\sigma}$$

Let $Z = \sqrt{n}(\bar{x} - \mu)/\sigma$. We know that Z has a standard normal distribution. We can write

$$T = \frac{Z}{s_2/\sigma}$$

Let's make up a new random variable $Y_2{}^2$:

$$Y_2{}^2 = \frac{n-1}{\sigma^2} s_2{}^2$$

Since

$$s_2{}^2 = \frac{n}{n-1} s_1{}^2$$

and

$$\frac{n}{\sigma^2} s_1{}^2 = Y_1{}^2$$

it follows that

$$s_2{}^2 = \frac{\sigma^2}{n-1} Y_1{}^2$$

so $Y_2{}^2 = Y_1{}^2$. (In other words, $Y_2{}^2$ is the same random variable as $Y_1{}^2$ masquerading under a different disguise.) Therefore, we know that $Y_2{}^2$ has a chi-square distribution with $n-1$ degrees of freedom. Then we can write T like this:

$$T = \frac{Z}{\sqrt{Y_2{}^2/(n-1)}}$$

At first this complicated expression seems pretty strange and not very helpful. What good does it do to have a standard normal random variable divided by the square root of a chi-square random variable? However, that combination does suddenly ring a bell—we have already calculated the distribution of that strange random variable in Chapter 12. We called it the t distribution with $n-1$ degrees of freedom.

Now we can calculate the width of the confidence interval. We need to find the value of c that satisfies the equation

$$\Pr(\bar{x} - c < \mu < \bar{x} + c) = .95$$

Change that to:

$$\Pr(\mu - c < \bar{x} < \mu + c) = .95$$
$$\Pr(-c < \bar{x} - \mu < c) = .95$$
$$\Pr\left(\frac{-c\sqrt{n}}{s_2} < \sqrt{n}\left(\frac{\bar{x} - \mu}{s_2}\right) < \frac{c\sqrt{n}}{s_2}\right) = .95$$

Using our definition of the statistic T, we have

$$\Pr\left(\frac{-c\sqrt{n}}{s_2} < T < \frac{c\sqrt{n}}{s_2}\right) = .95$$

Now we have to look in a table of the t distribution. We have to find a value of a such that

$$\Pr(-a < T < a) = .95.$$

For example, if $n - 1 = 8$, we can see from Table A3-5 that $a = 2.306$. Once we find a, we can find c from the formula

$$c = s_2 \frac{a}{\sqrt{n}}$$

Therefore, the 95 percent confidence interval for μ is from $\bar{x} - s_2 a/\sqrt{n}$ to $\bar{x} + s_2 a/\sqrt{n}$.

EXAMPLE Let's look at the number of seats in the House of Representatives that the President's party loses in midterm elections. (See Table 16-2.)

TABLE 16-2: House of Representatives Seats Lost by President's Party

Year	President's party	Seats lost
1942	Democrat	50
1946	Democrat	54
1950	Democrat	29
1954	Republican	18
1958	Republican	47
1962	Democrat	5
1966	Democrat	48
1970	Republican	12
1974	Republican	48
1978	Democrat	16
1982	Republican	26

sample average: 32.09
sample standard deviation (s_2): 17.807

Let's assume that the number of seats lost has a normal distribution with unknown mean μ and unknown variance σ^2. We'll calculate a 95 percent confidence interval for μ. First, we find $\bar{x} = 32.09$. Then, we find $s_2 = 17.8$. Since we have 11 observations, we need to look in Table A3-5 at the t distribution with 10 degrees of freedom. We can find that the value of a is 2.228. Then the confidence interval is from 20.1 to 44.1.

In general, here is the procedure to calculate confidence intervals using the t distribution if you have n observations of the random variable X.

1. Decide on the confidence level. (.95 is one of the most common levels.)
2. Calculate $\bar{x}$:

$$\bar{x} = \frac{x_1 + x_2 + \cdots + x_n}{n}$$

3. Calculate s_2:

$$s_2 = \sqrt{\frac{(x_1 - \bar{x})^2 + (x_2 - \bar{x})^2 + \cdots + (x_n - \bar{x})^2}{n - 1}}$$

$$= \sqrt{\frac{n}{n-1}(\overline{x^2} - \bar{x}^2)}$$

4. Look up the value of a in Table A3-5. (Note that if n is larger than 30, the t distribution is almost the same as the standard normal distribution.)
5. The confidence interval for μ is from $\bar{x} - s_2 a/\sqrt{n}$ to $\bar{x} + s_2 a/\sqrt{n}$.

The Distribution of the Sample Variance

 WARNING: mathematical section

Now we have to show that the distribution of the sample variance $s_1{}^2$ is related to the chi-square distribution. To start with, we'll assume that now we do know the true value of μ, the mean. We'll define the statistic s^2 like this:

$$s^2 = \frac{(X_1 - \mu)^2 + (X_2 - \mu)^2 + \cdots + (X_n - \mu)^2}{n}$$

s^2 is an estimator for the variance of X. We will rewrite the formula for s^2 as follows. (You may object that we shouldn't put σ into that formula, since we don't know the value of σ, but we're going to do it anyway.)

$$s^2 = \frac{\sigma^2}{n}\left[\frac{(X_1 - \mu)^2 + (X_2 - \mu)^2 + \cdots + (X_n - \mu)^2}{\sigma^2}\right]$$

$$= \frac{\sigma^2}{n}\left[\left(\frac{X_1 - \mu}{\sigma}\right)^2 + \left(\frac{X_2 - \mu}{\sigma}\right)^2 + \cdots + \left(\frac{X_n - \mu}{\sigma}\right)^2\right]$$

If we let $Z_1 = (X_1 - \mu)/\sigma$, $Z_2 = (X_2 - \mu)/\sigma$, and so on, then each Z has a standard normal distribution. That means that Z^2 has a chi-squared distribution with one degree of freedom. Therefore, if we define Y^2 like this:

$$Y^2 = \left(\frac{X_1 - \mu}{\sigma}\right)^2 + \left(\frac{X_2 - \mu}{\sigma}\right)^2 + \cdots + \left(\frac{X_n - \mu}{\sigma}\right)^2$$

then Y^2 has a χ_n^2 distribution. Since

$$s^2 = \frac{\sigma^2}{n} Y^2$$

we can tell that $(n/\sigma^2)s^2$ has a χ_n^2 distribution.

However, in general we cannot use s^2 as an estimate of the variance, since we often don't know the true value of μ. However, we did discuss the statistic s_1^2, the sample variance, which is calculated using $\bar{x}$ as an estimator for the population mean:

$$s_1^2 = \frac{(X_1 - \bar{x})^2 + (X_2 - \bar{x})^2 + \cdots + (X_n - \bar{x})^2}{n}$$

Now we'll try to find the distribution of s_1^2. We know about the distribution of Y^2, so we'll start by looking at that:

$$Y^2 = \left(\frac{X_1 - \mu}{\sigma}\right)^2 + \left(\frac{X_2 - \mu}{\sigma}\right)^2 + \cdots + \left(\frac{X_n - \mu}{\sigma}\right)^2$$

We can change it around into a form that is more meaningful. Unfortunately, we have to make the expression worse before we can make it better.

$$Y^2 = \frac{1}{\sigma^2} [(X_1 - \bar{x} + \bar{x} - \mu)^2 + \cdots + (X_n - \bar{x} + \bar{x} - \mu)^2]$$

$$= \frac{1}{\sigma^2} [(X_1 - \bar{x})^2 + 2(X_1 - \bar{x})(\bar{x} - \mu) + (\bar{x} - \mu)^2$$

$$+ \quad (X_2 - \bar{x})^2 + 2(X_2 - \bar{x})(\bar{x} - \mu) + (\bar{x} - \mu)^2 + \cdots$$

$$+ \quad (X_n - \bar{x})^2 + 2(X_n - \bar{x})(\bar{x} - \mu) + (\bar{x} - \mu)^2]$$

All of those terms starting with 2 in the middle column quite conveniently add up to zero. Therefore,

$$Y^2 = \frac{1}{\sigma^2} [(X_1 - \bar{x})^2 + (X_2 - \bar{x})^2 + \cdots + (X_n - \bar{x})^2] + \frac{n}{\sigma^2} (\bar{x} - \mu)^2$$

We defined the statistic s_1^2 as follows:

$$s_1^2 = \frac{(X_1 - \bar{x})^2 + (X_2 - \bar{x})^2 + \cdots + (X_n - \bar{x})^2}{n}$$

Therefore, after all the dust clears, we can rewrite the expression for Y^2:

$$Y^2 = \frac{n}{\sigma^2} s_1^2 + \frac{n}{\sigma^2} (\bar{x} - \mu)^2$$

Remember that $\bar{x}$ has a normal distribution with mean μ and variance σ^2/n, so

$$Z = \sqrt{n}\left(\frac{\bar{x} - \mu}{\sigma}\right)$$

has a standard normal distribution. Therefore,

$$Z^2 = \frac{n(\bar{x} - \mu)^2}{\sigma^2}$$

has a χ_1^2 distribution. Then

$$\frac{n}{\sigma^2} s_1^2 = Y^2 - Z^2$$

where Y^2 has a chi-square distribution with n degrees of freedom, and Z^2 has a chi-square distribution with 1 degree of freedom. If you know something about chi-square random variables, you're likely to guess that ns_1^2/σ^2 has a chi-square distribution with $n - 1$ degrees of freedom. And, in fact, that guess turns out to be right.

NOTES TO CHAPTER 16

It is important to note that there is a subtle point involved with the calculation of confidence intervals. If you calculate a 95 percent confidence interval, that does not exactly mean that there is a 95 percent chance that μ is contained in the interval. The mean μ is a constant, even if we don't know its value. Instead, it is the interval $\bar{x} - c$ to $\bar{x} + c$ itself that is a random interval, so we are calculating the probability that this random interval will be chosen so that it happens to contain μ.

One more important point about the t distribution needs to be made. The definition of the t distribution requires that the standard normal random variable Z and the chi-square random variable Y^2 must be independent. But if we look at these expressions:

$$Z = \frac{\sqrt{n}(\bar{x} - \mu)}{\sigma}$$

$$Y_2^2 = \left(\frac{n-1}{\sigma^2}\right)s_2^2$$

we can see that Z depends on the sample mean and Y_2^2 depends on the sample variance. Since these two quantities are both calculated from the same sample, it doesn't seem as if they could be independent. However, when a sample is taken from a normal distribution it has the amazing property that the sample mean and the sample variance *are* independent. The proof of this fact is too hard and boring to include in this book, though. And you should note that, in general, when you are sampling from a distribution that is not a normal distribution the sample mean and the sample variance will *not* be independent.

EXERCISES

1. Calculate a 95 percent confidence interval for the mean for the following random sample taken from a normal distribution with variance 11: 1.1, 0.2, 1.9, 4.1, 5.3, −6, .5, −.6

2–6. Calculate 95 percent confidence intervals for the means of the sets of numbers from Chapter 15, Exercises 2–6.

7. Calculate 95 percent confidence intervals for the test scores from the four subjects discussed in Chapter 3.

Calculate 99 percent confidence intervals for the mean if you have these observations for a random variable with a normal distribution with unknown mean and variance:

8. 18, 9, 15, 10, 16, 8, 7, 20, 13, 8, 12

9. 17, 13, 9, 8, 10, 13, 16, 17, 12, 11, 17

10. 15, 13, 13, 14, 15, 20, 15, 14, 9, 16, 12

11. 16, 12, 13, 12, 14, 11, 8, 13, 17, 15, 14

12. Show that s_2^2 is an unbiased estimator for the variance for a random sample.

13. Suppose a random sample of size 2 (X_1, X_2) is taken for a random variable with an unknown distribution. Calculate the expectation value of

$$\frac{(X_1 - \bar{x})^2 + (X_2 - \bar{x})^2}{n - 1}$$

☆ 14. Show that $\sum_{i=1}^{n} 2(X_i - \bar{x})(\bar{x} - \mu) = 0$.

15. Write a program that reads in a set of numbers selected from a normal distribution and then calculates a 95 percent confidence interval for the mean.

16. Toss two dice 15 times. In this case we know that the mean of each observation is 7. However, pretend for now that you don't know the mean, and then calculate a 95 percent confidence

interval for the mean, using the available data. Then, repeat the entire procedure 100 times. How many times did your estimated confidence interval contain the true value for the mean?

17. Estimate a 95 percent confidence interval for your grocery bill for several weeks.

18. Keep a record of the high temperature in your town every day this month. Then calculate a 95 percent confidence interval for the mean.

CHAPTER 17

HYPOTHESIS TESTING

In Chapter 2 we considered a specific hypothesis testing problem: If you toss a coin many times, how can you tell whether or not the coin is fair? Now we'll consider a more general treatment of the methodology that statisticians use when they formulate and test hypotheses.

Remember that the hypothesis that we want to test is called the null hypothesis (or H_0), and the hypothesis that says, "The null hypothesis is wrong" is called the alternative hypothesis. Examples of null hypotheses include:

- A coin is fair.

- The mean number of raisins in boxes of a particular brand of raisin cereal is 7.

- The difference in effectiveness between four cold medicines occurred entirely by chance.

- The rate of appointments to the U.S. Supreme Court fits the Poisson distribution.

If we decide to reject the null hypothesis, that means that we are almost sure the hypothesis is not true. More specifically, we usually design our test so that there is only a 5 percent chance that we would have rejected the hypothesis if it were really true. However, if we decide to accept the hypothesis, that does not mean for sure that the hypothesis is true. It just means that we have not yet found statistical evidence to reject it.

Test Statistics

The normal procedure in statistics is to calculate a specific quantity called a *test statistic*. There are several common test statistics. The one that you use depends on the problem you are facing. We will consider several examples in this chapter.

The test statistic is designed so that *if* the null hypothesis is true, you know exactly what the distribution of the test statistic is. Then you have to ask yourself: Suppose the null hypothesis is true. In that case, is the observed value of the test statistic a very plausible value? If the observed test statistic value is very unlikely to have occurred, then you figure that most likely the hypothesis is false.

For example, suppose you are testing a null hypothesis using a test statistic Z. Suppose you know that Z will have a standard normal distribution if the null hypothesis is true. Calculate the value of Z. If, for example, the value of Z turns out to be .878, then everything is fine. There is a reasonably good chance of drawing the number .878 from a standard normal distribution. Since the observed value is not particularly implausible, you have no grounds for rejecting the hypothesis.

However, suppose the observed value of the test statistic Z turned out to be 3. Then you should begin to get suspicious. You can see from the standard normal table that there is a probability of only .0026 that a standard normal random variable will be outside 3. (We will use the terms inside and outside in the following fashion. We will say that Z is *inside* a value c if $-c < Z < c$. We will say that Z is *outside* a value c if $Z < -c$ or if $Z > c$. In other words, Z is inside c if $|Z| < c$, and Z is outside c if $|Z| > c$.) You should say to the advocates of the null hypothesis, "You can't pull the wool over my eyes. I know that this test statistic value is very unlikely to have occurred if the null hypothesis were true, so I'm going to reject the hypothesis."

The null hypothesis advocates might respond, "If you reject the null hypothesis then you will be committing a type 1 error, since we think that the null hypothesis is really true. We admit that we had bad luck with our test statistic, and it turned out to have an implausible value. But it is still possible that you might draw the number 3 from a standard normal distribution."

Of course, there is no way that you can prove them wrong. There still is a slight possibility that the null hypothesis might be true, so you could commit a type 1 error by erroneously rejecting the hypothesis. But that is the risk that you will have to take. (Remember that a type 1 error occurs if you reject the null hypothesis when it is really true. A type 2 error occurs if you accept the null hypothesis when it is really false. See Chapter 2.) Normally, we design our test so that the risk of committing a type 1 error is less than 5 percent. The risk of committing a type 1 error is called the *level of significance* of the test. Therefore, we can say that our test is designed to be at the 5 percent significance level.

From the standard normal tables we can see that there is a 95 percent chance that Z will be inside 1.96, so we will design our test so that the null hypothesis is accepted if Z is inside 1.96 and rejected otherwise.

Therefore, we will call the region inside 1.96 the zone of acceptance and the region outside 1.96 the critical region. (See Figure 17-1.) Sometimes the number that is the boundary between the critical region and the zone of acceptance is called the *critical value* of the test statistic. In this case the critical values are 1.96 and -1.96.

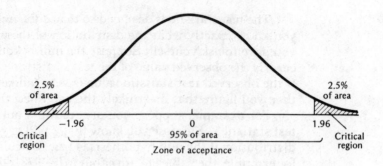

FIGURE 17-1

We can see that with this test

$$\text{Pr(rejecting } H_0 \text{ if it is really true)}$$
$$= \text{Pr}[(Z > 1.96) \text{ or } (Z < 1.96)]$$
$$= .025 + .025$$
$$= .05$$

which is the result we want. If the observed value of the test statistic turns out to be outside 1.96, then we will say that we can reject the hypothesis at the 5 percent significance level.

However, suppose that we want to be more cautious. Suppose that it is very costly for us to reject the hypothesis erroneously, so we want to make sure that the probability of this event happening is only 1 percent. Then we need to widen the zone of acceptance. (See Figure 17-2.) There is a 99 percent chance that Z will be inside 2.58. There-

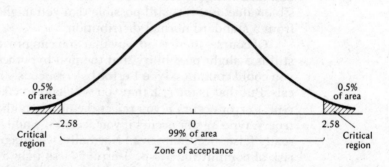

FIGURE 17-2

fore, we can ensure that there is only a 1 percent chance of committing a type 1 error if we design our test so that the zone of acceptance runs from −2.58 to 2.58. If the value of the test statistic turns out to be −2.6, we can reject the hypothesis at the 1 percent significance level. (This is poor terminology, since a *more* significant test corresponds to a *lower* significance level.)

However, suppose the value of the test statistic Z turns out to be 2. In that case we cannot reject the hypothesis at the 1 percent level. If we want a test at that level, we must accept the hypothesis. However, as we saw earlier, with a test statistic of 2 we can reject the hypothesis at the 5 percent level. Test statistics like this one are in a sort of gray area. Is the hypothesis really true? Nobody knows, and this time we are not even sure whether or not to accept the hypothesis. If you're willing to risk a 5 percent chance of a type 1 error, then you can reject the hypothesis. However, if you are more cautious you will have to accept the hypothesis.

The situation is much more clear-cut when you get a test statistic such as 3 or larger. In that case you can reject the hypothesis at every significance level.

It will be helpful to remember these critical values:
If Z has a standard normal distribution when the null hypothesis is true, then

- if $-1.96 < Z < 1.96$, accept the hypothesis at the 5 percent level.

- if $-2.58 < Z < 2.58$, accept the hypothesis at the 1 percent level.

Testing the Value of the Mean

Now we'll see what test statistics arise in actual practice. Suppose we can observe a sequence of numbers drawn from a normal distribution. Suppose that we know the variance, but not the mean, of the distribution. We need to test the hypothesis that μ equals a particular value μ^*.

For example, suppose that we're quality control inspectors investigating the number of raisins in each (small) box of a raisin cereal. If there are too few raisins in the box, customers will complain. If there are too many, then the company will lose money on each box of cereal sold. The raisins are put into the boxes by an Automatic Raisin Packer. We know that the machine works in such a way that the number of raisins in each box has a normal distribution with variance 16.16. On the average, the boxes are supposed to have 7 raisins. Our mission is to test the null hypothesis that the mean μ is equal to 7. We have $n = 13$ observations for the mean:

$$9, 11, 6, 10, 7, 4, 0, 7, 8, 6, 8, 2, 18$$

The sample average $\bar{x}$ is 7.38. Is that close enough to 7 so that we should accept the hypothesis? Or is it too far away? We know that if the hypothesis is true, then $\bar{x}$ will have a normal distribution with mean $\mu = 7$ and variance $16.16/n$. Therefore,

$$Z = \frac{\sqrt{n}\,(\bar{x} - 7)}{\sigma} = \frac{\sqrt{13}\,(7.38 - 7)}{4.02}$$

will have a standard normal distribution. Therefore, Z will be our test statistic. In our case, the computed value of Z is .341, which is well within the zone of acceptance. So we can accept the hypothesis that $\mu = 7$.

Of course, in general we cannot use the statistic $z = (X - \mu^*)/\sigma$, because we ordinarily won't know the true value of σ. However, if the null hypothesis $\mu = \mu^*$ is true, then the test statistic

$$t = \sqrt{n}\left(\frac{x - \mu^*}{s_2}\right)$$

will have a t distribution with $n - 1$ degrees of freedom. (See Chapter 16.)

For example, suppose that you have the following data points representing the weights of 27 sample players on a particular football team:

160, 185, 235, 208, 170, 185, 204, 180, 205, 215,
185, 188, 180, 220, 220, 221, 205, 235, 225, 190,
180, 205, 250, 210, 230, 210, 218

You want to test the hypothesis that these weights were selected from a normal distribution with mean 220. You need to calculate the two statistics $\bar{x} = 204.4$ and $s_2 = 22.1$. Then you can calculate the test statistic t:

$$t = \frac{(204.4 - 220)}{22.2} \sqrt{27} = -3.65.$$

If the hypothesis is true, t will have a t distribution with 26 degrees of freedom. If you look up the results in a t table you can see that the critical value for a 1 percent test is 2.779. In other words, you can reject the null hypothesis at the 1 percent level if the value of the test statistic is outside 2.779. Since -3.65 is in the critical region, you have good statistical evidence to reject the hypothesis that the sample of football players was selected from a population with mean 220.

General procedure to test the hypothesis that the mean $\mu = \mu^*$, when you have observed n values taken from a normal distribution:

Method 1. Use this method if you *know* the variance (σ^2) of the distribution.
1. Calculate the sample average $\bar{x}$.
2. Calculate the test statistic Z:

$$Z = \frac{\sqrt{n}\,(\bar{x} - \mu^*)}{\sigma}$$

3. If you want to test the hypothesis at the 5 percent significance level, then accept the hypothesis that $\mu = \mu^*$ if Z is between -1.96 and 1.96; otherwise reject the hypothesis.
4. If you want to test the hypothesis at another significance level, then look in Table 16-1 or A3-2 to find the critical value for Z.

Method 2. Use this method if you *don't know* the variance of the distribution.
1. Calculate the sample average $\bar{x}$.
2. Calculate the sample variance s_2^2:

$$s_2^2 = \frac{(X_1 - \bar{x})^2 + (X_2 - \bar{x})^2 + \cdots + (X_n - \bar{x})^2}{n - 1}$$

3. Calculate the statistic t:

$$t = \sqrt{n}\, \frac{(\bar{x} - \mu^*)}{s_2}$$

4. The t statistic will have a t distribution with $n - 1$ degrees of freedom. Look in Table A3-5 to find the critical value for the t distribution with the appropriate degrees of freedom.

One-tailed Tests

Suppose that you are a quality control inspector for a semiconductor firm that buys silicon wafers from a particular supplier. Each wafer has a certain number of defects. If there are too many defects, you must reject the wafer. The supplier tells you that, on the average, there are 14 defects per wafer. Your job is to find out whether or not the supplier is right. You have checked the number of defects for a sample of 17 wafers, with these results:

7, 16, 19, 12, 15, 9, 6, 16, 14, 7, 2,
15, 23, 15, 12, 18, 9

You want to test the hypothesis that the number of defects on each wafer has a normal distribution with mean $\mu = 14$. However, suppose it turns out that you can reject the hypothesis that $\mu = 14$ because the sample average is significantly *less* than 14. In that case you'll be totally happy—you surely won't complain to the supplier if the number of defects is less than is advertised. So you don't really want to test the null hypothesis that $\mu = 14$. Instead, you want to test the null hypothesis that $\mu \leq 14$. If you can reject this null hypothesis, then you will complain to the supplier. You can use the same t statistic again. The only difference is that, this time, you will only reject the null hypothesis if the value of the t statistic is in the region where the top 5 percent of the area is located. Figure 17-3 illustrates the critical region and the zone of acceptance for this test. In our case, we will have a t distribution with 16 degrees of freedom. If we look in Table A3-4 we can see that the critical region is located for values of t above 1.746.

This type of test is called a *one-tailed test*, because the critical region consists of only one tail of the distribution. In a one-tailed test the null hypothesis is rejected only if the test statistic has a value significantly greater than expected. (C   '   do a one-tailed test

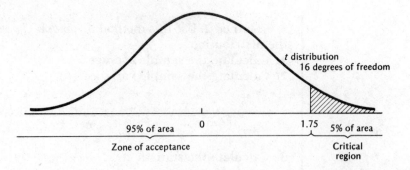

FIGURE 17–3

using only the left-hand tail, in which case the null hypothesis is rejected only if the test statistic value is significantly less than expected.)

The tests that we did before are called *two-tailed tests*. In a two-tailed test, you reject the null hypothesis if the test-statistic value is either very low or very high. Which type of test you should use depends on your situation. Normally, if the null hypothesis involves an inequality, such as $\mu > \mu^*$, you will want to use a one-tailed test. If the null hypothesis involves an equality, such as $\mu = \mu^*$, then you will use a two-tailed test.

In the semiconductor case, the sample average $\bar{x} = 12.647$, so obviously you cannot reject the hypothesis that $\mu < 14$. The value of s_2 is 5.396, so the test statistic value is:

$$T = \sqrt{n}\left(\frac{\bar{x} - 14}{s_2}\right) = -1.033.$$

Testing Hypotheses About the Probability of Success

Now we return to the problem of attempting to tell whether or not a coin is fair. To make things easier, let's assume that we have performed enough tosses so that we can approximate the binomial distribution by the normal distribution. In that case, if the hypothesis $p = p^*$ is true, then the number of heads (X) will have a normal distribution with mean $\mu = p^*N$ and variance $\sigma^2 = Np^*(1 - p^*)$. The variable $Z = (X - \mu)/\sigma$ will have a standard normal distribution.

Now, suppose that we have tossed the coin 10,000 times, and we ended up with 5,056 heads. Should we accept the hypothesis that the coin is fair? The fair-coin hypothesis says that $p = .5$, so X will have a normal distribution with $\mu = 5,000$ and $\sigma^2 = 10,000/4$. We need to calculate the test statistic Z:

$$Z = \frac{X - 5,000}{\sqrt{10,000/4}} = \frac{56}{50} = 1.12.$$

This value is within the 95 percent zone of acceptance, so we can accept this hypothesis at the 5 percent significance level.

For another example, suppose there were 4,884 heads that resulted from the 10,000 tosses. In that case the value of the test statistic is $-116/50 = -2.32$. This value is outside 1.96, so we can reject the fair coin hypothesis at the 5 percent level (and the person who supplied the coin has some explaining to do). However, the value −2.32 is not outside the zone of acceptance at the 1 percent level, so if we want to be more cautious we cannot reject the fair-coin hypothesis.

Return to the first situation, in which 5,056 heads appeared in 10,000 flips. Suppose that we don't actually believe that the coin is fair. Instead, we think that the coin is unbalanced so that heads are slightly more likely to appear. In particular, we'll test the hypothesis that $p = .51$. If this null hypothesis is true, then X will have a normal distribution with mean 5,100 and variance $10,000 \times .51 \times .49 = 2,499$. In this case the value of our test statistic is $-44/49.98 = -0.880$. This value is well within the zone of acceptance, so we can't reject the hypothesis that $p = .51$. However, we have already found that we also can't reject the hypothesis that $p = .5$. There is no way that both of these hypotheses can be right, but we have no way to tell the two apart using only the information available to us. You probably could have guessed that it would be very difficult to tell the difference between these two hypotheses.

This fact illustrates that hypothesis testing methods can do a good job of proving hypotheses wrong, but they often can't do a very good job of proving hypotheses right. Even if you decide to accept the null hypothesis, that does not mean that there is not some other hypothesis that can also adequately account for the data. If you want to make a very convincing case that your hypothesis is true, then you will have to be able to reject all of the likely competing hypotheses. Since we haven't been able to do that in the coin example, we cannot say for sure that the coin is fair.

We have only one hope—if we flip the coin many, many times, then finally we will reach the point where we can tell the difference between the hypotheses $p = .5$ and $p = .51$. However, in the real world you often cannot increase your sample size by a lot. If you find yourself with two competing hypotheses neither of which can be rejected by the available data, then you're stuck.

The Chi-square Test

Let's suppose that we are trying to test whether there is any difference between four competing cold-prevention medicines. None of the medicines is guaranteed to work—instead, they just promise to reduce your chances of getting a cold. Therefore, the number of people who try each kind of medicine and then get colds can be regarded as a random variable. Suppose we have checked with a sample of 495 people. We asked them what kind of medicine they used, and then whether or not they got colds. The results were:

	Medicine 1	Medicine 2	Medicine 3	Medicine 4	Total
How many got colds	15	26	9	14	64
How many did not	111	107	96	117	431
Total	126	133	105	131	495

(This type of table is called a *contingency table*—in this case with two rows and four columns.)

We can see from the table that medicine 3 seemed to be the most effective. Only 8.5 percent of the people who tried medicine 3 got colds. However, there are many other things that could have determined whether or not those people got colds. Maybe the people who used medicine 3 just happened to be exposed to fewer cold germs, so the fact that they got fewer colds is just a chance happening that has nothing to do with the fact that they used medicine 3.

Therefore, our null hypothesis will be as follows: There is basically no difference between the four medicines. In that case, the observed differences between the two medicines arose solely by chance.

Now we need to develop a test statistic to check this hypothesis. We can observe that in the total sample the fraction of people who got colds was .129 and the fraction who did not was .871. If there really was no difference between the medicines, then the fraction of people who got colds or did not get colds in each group should be close to these fractions. We can make a table comparing the actual and observed values for the number of people in each group:

	Medicine 1	Medicine 2	Medicine 3	Medicine 4
Number with colds				
actual	15	26	9	14
predicted	16.254	17.157	13.545	16.899
Number without colds				
actual	111	107	96	117
predicted	109.746	115.843	91.455	114.101

(Each location in the table is called a *cell*. This table has 8 cells.)

We want to base our test statistic on the difference between the observed frequencies and the frequencies that are predicted if there is in fact no difference between the medicines. If this difference is small, we can reasonably accept the no-difference hypothesis. If this difference is large, then we should reject the hypothesis.

Let f_i represent the observed frequency in cell i and let f_i^* represent the predicted frequency for cell i. Then, if there are n cells, we will use this test statistic:

$$S = \frac{(f_1 - f_1^*)^2}{f_1^*} + \frac{(f_2 - f_2^*)^2}{f_2^*} + \cdots + \frac{(f_n - f_n^*)^2}{f_n^*}$$

$$= \sum_{i=1}^{n} \frac{(f_i - f_i^*)^2}{f_i^*}$$

In our case we have 8 cells, and the value of the test statistic is

$$\frac{(15 - 16.254)^2}{16.254} + \frac{(26 - 17.157)^2}{17.157} + \frac{(9 - 13.545)^2}{13.545} + \frac{(14 - 16.899)^2}{16.899}$$

$$+ \frac{(111 - 109.746)^2}{109.746} + \frac{(107 - 115.843)^2}{115.843} + \frac{(96 - 91.455)^2}{91.455}$$

$$+ \frac{(117 - 114.101)^2}{114.101} = 7.666$$

As it turns out, if the null hypothesis is true this test statistic has a chi-square distribution, so it is called the chi-square statistic. The degrees of freedom is given by

(degrees of freedom)

= (Number of rows − 1) × (Number of columns − 1)

In our case, we have 2 rows and 4 columns, so our chi-square statistic has $(2 - 1) \times (4 - 1) = 3$ degrees of freedom. (In fact, the statistic described here has only approximately a chi-square distribution.)

Now that we have the test statistic, we need to look up the critical values in the chi-square tables. A χ_3^2 random variable has a 5 percent chance of being greater than 7.8. Since our test statistic is less than this value, we cannot reject the hypothesis at the 5 percent level. Using these data we cannot establish that there is any difference between the four medicines. However, the observed test statistic value of 7.666 is almost as large as 7.8, so these data indicate that there is almost more variation between the medicines than would be expected to happen by pure chance. So these data do tend to suggest that we should investigate this question further.

General procedure for chi-square test:
Suppose you are given a contingency table with m rows (categories) and n columns (groups):

	Group 1	Group 2	Group 3	$\cdots$	Group n
Category a	a_1	a_2	a_3	$\cdots$	a_n
Category b	b_1	b_2	b_3	$\cdots$	b_n
Category c (and so on)	c_1	c_2	c_3	$\cdots$	c_n

The chi-square test is used to test the hypothesis that there is *no* significant difference between the groups. In other words, any observed difference in the proportion of each group belonging to a particular category arose solely by chance.

1. Calculate the total number of observations in each category:

$$a_{\text{total}} = a_1 + a_2 + \cdots + a_n$$
$$b_{\text{total}} = b_1 + b_2 + \cdots + b_n$$

and so on.

2. Calculate the total number of observations in each group:

$$t_1 = a_1 + b_1 + c_1 + \cdots$$

$$t_2 = a_2 + b_2 + c_2 + \cdots$$

$$\cdots \cdots \cdots \cdots \cdots \cdots$$

$$t_n = a_n + b_n + c_n + \cdots$$

3. Calculate the grand-total number of observations:

$$T = t_1 + t_2 + t_3 + \cdots + t_n$$

4. Calculate the proportion in each category:

$$p_a = \frac{a_{\text{total}}}{T}$$

$$p_b = \frac{b_{\text{total}}}{T}$$

and so on.

5. Calculate the predicted frequency of occurrence for each cell:

$$f_{a1} = p_a t_1 \quad f_{a2} = p_a t_2 \quad \cdots \quad f_{an} = p_a t_n$$

$$f_{b1} = p_b t_1 \quad f_{b2} = p_b t_2 \quad \cdots \quad f_{bn} = p_b t_n$$

$$\cdots$$

6. Calculate the value of the chi-square statistic S:

$$S = \frac{(a_1 - f_{a1})^2}{f_{a1}} + \frac{(a_2 - f_{a2})^2}{f_{a2}} + \cdots + \frac{(a_n - f_{an})^2}{f_{an}}$$

$$+ \frac{(b_1 - f_{b1})^2}{f_{b1}} + \frac{(b_2 - f_{b2})^2}{f_{b2}} + \cdots + \frac{(b_n - f_{bn})^2}{f_{bn}} + \cdots$$

7. If the null hypothesis is true, the statistic S will have a chi-square distribution with $(m - 1) \times (n - 1)$ degrees of freedom. Look up the critical value in Table A3-3. If the observed value is greater than the critical value, then you should reject the hypothesis.

Goodness-of-fit Tests

The chi-square test can also be used to test whether or not a particular probability distribution fits the observed data very well. This type of test is called a *goodness-of-fit test*. Once again, we want to compare the observed frequencies f of a particular occurrence with the frequencies f^* that are predicted to occur if the alleged distribution really does fit the data well. Once again, we compute the statistic

$$\sum_{i=1}^{n} \frac{(f_i - f_i^*)^2}{f_i^*}$$

If the null hypothesis is true, this statistic will have approximately a chi-square distribution. If the value of the test statistic turns out to be too large, that means there is too much of a discrepancy between the actual results and the predicted results, so we can reject the hypothesis that the predicted distribution fits the data. The number of degrees of freedom for the chi-square statistic is

$$n - 1 - (\text{number of parameters that you have to estimate using the sample})$$

For example, if you use the sample to estimate the mean of the distribution you are using, then the χ^2 statistic will have $n - 2$ degrees of freedom.

Let's perform a goodness-of-fit test to see if the Poisson distribution is appropriate for predicting the number of United States Supreme Court justices that will be appointed in a five-year period. Table 17-1 shows the number of Court appointments that have been made during each five-year period in U.S. history.

TABLE 17-1: Appointments to United States Supreme Court

Period	Number of appointments	Period	Number of appointments
1790–94	3	1895–99	2
1795–99	4	1900–04	2
1800–04	2	1905–09	2
1805–09	2	1910–14	6
1810–14	2	1915–19	2
1815–19	0	1920–24	4
1820–24	1	1925–29	1
1825–29	2	1930–34	3
1830–34	1	1935–39	4
1835–39	5	1940–44	5
1840–44	1	1945–49	4
1845–49	3	1950–54	1
1850–54	2	1955–59	4
1855–59	1	1960–64	2
1860–64	5	1965–69	3
1865–69	0	1970–74	3
1870–74	4	1975–79	1
1875–79	1		
1880–84	4		
1885–89	3		
1890–94	4		

The mean is 2.605, so that on average 2.605 Supreme Court appointments are made in a five-year period. Here is the frequency distribution of these data. The upper figure is the number of appointments, the lower figure the number of periods in which there were that many appointments.

0	1	2	3	4	5	6
2	8	10	6	8	3	1

If the number of Supreme Court appointments is really given by a Poisson distribution with mean = 2.605, the predicted frequency distribution is

0	1	2	3	4	5	6
2.77	7.30	9.50	8.25	5.36	2.77	1.22

We can now calculate the chi-square test statistic:

$$\frac{(2 - 2.77)^2}{2.77} + \frac{(8 - 7.30)^2}{7.30} + \frac{(10 - 9.50)^2}{9.50}$$

$$+ \frac{(6 - 8.25)^2}{8.25} + \frac{(8 - 5.36)^2}{5.36} + \frac{(3 - 2.77)^2}{2.77}$$

$$+ \frac{(1 - 1.22)^2}{1.22} = 2.28$$

It looks as though the observed frequencies match the predicted frequencies quite well. We have $n = 7$ categories, and we had to use the sample data to estimate the mean, so that leaves us with $7 - 1 - 1 = 5$ degrees of freedom. We can see from a chi-square table that a χ_5^2 random variable has a 95 percent chance of being less than 11.07, so the critical region occurs for values of the test statistic above 11.07. The observed value is well within this limit, so we will accept the hypothesis that the rate of Supreme Court appointments can be described by the Poisson distribution. (Note that this was a one-tailed test, since we only wanted to reject the hypothesis if the test statistic was larger than expected. If the test statistic is very small, that means that the predicted frequencies are very close to the observed frequencies.)

Analysis of Variance

Suppose that we have observed scores on a particular aptitude test for three different groups of ten people each. The results were:

Group a: 88, 92, 91, 89, 89, 86, 92, 86, 89, 89
Group b: 91, 92, 85, 94, 93, 87, 87, 92, 91, 89
Group c: 87, 88, 95, 88, 92, 87, 89, 88, 87, 88

The average scores for the three groups are close together. It seems reasonable to suppose that there is in fact no difference in aptitude between the groups, and that the observed difference in the average score has arisen solely by chance.

Suppose that we check the scores for three different groups and find these results:

Group d: 87, 94, 91, 89, 89, 84, 92, 86, 89, 89
Group e: 82, 76, 84, 79, 77, 84, 81, 69, 79, 74
Group f: 69, 79, 67, 64, 65, 69, 69, 64, 72, 66

In this case it seems clear that there is a real difference in aptitude between the three groups. In other words, we can reject the hypothesis that the observed differences between the groups arose solely by chance.

In both of these cases it was obvious whether or not there was a significant difference between the average scores for the groups. However, in general it will be more difficult to tell if the observed differences in scores is significant or random. We need to develop a new method that is called *analysis of variance*. For now, let's assume that we have $m = 3$ groups (call them group a, group b, and group c), and that there are n people in each group. Assume that we know that the aptitude scores for the people in each group are selected from a normal distribution, and assume that the variance of the distribution is the same for all three groups.

Let's say that μ_a is the unknown mean aptitude test score for group a, μ_b is the mean for group b, and μ_c is the mean for group c. Our mission is to test the null hypothesis:

$$\mu_a = \mu_b = \mu_c = \mu$$

In other words, the null hypothesis states that the mean score for each group is the same. The alternative hypothesis simply states that the means are not all the same.

First, one obvious thing to do is calculate $\bar{a}$, $\bar{b}$, and $\bar{c}$ (the sample averages for each sample). If $\bar{a}$, $\bar{b}$, and $\bar{c}$ are close to each other, we will be more willing to accept the hypothesis that μ_a, μ_b, and μ_c are all equal. We can calculate $\bar{x}$, the average for all the numbers:

$$\bar{x} = \frac{\bar{a} + \bar{b} + \bar{c}}{m} = \frac{\bar{a} + \bar{b} + \bar{c}}{3}$$

We can also calculate the sample variance (version 2) for these three averages (we'll call that variance S^{*2}):

$$S^{*2} = \frac{(\bar{a} - \bar{x})^2 + (\bar{b} - \bar{x})^2 + (\bar{c} - \bar{x})^2}{m - 1}$$

The larger S^{*2} is, the *less* likely we will be to accept the no-difference null hypothesis.

We should also look at the sample variance for each individual sample:

$$s_a^2 = \sum_{i=1}^{n} \frac{(a_i - \bar{a})^2}{n - 1}, \qquad s_b^2 = \sum_{i=1}^{n} \frac{(b_i - \bar{b})^2}{n - 1}, \qquad s_c^2 = \sum_{i=1}^{n} \frac{(c_i - \bar{c})^2}{n - 1}$$

It will turn out to be useful to calculate the average of the three sample variances (call it S^2):

$$S^2 = \frac{s_a^2 + s_b^2 + s_c^2}{3}$$

The larger these three variances are, the more likely we are to see $\bar{a}, \bar{b}$, and $\bar{c}$ spread out, even if they really do come from distributions with the same mean. For example, suppose that the observed values of $\bar{a}, \bar{b}$, and $\bar{c}$ are 500, 400, 450. If $s_a^2 = s_b^2 = s_c^2 = 1$, we know right away that it is extremely unlikely that $\bar{a}, \bar{b}$, and $\bar{c}$ could have the observed values if they really did come from distributions with the same mean. On the other hand, if $s_a^2 = s_b^2 = s_c^2 = 10{,}000$, then it would be quite likely to see $\bar{a}, \bar{b}$, and $\bar{c}$ spread out by this much even if the null hypothesis is true. Therefore, the larger S^2 is, the *more* likely we will be to accept the null hypothesis.

We will calculate the following statistic (call it F):

$$F = \frac{n\,S^{*2}}{S^2}$$

If the value of F is large, we will reject the null hypothesis. We can show that the F statistic will have an F distribution with $(m - 1)$ and $m(n - 1)$ degrees of freedom. (m is the number of groups and n is the number of items in each group.) The F distribution is described in Chapter 12, and Table A3-6 lists some values for the cumulative distribution function.

In the examples we discussed earlier, we had $m = 3$ and $n = 10$. Therefore, the F statistic will have 2 and 27 degrees of freedom. Table A3-6 shows that this type of F statistic has a 95 percent chance of being less than about 3.3. Therefore, if the observed F statistic value is greater than 3.3, we will reject the null hypothesis; otherwise we will accept the null hypothesis.

In the first example, the F statistic is $4.133/6.693 = .6175$. Just as we suspected all along, we should accept the hypothesis. In the second example, the F value is $1061/16.996 = 62.426$, so we should reject the hypothesis.

Here is the general procedure for an analysis-of-variance test. (Assume that you have m groups, each with n members.)

1. Calculate the sample average for each group:

$$\bar{a} = \frac{a_1 + a_2 + \cdots + a_n}{n}$$

$$\bar{b} = \frac{b_1 + b_2 + \cdots + b_n}{n}$$

$$\bar{c} = \frac{c_1 + c_2 + \cdots + c_n}{n}$$

and so on.

2. Calculate the average of all the averages:

$$\bar{x} = \frac{\bar{a} + \bar{b} + \bar{c} + \cdots}{m}$$

3. Calculate the sample variance of the averages:

$$S^{*2} = \frac{(\bar{a} - \bar{x})^2 + (\bar{b} - \bar{x})^2 + (\bar{c} - \bar{x})^2 + \cdots}{m - 1}$$

4. Calculate the sample variance for each group:

$$s_a^2 = \frac{(a_1 - \bar{a})^2 + (a_2 - \bar{a})^2 + \cdots + (a_n - \bar{a})^2}{n - 1}$$

$$s_b^2 = \frac{(b_1 - \bar{b})^2 + (b_2 - \bar{b})^2 + \cdots + (b_n - \bar{b})^2}{n - 1}$$

$$s_c^2 = \frac{(c_1 - \bar{c})^2 + (c_2 - \bar{c})^2 + \cdots + (c_n - \bar{c})^2}{n - 1}$$

and so on.

5. Calculate the average of all of the sample variances:

$$S^2 = \frac{s_a^2 + s_b^2 + s_c^2 + \cdots}{m}$$

6. Calculate the value of the F statistic:

$$F = \frac{n\,S^{*2}}{S^2}$$

7. Look in Table A3-6 to find the critical value for an F distribution with $(m - 1)$ and $m(n - 1)$ degrees of freedom.

8. If the observed value of the F statistic is greater than the critical value, reject the null hypothesis. Otherwise accept it.

EXAMPLE To illustrate, let's investigate the effects that two different surgical procedures have on the rate of growth of laboratory rats. The two procedures we will investigate are area postrenal lesion and ovariectomy. We will need four groups of rats: one group that has both procedures; one group that has neither procedure; and two groups that of which has only one of the procedures. Then we will investigate their rates of growth.

The rates of growth coming from experiments performed by Liz Ashburn at Yale University are:

Group 1 (both): −0.088; −0.165; −0.099; 0.031; 0.030; 0.046; −0.010; −0.070; −0.099; 0.028; 0.019; 0.059; −0.037; 0.066; −0.044; −0.038; 0; −0.034; 0; −0.013; 0.014

Group 2 (ap lesion): -0.051; -0.079; -0.120; -0.017; -0.019; -0.065; 0.001; -0.038; 0.027; -0.030; -0.013; -0.012; 0.001; 0; -0.074; -0.104; -0.050; 0.033; 0.009; 0.039; 0.022

Group 3 (ovariectomy): $.152$; $-.120$; $.018$; 0; $.032$; $.031$; $-.020$; -0.143; 0.009; 0.012; 0.023; -0.014; 0.047; -0.007; -0.061; 0.137; 0.010; -0.136; 0.132; 0; 0.048

Group 4 (neither): -0.006; 0.047; 0.030; 0.016; 0.060; -0.045; 0.004; 0.018; 0.038; 0.006; 0.021; 0.006; 0.012; 0.031; 0.044; 0.009; 0.029; -0.029; 0.05; -0.027; 0.068

We need to calculate the sample average and the standard deviation s_2 for each group:

Group 1: $\bar{x} = -0.0192$, $s_2 = 0.0596$; Group 2: $\bar{x} = -0.0257$, $s_2 = 0.0445$;

Group 3: $\bar{x} = 0.0071$, $s_2 = 0.0786$; Group 4: $\bar{x} = 0.0182$, $s_2 = 0.0292$.

Then we can calculate the variance between the four averages: $s^{*2} = 0.000436$. The value of the test statistic is

$$\frac{21 \times 0.000436}{0.00314} = 2.92$$

If the null hypothesis is true, the test statistic will have an F distribution with $m - 1 = 3$ and $m(n - 1) = 80$ degrees of freedom. The F table shows that this random variable has a 95 percent chance of being less than about 2.7, so our observed statistic is just within the critical region and we can therefore reject the null hypothesis that the procedures have no effect on growth. However, these results consist of body-weight measurements within the first two weeks of the procedures and the differences between the different groups of rats become less when more time has elapsed since the procedures were done.

Derivation of the F Statistic

 WARNING: mathematical area

We now have to show that the F statistic we used in the last section really does have an F distribution. Let's assume that we have $m = 3$ groups (call them group a, group b, and group c), and that there are n people in each group.

Let's say that μ_a is the unknown mean for group a, μ_b is the mean for group b, and μ_c is the mean for group c. Calculate the averages $\bar{a}, \bar{b}$, and $\bar{c}$. $\bar{a}$ will have a normal distribution with mean μ_a and variance σ^2/n. If the null hypothesis is true, then $\bar{a}, \bar{b}$, and $\bar{c}$ act like three observations taken from a normal distribution with mean μ and variance σ^2/n.

We can estimate the variance σ^2 by using the sample variance for these three averages. (We'll call that variance S^{*2}.)

$$S^{*2} = \frac{(\bar{a} - \bar{x})^2 + (\bar{b} - \bar{x})^2 + (\bar{c} - \bar{x})^2}{m - 1}$$

We know from Chapter 16 that this statistic:

$$Z^{*2} = \frac{n(m - 1) S^{*2}}{\sigma^2}$$

will have a chi-square distribution with $m - 1$ degrees of freedom. If the mean for each group really is different, then we would expect that the variance across $\bar{a}$, $\bar{b}$, and $\bar{c}$ should be greater than the variance within each sample. However, if the mean of each group is the same, then s_a^2, s_b^2, and s_c^2 can all be used as estimators for the variance of the whole population. Or we could use the average of these three variances (which we called S^2):

$$S^2 = \frac{s_a^2 + s_b^2 + s_c^2}{m} = \frac{s_a^2 + s_b^2 + s_c^2}{3}$$

We know that $[(n-1)/\sigma^2] S_a^2$ has a chi-square distribution with $n - 1$ degrees of freedom, so

$$Z^2 = \frac{m(n-1)}{\sigma^2} \times \frac{s_a^2 + s_b^2 + s_c^2}{m}$$

will have a chi-square distribution with $m(n-1)$ degrees of freedom.

Now, we'll compare these two statistics Z^2 and Z^{*2} by calculating their ratio:

$$F = \frac{Z^{*2}/(m - 1)}{Z^2/m(n - 1)}$$

F is equal to the ratio of two chi-square random variables divided by their degrees of freedom, so it will have an F distribution.

Now all we have to do is show that this expression for the F statistic is really the same as the expression we used in the last section.

$$F = \frac{nS^{*2}/\sigma^2}{S^2/\sigma^2} = \frac{nS^{*2}}{S^2}$$

And therefore we have reached the result that we wanted.

EXERCISES

Given the following samples, test the hypothesis that the mean is as given:

1. 1, 5, 17, 9, 23, 17, 4, 3, 8, 8, 7, 8, 6, 0, −1: mean 7

2. 4, 30, −17, −29, 8, 7, −5, 4, 3, −6: mean −2

3. 15, 22, −19, 0, 1, 2, 4, 3, −3, 7: mean 14

4. 17, −9, −8, −10, 8, 5, 4, −7, 3, 4, −5, −7, −3, 2, 3: mean 0

5. Suppose four new pesticides are being tested in a laboratory, with the following results:

	Type 1	Type 2	Type 3	Type 4	Total
Insects killed	139	100	73	98	410
Insects surviving	15	50	80	47	192
Total tested	154	150	153	145	602

Is pesticide 1 significantly better than the rest?

6. Suppose five different meteorological theories are tested to see if they predict the weather correctly. The results are:

	Theory 1	Theory 2	Theory 3	Theory 4	Theory 5	Total
Reports correct	50	48	53	47	46	244
Reports incorrect	76	74	75	76	77	378
Total reports	126	122	128	123	123	622

Is theory 3 significantly better than the rest?

7. Estimate the mean of the scores of your favorite football team last year. Test the hypothesis that the mean score is greater than 14.

8. Test the hypothesis that the mean number of pages in your favorite daily newspaper is greater than 50.

9. Estimate the mean price of a gallon of milk in your city over the past month. Test the hypothesis that the price this month is significantly greater than the price last month.

10. Consider a random variable with a binomial distribution with p unknown. How big does n have to be for you to be able to tell the difference (at the 5 percent significance level) between the hypothesis $p = .5$ and the hypothesis $p = .51$?

11. Perform a goodness-of-fit test to see if the normal distribution is appropriate for the heights of a sample of people you know.

12. Perform a goodness-of-fit test to see if the Poisson distribution is appropriate for the number of phone calls that you receive at your house.

13. Perform a goodness-of-fit test to see if the uniform distribution is appropriate for the numbers that you roll on a die.

14. Test the hypothesis that there is no significant difference between groups a, b, c, and d:

	Group a	Group b	Group c	Group d
Number of successes	16	12	7	13
Number of failures	54	94	66	49

15. Perform an analysis-of-variance test to see if the following sets of numbers were selected from distributions with the same mean:

Group 1: 18, 9, 15, 10, 16, 8, 7, 20, 13, 8, 12

Group 2: 17, 13, 9, 8, 10, 13, 16, 17, 12, 11, 17

Group 3: 15, 13, 13, 14, 15, 20, 15, 14, 9, 16, 12

Group 4: 16, 12, 13, 12, 14, 11, 8, 13, 17, 15, 14

16. Make a list of the first letters of the last names of 20 people you know and assign each letter a number ($A = 1, B = 2$, etc.) Test the hypothesis that the resulting numbers come from a distribution with mean 13.

17. Repeat the same procedure as in Exercise 15, only this time use the first names, and assume that the variance of the distribution is 25.

18. Divide your friends into categories by hair color and eye color. Perform a chi-square test to see if there is a significant difference in eye color for people with different hair colors.

19. Perform a goodness-of-fit test to see if the weights of a group of your friends fit the normal distribution.

20. Perform an analysis-of-variance test to see if people you know with different hair colors have the same height.

21. Look through some old newspapers to find some predictions from some well-known psychic. Test the hypothesis that the psychic could have made the predictions by pure guessing.

CHAPTER 18

POLLS AND SAMPLING

How can we find out how many people in a population have a particular characteristic? For example, we might want to know how many voters support our favorite presidential candidate. Or we might be interested in some general characteristics of people in a certain state—for example, how many are children, how many live in cities, how many are employed, and so on.

One way to find the answers to these questions is to check with everybody. This method will be very accurate. Since we're asking *everybody*, we can get a detailed view of the entire population. This method is used sometimes. An election is held every four years in the United States to find out the presidential preferences of all voters. Every ten years a census is held to obtain detailed information about all of the people in the country.

However, there are disadvantages to the ask-everybody method. The main one is that this method is very expensive. Elections and censuses are costly. There will often be times when we would like to obtain information about the population but we can't wait until the next census or the next election.

Another possible method is to ask some people who are part of a sample. If the sample is representative of the entire population, we can use the characteristics of the people in the sample to estimate the characteristics of the people in the population. For example, the Gallup Poll interviewers check with approximately 3,000 to 4,000 people in an attempt to estimate the opinions of all 200 million people in the country.

Are these results likely to be accurate? At first glance you might be suspicious. The poll takers are only talking to one out of every 40,000 people. You probably think it is unlikely that each person in the poll has the same opinions as his or her 40,000 closest neighbors. However, polls do seem to be fairly accurate. The election results predicted by polls are usually close to the actual results of the election (with a few notable exceptions).

Now we will look at the theory that explains why these results tend to be accurate. We'll let N stand for the number of people in the population we are investigating. We'll assume that M of these people favor our candidate and $N - M$ favor the opposing candidate. (We'll ignore the people who are undecided.) Our goal is to estimate M/N—the fraction of people who support our candidate. Let $p = M/N$. We'll ask a sample of n people. X will represent the number of people in the sample that favor our candidate. If our poll is any good, X/n will be close to M/N.

For example, suppose that we are trying to estimate the preferences of people in a town with 30,000 people. We will ask all the people in a sample of 500 which candidate they support. Suppose that in reality there are 16,500 people who support our candidate. (16,500 is 55 percent of the total population.) If it turns out that 270 people (54 percent) in the sample support our candidate, then the sample did a good job of representing the entire population. On the other hand, if 330 people (66 percent) in the sample are on our side, then the sample is quite unrepresentative and our poll will give us very misleading results.

It makes a big difference how the sample is selected, since the value of X will depend on exactly who is in the sample. We need to figure out a good system for choosing the sample so that it will be representative of the population as a whole. We can't just start asking our friends, since our friends might be more likely to be on our side. We can't select just one neighborhood and interview everyone there, since people in one particular neighborhood are not likely to be representative of the diverse characteristics of all of the people in the town.

There are subtle problems with other systems as well. We can't just mail out a lot of postcards and ask people to return them, since the people on our side might be more likely to take the trouble to send the cards back. We might decide that we can make our sample representative by deciding in advance that we want our sample to contain certain quotas of people with particular characteristics. For example, we might decide that we want our sample to contain 50 percent women, 15 percent minorities, and 0.5 percent veterinarians. However, that method still doesn't answer the question about how to select the sample, since it doesn't tell us which minorities or which women or which veterinarians to include in the sample. We obviously can't set in advance a quota for the number of people in the sample who favor our candidate, since we don't know what that fraction is until after we've taken the sample.

It turns out that the best system for selecting the sample is to have no system at all—in other words, select the sample completely at random. We should design the sampling system so that each person has an equal chance of being selected. Not only that, we should design the system so that every single possible sample that we might conceive of has an equal chance of being the sample that we actually choose.

How are we going to do this? One way is to write everyone's name on a slip of paper, put the papers in little capsules, and then put all of the capsules in a large drum. If we mix up the capsules very thoroughly and then pull n capsules out of the drum, we will have a random sample of n people. However, even this approach is difficult if N is very large. For one thing, we would need a very large drum. Another problem is that it is difficult to mix the capsules well if there are a large number of them. If the capsules are not mixed well, then the people whose names were put in last have a greater chance of being selected and we will no longer have a pure random sample.

An easier method is to give everyone in the population a number. Then we can select a bunch of random numbers and interview the people whose numbers we've chosen. How do we select the random numbers? It's not as easy as it sounds. We can't just start making up numbers, since it is hard for a person to make up a long string of numbers without falling into some sort of pattern. (Try it yourself sometime.) We could use a die if we only needed numbers from 1 to 6, but to get a larger group of numbers we need a better system. In the old (precomputer) days, the best way was to use a table of random digits. A random-digit table is a table that has been created by someone whose job it is to create random numbers. The numbers have been tested to make sure that they pass certain tests of randomness. In these days, you can have a computer generate the random numbers. Most computer systems have built-in random number generators. The numbers that they generate are not true random numbers, since they are generated according to a fixed rule. However, the rule is unpredictable enough that for all practical purposes the numbers seem to have been selected totally at random.

Now we need to calculate the number of possible ways of selecting our random sample. We discussed this question in Chapter 5. We found that if you are going to select a sample of n objects without replacement from a population of size N, there are

$$\binom{N}{n} = \frac{N!}{n!(N - n)!}$$

ways of selecting the sample. In a pure random sample each of these possibilities is equally likely. For example, if you're selecting a sample of size 6 from a population of size 10, then there are $10!/(4!\, 6!) = 210$ ways of selecting the sample.

Out of all of these possible samples, how many have X equal to a particular value k? X is a random variable, since it depends on which random sample we select. First, we can establish that there are $\binom{M}{k}$ ways of selecting the k people in the sample who favor our candidate.

For each of these possibilities there are $\binom{N - M}{n - k}$ ways of selecting the other $n - k$ people in the sample who are opposed to our candidate. Therefore, there are

$$\binom{M}{k}\binom{N - M}{n - k}$$

ways of selecting a sample such that k people in the sample support our candidate. Thus, the probability that X will equal k is

$$\frac{\binom{M}{k}\binom{N - M}{n - k}}{\binom{N}{n}}$$

For example, if $N = 10$, $M = 4$, and $n = 6$, then there are

$$\binom{4}{3}\binom{6}{3} = 80$$

ways of selecting a sample with $X = 3$, so the probability of this event happening is $80/210 = .381$.

We developed this formula before and gave it an intimidating name. We called it the density function for a random variable with the hypergeometric distribution. (See Chapter 9.)

We found that the expectation of X is nM/N, so we expect that X will likely be close to nM/N, which is what we want. However, X probably won't be exactly equal to its expected value.

We can figure out how close X will be to nM/N. Suppose that we're trying to estimate how many people out of a population of 200 million people support our candidate. Suppose that 1/2 of the people actually do support our candidate and 1/2 are on the other side. We'll interview 100 randomly selected people. Then X has a hypergeometric distribution with $N = 200$ million, $M = 100$ million, $p = 1/2$, and $n = 100$. Table 18-1 shows the probabilities.

TABLE 18-1: Hypergeometric Probabilities with $N = 200,000,000$, $M = 100,000,000$, and $n = 100$

k	$Pr(X = k)$	k	$Pr(X = k)$
40	.0108	51	.0780
41	.0159	52	.0735
42	.0223	53	.0665
43	.0300	54	.0579
44	.0389	55	.0484
45	.0484	56	.0389
46	.0579	57	.0300
47	.0665	58	.0223
48	.0735	59	.0159
49	.0780	60	.0108
50	.0795		

If our sample represented the population perfectly, X would equal 50. (In other words, exactly half of the sample would be on our side.) The table shows that there is only a .0795 probability that X will be exactly equal to 50. However, there is about a 63 percent chance that X will be between 46 and 54, and a 95 percent chance that X will be between 40 and 60. That means that it would be extremely unlikely for the sample proportion X/n to be more than 10 percentage points away from the true proportion M/N.

However, we want the poll to be even more accurate than that. It makes a big difference to us whether the proportion that supports our candidate is 40 percent or 60 percent. We will try to make the sample more accurate by interviewing more people. We'll now ask 1,000 people. Table 18-2 shows the results.

TABLE 18-2: Hypergeometric Probabilities with $N = 200,000,000$, $M = 100,000,000$, and $n = 1,000$

k	Pr(X = k)	k	Pr(X = k)
484	.0141	501	.0235
485	.0150	502	.0233
486	.0159	503	.0231
487	.0168	504	.0228
488	.0176	505	.0224
489	.0185	506	.0219
490	.0192	507	.0213
491	.0200	508	.0207
492	.0207	509	.0200
493	.0213	510	.0192
494	.0219	511	.0185
495	.0224	512	.0176
496	.0228	513	.0168
497	.0231	514	.0159
498	.0233	515	.0150
499	.0235	516	.0141
500	.0235		

The table shows that there is a 65 percent chance that X will be between 516 and 484. Suppose X actually did equal 484. Then we would estimate that the proportion of the population supporting our candidate was .484. We would be in error by .500 − .484 = .016. Therefore, there is a 65 percent chance that our estimated poll result will be within 1.6 percentage points of the true value. In that situation we can predict with a fair degree of confidence what the opinions of the population are, based on the opinions of the 1,000 people in the sample.

The poll results become even more accurate if the population proportion p is very small or very large. For example, suppose $p = .1$ (meaning that our candidate is supported by only 10 percent of the population.) Table 18-3 shows the probabilities.

The table indicates that there is a 96 percent chance that the sample proportion will be between .081 and .119.

Looking at the extreme cases, you can see that if $p = 0$ or $p = 1$ there is a 100 percent chance that X will exactly equal nM/N.

These results illustrate the basic ideas of why polls work. It turns out that even with relatively small samples it is highly unlikely that the sample proportion will be very far away from the true proportion.

We can extend these results to obtain the probabilities for samples of different sizes. However, the hypergeometric calculations are very cumbersome to deal with. To make the calculations easier, let's change our sampling procedure slightly. We'll still select 1,000 names from the drum. However, this time after we select each name we'll put it back in the drum and mix all of the names again. That means that a person who has been selected once in the sample might be selected again, and would thus be interviewed twice. (That person

TABLE 18-3: Hypergeometric Probabilities with
$N = 200,000,000$, $M = 20,000,000$, and $n = 1000$

k	Pr(X = k)	k	Pr(X = k)
81	.0055	101	.0415
82	.0068	102	.0407
83	.0084	103	.0394
84	.0102	104	.0378
85	.0122	105	.0358
86	.0144	106	.0336
87	.0168	107	.0312
88	.0194	108	.0286
89	.0220	109	.0260
90	.0248	110	.0234
91	.0275	111	.0209
92	.0302	112	.0184
93	.0328	113	.0161
94	.0352	114	.0139
95	.0373	115	.0119
96	.0390	116	.0101
97	.0404	117	.0085
98	.0414	118	.0070
99	.0419	119	.0058
100	.0419		

probably will be annoyed, which is one reason why this method is not used in practice.) There is even a minuscule chance that we will select the same person 1,000 times.

Once again we'll let X represent the number of people in the sample who favor our candidate. Let's call it a "success" if a particular person in the sample favors our candidate. Then we know exactly what the distribution of X looks like—it has a binomial distribution with parameters n and $p = M/N$.

It turns out that if the population size is much larger than the sample size we can use the binomial distribution even if we sample without replacement. For example, let's suppose that, in a population of 200 million, half of the people are on our side and half are on the other side. Then there is a probability of 1/2 that the first person we select will support our candidate. Suppose that the first person we select does support our candidate. If we sample with replacement, there is a probability of .5 that the second person we select will also be on our side. If we sample without replacement then there is a probability of

$$\frac{99,999,999}{199,999,999} = .4999999975$$

that the second person will support our candidate. So it does make a little bit of difference whether we sample with replacement or without replacement—but not much. Therefore, we can approximate the hypergeometric distribution by a binomial distribution. Since the variance of the hypergeometric distribution is

$$\frac{n(M/N)(1 - M/N)(N - n)}{N - 1}$$

we will use a binomial distribution with this same variance. Note that the variance of the hypergeometric distribution is the same as the variance of the binomial distribution except for the factor $(N - n)/(N - 1)$, which is called the *correction factor* or the *finite population correction factor*. We can think of it as correcting for the fact that we are selecting the sample without replacement. As you can see, if N is much larger than n the value of the correction factor is close to 1, meaning that we can ignore it. For example, if $N = 200$ million and $n = 1,000$, then the value of the correction factor is .999995005.

The binomial distribution itself is rather cumbersome, so while we're making approximations we may as well go all the way and approximate the binomial distribution with a normal distribution. We know that this works when n becomes large. (See Chapter 14.) Therefore, we will represent the density of X as being a normal density function with mean $\mu = nM/n$ and variance

$$\sigma^2 = n \frac{M}{N} \left(1 - \frac{M}{N} \right) \left(\frac{N - n}{N - 1} \right) = np(1 - p) \left(\frac{N - n}{N - 1} \right)$$

Let's find out what intervals have a 95 percent chance of containing X for different values of N, n, and p. We'll let c stand for half the width of the interval. Then we know that the value of c is given by the equation

$$\Pr(\mu - c < X < \mu + c) = .95$$

which we can change to

$$\Pr\left(\frac{-c}{\sigma} < \frac{X - \mu}{\sigma} < \frac{c}{\sigma} \right) = .95$$

As we saw in Chapter 16, in this case $c = 1.96\sigma$. Now we can make a table of these results. (See Table 18-4.)

TABLE 18-4: Percent Error for Sample

N	$n = 100$	$n = 500$	$n = 1,000$	$n = 5,000$	$n = 10,000$	$n = 50,000$
10,000	9.8	4.3	2.9	1.0	0	—
50,000	9.8	4.4	3.1	1.3	0.9	0
100,000	9.8	4.4	3.1	1.4	0.9	0.3
500,000	9.8	4.4	3.1	1.4	1.0	0.4
50,000,000	9.8	4.4	3.1	1.4	1.0	0.4
200,000,000	9.8	4.4	3.1	1.4	1.0	0.4

The table assumes that $p = .5$. If the true value of p is different from .5, then the errors will be less than the values listed in the table. The table lists the percentage-point error. For example, with population size 50,000 and sample size 5,000, the table lists the value 1.3. That means that there is a 95 percent chance that the sample proportion will be within 1.3 percentage points of the true value (in other words, between .487 and .513).

If you check the results for $N = 200$ million and $n = 100$ you can see that the calculations performed using the normal approximation give the same results as the exact calculations did.

There are some interesting results that you can see if you scan through the table. If you take a sample of 1,000 people there is a 95 percent chance that the poll result will be within 3.1 percentage points of the true value. If you increase the sample size to 5,000, the error falls to only 1.4 percent. So the table does tend to reinforce one's faith in polls.

Another interesting result you can see is that a sample of 1,000 does just as well when the population is 200 million as it does when the population is 50,000. You might expect that the sample would become less accurate as the population becomes larger, but it doesn't work that way.

However, the reverse is also true. If you want to get an accurate sample of a population of 50,000, you need just as large a sample as you would if you had a population of 200 million. Making the population smaller does not reduce the number of people you need in the sample in order to get a representative sample. You can get a good cross section of 200 million people by interviewing one person in every 40,000, but if you try to interview one person in 40,000 when the population is 50,000 you will end up with a very unrepresentative sample. What this means is that if you want an accurate view of the opinions of people in every state you will need a much larger sample than you would if you only needed to know the opinions of the entire country.

Another important fact to note is that, although the error does go down as the sample size becomes larger, it reaches a point where large increases in the sample size lead to only small decreases in the error. When you decide on what size sample to use, you need to take two factors into consideration. Adding more people will make the sample a bit more accurate, but the cost of taking the sample becomes larger if more people are included.

It is very important to remember that all of these results work only when the sample is a pure random sample. If the sample is not a pure random sample, all bets are off. A good example of a nonrandom sample was the 1936 *Literary Digest* presidential election poll. The *Literary Digest* had two million people respond to its poll, which is a much larger number than would have been needed to get an accurate result if the sample had been selected randomly. However, the poll predicted that Alf Landon would be an easy winner, whereas in fact Franklin Roosevelt won by a landslide. The problem came about because the *Digest* sample was not a random sample. The magazine mailed out cards to people whose names were obtained from telephone lists and other sources, but at that time the people who had telephones were not representative of the population as a whole. If the sample is not selected randomly there is no way to estimate how far off it might be.

In practice, modern opinion polls are not able to select pure random samples. You can't put the name of everyone in the country into a hat. For one thing, there is no such thing as a list of names for the whole country. Even if there were, it would be very expensive to interview 3,000 randomly selected people scattered all over the country. Instead, the pollsters select some regions at random, then they select some subregions, and finally they select some households to interview. This procedure guarantees that the people in the sample will live in clusters, making it possible for one interviewer to interview quite a few people. However, this procedure does have the effect of making the predicted errors larger, as you will notice if you look at the reported errors for opinion polls.

Opinion polls that try to predict the results of elections have even bigger problems. Not everyone votes, so the poll would rather not count the opinion of anyone who decides not to vote. Therefore, the polls ask some questions that they use to guess whether or not a person will vote. And there is another obvious problem. If a lot of people change their minds after the poll but before the election, then the poll will not be able to predict the election results very well.

Another example of a national sample is the Current Population Survey, which is conducted each month by the Census Bureau for the Bureau of Labor Statistics. Among other things, the Survey is used to calculate the unemployment rate every month. The Bureau of Labor Statistics wants to know about the characteristics of the unemployed—how long they have been unemployed, what kind of jobs they used to have, and so on. In order to get data on that many different categories, the Current Population Survey needs to use a much larger sample than it would need if it just wanted to know the total number of unemployed people in the country. For this reason, the Current Population Survey uses a sample of more than 100,000 people.

EXERCISES

1. Estimate the frequency of occurrence of the letters of the alphabet in your favorite book by examining a sample of a few pages. How accurate do you think your results are?

2. Estimate the frequency of the different first names in your city by looking at a random sample of names in the phone book.

3. Suppose you have 60 red marbles and 40 blue marbles in a box. If you pick out 10 marbles at random with replacement, what is the probability that you will pick 6 red marbles? If you select 10 marbles without replacement, what is the probability that you will select 6 red marbles?

4. Suppose that 55 percent of the people in a population of 500,000 support your candidate. If you conduct a poll of 1,000 people, what is the interval that has a 95 percent chance of containing the results of your poll?

In each of the following exercises, you are given the number of people (N) in the group and the number of people (M) who support your candidate. If you ask a sample of n people whom they support, what is the probability that the number of people in the sample on your side will have the values listed?

	N	M	n	People in sample on your side
5.	15	8	5	1, 2, 3, 4
6.	15	3	5	1, 2, 3, 4
7.	15	10	5	1, 2, 3, 4
8.	40	25	5	1, 2, 3, 4
9.	40	25	10	4, 5, 6, 7
10.	40	25	20	9, 10, 11, 12
11.	30	15	20	8, 9, 10, 11, 12
12.	50	25	20	8, 9, 10, 11, 12
13.	100	50	20	8, 9, 10, 11, 12

CHAPTER 19

LINEAR REGRESSION

Often in statistics we want to investigate the question: How much does one quantity affect another quantity? For example, we might want to find out how much personal income affects personal spending, or how much the money supply affects the price level, or how much the state-wide average income affects the number of marriages in a state. There are many other situations in which one quantity (called the *independent variable*) has a big effect on another quantity (called the *dependent variable*). Once we've figured out the relationship between the two variables, we can predict the value of the dependent variable if we know the value of the independent variable. For example, suppose we used data from 1973 to 1983 to estimate the relation between income and spending. Then, once we know what income will be in 1984, we can guess what spending will be in 1984.

First we'll need to collect a list of observations of the quantities that we're interested in. For example, Table 19-1 shows personal income and personal consumption expenditures each year for a few recent years. In order to present the data in a more meaningful form,

TABLE 19-1: Disposable Personal Income and Consumption Expenditure

Year	Disposable income per capita	Consumption expenditure per capita
1960	1934	1798
1965	2430	2214
1970	3348	3020
1972	3837	3510
1973	4285	3849
1974	4646	4197
1975	5088	4584
1976	5504	5064
1977	6017	5579
1978	6672	6179
1979	7367	6848

we can make a picture. We'll put total income on the horizontal axis and consumption spending on the vertical axis, and then put a dot to correspond to each year in the table. Figure 19-1 shows the result.

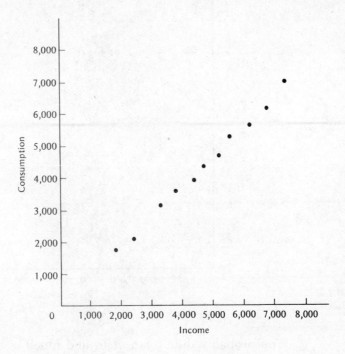

FIGURE 19–1

The diagram clearly shows that there is a very strong relationship between income and spending, which suggests that if we knew income in a given year we would have a very good chance of being able to predict consumption spending correctly.

Figure 19-2 shows the relationship between income per capita and marriages per capita for nine northeastern states in a recent year.

TABLE 19-2

State	1981 per capita income	Marriages per 1,000 people
Connecticut	12,816	8.21
Maine	8,535	11.16
Massachusetts	11,128	8.07
New Hampshire	9,994	10.77
Rhode Island	10,153	7.96
Vermont	8,723	10.18
Delaware	11,095	7.66
D.C.	13,539	8.33
Maryland	11,477	11.11
New Jersey	12,127	7.82
New York	11,466	8.54
Pennsylvania	10,370	7.78

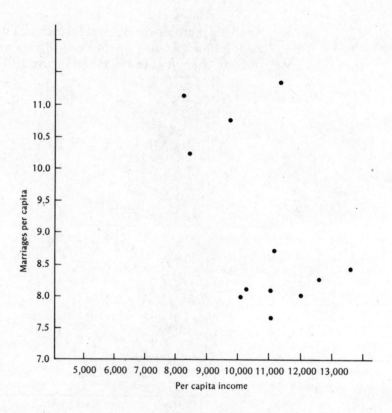

FIGURE 19–2

You probably didn't expect to find much of a connection, and the graph does indeed indicate that there is not a very close relationship. Knowing the per capita income in a state does not help you guess the number of marriages that will take place in that state.

Figure 19-3 illustrates a case that is between these two extremes.

TABLE 19-3: Money Supply and Price Level

Year	Money supply (M1)	Consumer Price Index (1967 = 100)
1960	142	88.7
1965	169	94.5
1970	215	116.3
1973	264	133.1
1974	275	147.7
1975	288	161.2
1976	305	170.5
1977	328	181.5
1978	352	195.4
1979	370	217.4

The graph plots the relationship between the money supply and the price level (measured by the consumer price index). Clearly there is some relationship, but it is not as close as the relationship shown in Figure 19-1.

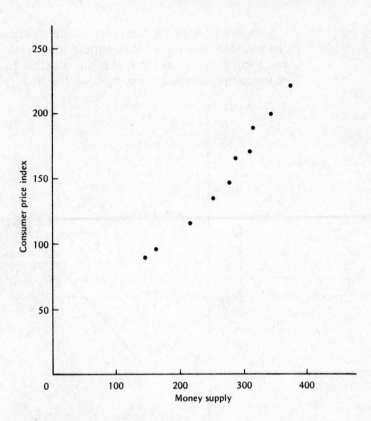

FIGURE 19–3

The Regression Line

We'll try to represent the relationship in each case by a straight line. If we take a ruler and set it down on the graph we can find the line that best represents the points on the graph. Figure 19-4 shows that we can find a line that does a very good job of representing the income/spending relationship.

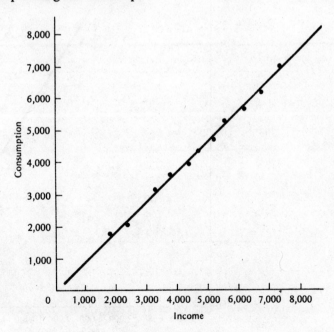

FIGURE 19–4

Figure 19-5 shows that it is possible to draw a line that represents the relation between money supply and price level reasonably well, but Figure 19-6 shows that it is not possible to represent the income/marriage relationship very well with a line.

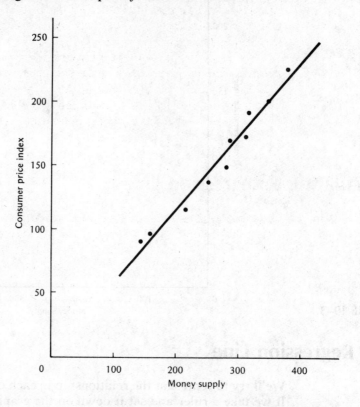

FIGURE 19–5

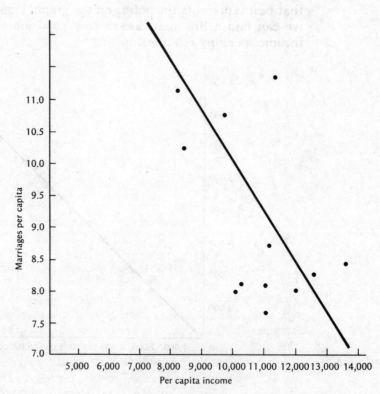

FIGURE 19–6

Such a line is called a *regression line*, and this type of analysis is called *regression analysis*. We need to calculate two numbers to summarize the line: the slope and the vertical intercept. We also would like some way to measure whether the line fits the data very well, as does the line in Figure 19-4, or whether it fits the data poorly, as does the line in Figure 19-6.

We could, in principle, solve every regression problem by making a graph of all of the points and then using a ruler to determine by trial and error which line seems to fit the data points the best. However, plotting a lot of points on a graph can be tedious, so there's got to be a better way. We'll work out a mathematical technique that allows us to determine which line is best.

Calculating a Regression Line

Figure 19-7 illustrates the general situation. Suppose that x represents the independent variable and y represents the variable that depends on x. We want to find the line that best fits the four points shown in the diagram: (x_1, y_1), (x_2, y_2), (x_3, y_3), (x_4, y_4). We'll let m represent the slope of the line and b represent the y-intercept. Our mission is to calculate m and b.

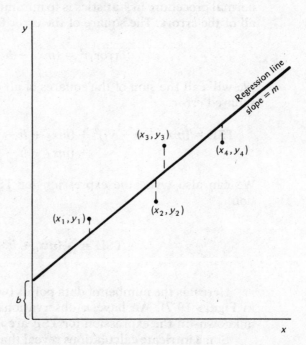

FIGURE 19–7

Suppose we guess that the best regression line is the line shown in Figure 19-8.

That line looks like a good choice, but it doesn't fit the data points perfectly. For each point there is a certain amount of vertical distance between the point and the line. We'll call that distance the *error* of the line relative to that point. A larger value for the error means that the line does a worse job of representing the points. Each point has its own error. (Call these error$_1$, error$_2$, error$_3$, and error$_4$.) We'd like to choose the line so that the total error is as small as possible. The

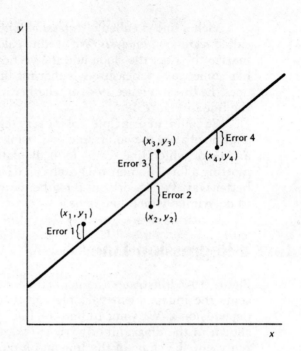

FIGURE 19–8

normal procedure in statistics is to minimize the sum of the *squares* of all of the errors. The square of the error for the point (x_1, y_1) is

$$(\text{error}_1)^2 = (mx_1 + b - y_1)^2$$

We will call the sum of the squares of all of the errors TSE, for total squared error:

$$TSE = (mx_1 + b - y_1)^2 + (mx_2 + b - y_2)^2$$
$$+ (mx_3 + b - y_3)^2 + (mx_4 + b - y_4)^2$$

We can also write the expression for TSE with summation notation:

$$TSE = \sum_{i=1}^{n} (mx_i + b - y_i)^2$$

Here n is the number of data points (which is four in the example in Figure 19-7). We have n observations for x and y, so the only unknowns in the expression for TSE are m and b.

Some intricate calculations reveal that the optimum values for m and b must satisfy these equations:

$$m\bar{x} + b - \bar{y} = 0$$
$$m\overline{x^2} + b\bar{x} - \overline{xy} = 0$$

The first equation simply staes a common-sense fact: The best line should pass through the point $(\bar{x}, \bar{y})$—the point that consists of the average values of x and y.

Now we can use these two equations to find the value for the slope:

$$m = \frac{\overline{xy} - \overline{x}\,\overline{y}}{\overline{x^2} - \overline{x}^2}$$

(Make sure you remember the difference between $\overline{x^2}$, the average value of all of the x^2's, and $\overline{x}^2$, the square of the average value of x. Also, note that $\overline{x}\,\overline{y}$ is the average of y multiplied by the average of x, while $\overline{xy}$ is the average value of the product of x and y.)

Once we know m, we can calculate b:

$$b = \overline{y} - m\overline{x}$$

When we're faced with a real problem in which we have to calculate these values, it is best to use a computer. Here are the results for the examples discussed above:

income/consumption relation:
slope = 0.9343
intercept = −84.397

income/marriage relation:
slope = -4.86×10^{-4}
intercept = 14.29

money supply/price level relation:
slope = 0.5575
intercept = −0.3331

The Accuracy of the Line

As we pointed out earlier, knowing the slope and the intercept of the regression line doesn't tell us anything about how well the line fits the data. So we need to develop another measure to tell how well the line fits. Our first inclination is just to use TSE, the total squared error, since that measures how much discrepancy there is between the points on the line and the actual data points:

$$\text{TSE} = \sum_{i=1}^{n} (\hat{y}_i - y_i)^2 \qquad (\hat{y}_i = mx_i + b)$$

If TSE is zero, then our line fits the data points perfectly. However, if the numerical value of TSE is greater than zero, then we need something to compare this number with so that we can tell whether or not the fit of the line is any good.

We can compare the predictions of our regression line with those of a very simple-minded prediction plan: We could always predict that the value of y will be $\overline{y}$. If we follow that prediction rule we're ignoring the values of x, so we're guessing that x does not affect y very much. We can calculate the total squared error of this method (call it SE_{av}, since it is the total squared error of y about its average):

$$\text{SE}_{av} = \sum_{i=1}^{n} (y_i - \overline{y})^2$$

We can hope that the TSE of our regression line is less than the SE_{av} which comes about from this simple-minded prediction plan. If TSE = SE_{av}, that means that our line does a pretty lousy job of predicting the value of y, since we could predict y just as well if we didn't know anything about the value of x. Therefore, we'll define our measure of the accuracy of the regression line as follows:

$$r^2 = 1 - \frac{TSE}{SE_{av}}$$

The quantity r^2 is called the *coefficient of determination*. This measure has the two features that we decided that our fitness measure should have:

(1) If TSE = 0, then $r^2 = 1$, and the line fits perfectly.

(2) If TSE = SE_{av}, then $r^2 = 0$, and the line fits very poorly.

The value of r^2 will always be between 0 and 1. The higher the value of r^2, the better the line fits. The symbol r^2 is used because r^2 is equal to the square of the sample correlation coefficient between these two variables.

For the examples given earlier, the r^2 value for the income/consumption relation is .9989; for the income/marriage relation r^2 is .2728; and for the money supply/price level relation r^2 is .9720.

Another important measure of the accuracy of the line is the *standard error of estimate*. In theory, we are supposing that the relationship $y = mx + b$ works reasonably well because the value of x is the major factor that determines the value of y. However, there might also be other factors that can influence y that are not related to x. The way statisticians handle these unaccounted-for factors is to assume that the true relationship between x and y is

$$y = mx + b + e$$

We use the letter e because it stands for error. In this case e is a random variable that covers all of the other factors that we are not accounting for. For example, in the money supply/price level equation there are lots of other things that will affect the price level—for example, weather conditions that affect crop prices and political conditions that affect international oil prices. All of these other factors will appear as part of the error term in our equation.

We can establish that the expectation of e is zero [$E(e) = 0$], because the error term is just as likely to cause the value of y to be above the regression line as it is to cause it to be below the regression line. In general, though, we won't know what the distribution of e looks like. Many times it is reasonable to assume that e has a normal distribution. We'll make that assumption here. We don't know in advance the variance of e, but we can use the data to estimate it.

If we have n data points, then we have n observations of the random variable e:

$$e_1 = y_1 - mx_1 - b$$
$$e_2 = y_2 - mx_2 - b$$
$$\cdots\cdots\cdots\cdots\cdots$$
$$e_n = y_n - mx_n - b$$

So we can calculate the sample variance, s^2:

$$s^2 = \frac{e_1{}^2 + e_2{}^2 + \cdots + e_n{}^2}{n}$$

(Note that this equation works because $E(e) = 0$.) The *standard error of estimate* is the square root of s^2.

There is one important point that must be kept in mind. Even if the regression line fits the data points very well, that does not prove that changes in the dependent variable are caused by changes in the independent variable. For example, if you carried out a regression you would probably find a strong association between the total number of cars purchased in a city and the total number of loaves of bread purchased. However, this does not mean that there is any connection between the two quantities. It just reflects the simple fact that in big cities there will be more people both to buy bread and to buy cars.

Even if you're sure that two quantities really are related, you're not sure which causes which. For example, you can find an association between investment and national income. But does that mean that changes in investment cause changes in income or does it mean that changes in income cause changes in investment or both? Whenever you perform a regression, you have to make sure that you perform some kind of analysis so that you know exactly what it is that you're doing. Don't follow the lead of some researchers whose motto is: "If it moves, run a regression on it!"

Several Independent Variables

The method we have discussed up to now is called *simple* linear regression, because we have only one independent variable. However, there will be times when we will think that more than one independent variable is required to explain the dependent variable. In that case we need to use the method of *multiple regression*. For example, suppose we are investigating the number of statistics books that are bought in different cities. We may expect that demand for statistics books will depend on two things: the average income in the city and the average price of the statistics books. Table 19-4 includes data for some hypothetical cities.

We can represent this relationship by an equation:

$$Y = B_1 X_1 + B_2 X_2 + B_3 + e$$

In this equation Y represents the number of statistics books bought, X_1 the average income, and X_2 the average price of statistics books. B_1, B_2, and B_3 are constants that we don't know but will estimate, and e is a random variable representing the error term (which takes into account all possible factors that might affect the demand for statistics books other than income and price). We expect that B_1 will be positive, since more books will be bought when income is higher, but that B_2 will be negative, since fewer books will be demanded when the price is higher.

TABLE 19-4

Statistics books demanded	Average income (thousand dollars)	Average statistics book price
166	20	10
180	21	9
73	12	10
81	16	14
229	24	8
182	24	15
233	23	6
102	15	10
190	20	7
150	19	10
221	25	11
137	21	15
173	19	8
150	20	12
92	14	10

In principle, we will proceed exactly as we did before. We will calculate the values of B_1, B_2, and B_3 that minimize the square of the error between the values predicted by the equation and the true values. There are only two differences: We can't draw a picture of the relationship (unless we're good at drawing multi-dimensional diagrams), and the calculation process is a bit harder. (But so what—we'll have the calculations done by a computer anyway.)

Multiple Regression Calculation

 WARNING: We are now coming to the last, and hardest, topic in the book. If you've made it this far, but the rest of the chapter looks too intimidating mathematically, then feel free to bail out now. You've already learned a lot about probability and statistics.

Let us consider the general case where y is determined by the equation

$$y = B_1x_1 + B_2x_2 + \cdots + B_{m-1}x_{m-1} + B_m + e$$

[We're assuming that we have $m - 1$ independent variables ($x_1, x_2, \ldots, x_{m-1}$.) Note that B_m is the coefficient of a constant term, analogous to the y intercept term in the simple linear case. The term e is a normal random variable with mean 0 and unknown variance.] We'll let n be the number of observations—that is, the number of data points.

(There are times when you expect a relationship between two or more quantities, but you feel that the relationship cannot be expressed as a linear equation. In that case, you can usually perform some tricky transformations involving logarithms to end up with a linear equation. Once you have a linear equation, you can use the methods described here.)

To save us a horrendous amount of work, we're going to use matrix notation. We will use boldface letters such as **y** or **X** to stand for matrices. We'll define **y** and **e** to be matrices with n rows and 1 column:

$$\mathbf{y} = \begin{pmatrix} y_1 \\ y_2 \\ y_3 \\ y_4 \end{pmatrix} \qquad \mathbf{e} = \begin{pmatrix} e_1 \\ e_2 \\ e_3 \\ e_4 \end{pmatrix} \qquad \text{(shown here for } n = 4)$$

B is a matrix with 1 column and m rows:

$$\mathbf{B} = \begin{pmatrix} B_1 \\ B_2 \\ B_3 \end{pmatrix}$$

We'll write all of the independent variables in one large matrix called **X**:

$$\mathbf{X} = \begin{pmatrix} x_{11} & x_{12} & 1 \\ x_{21} & x_{22} & 1 \\ x_{31} & x_{32} & 1 \\ x_{41} & x_{42} & 1 \end{pmatrix} \qquad \text{(assuming } m = 3)$$

Then we can write the whole equation like this:

$$\mathbf{y} = \mathbf{XB} + \mathbf{e}$$

If we wrote out all of the matrices explicitly, it would look like this (so you can see how much writing the matrix notation saves):

$$\begin{pmatrix} y_1 \\ y_2 \\ y_3 \\ y_4 \end{pmatrix} = \begin{pmatrix} x_{11} & x_{12} & 1 \\ x_{21} & x_{22} & 1 \\ x_{31} & x_{32} & 1 \\ x_{41} & x_{42} & 1 \end{pmatrix} \begin{pmatrix} B_1 \\ B_2 \\ B_3 \end{pmatrix} + \begin{pmatrix} e_1 \\ e_2 \\ e_3 \\ e_4 \end{pmatrix}$$

Here x_{12}, for example, is the observation of the variable x_2 in period 1.

It would be even worse if we wrote all of the equations out the long way:

$$y_1 = B_1 x_{11} + B_2 x_{12} + B_3 + e_1$$

$$y_2 = B_1 x_{21} + B_2 x_{22} + B_3 + e_2$$

$$y_3 = B_1 x_{31} + B_2 x_{32} + B_3 + e_3$$

$$y_4 = B_1 x_{41} + B_2 x_{42} + B_3 + e_4$$

To use matrix notation, we need to know three things: the *transpose* of a matrix **X** (we'll symbolize the transpose by **X′**), the product of two matrices, and the inverse of a matrix **A** (we'll symbolize the inverse of **A** by $\mathbf{A}^{-1}$).

We will use $\hat{\mathbf{B}}$ to stand for the matrix consisting of our estimates for the coefficients for $\mathbf{B}$. Then $\hat{\mathbf{y}}$, our predictions for $\mathbf{y}$, can be found from the equation

$$\hat{\mathbf{y}} = \mathbf{X}\hat{\mathbf{B}}$$

The vector of the errors is $(\hat{\mathbf{y}} - \mathbf{y})$, so the total squared error is

$$\text{TSE} = \sum_{i=1}^{n} (\hat{y}_i - y_i)^2$$

Rewrite the expression for TSE in matrix notation:

$$\text{TSE} = (\mathbf{XB} - \mathbf{y})'(\mathbf{XB} - \mathbf{y})$$

Note that $(\mathbf{XB} - \mathbf{y})'$ is an array with 1 row and t columns and $(\mathbf{XB} - \mathbf{y})$ is an array with t rows and 1 column, so the result of multiplying then will be an array with 1 row and 1 column (in other words, a regular number, or scalar, as it is sometimes called.)

We can rewrite the equation, using some tricks of matrices:

$$\text{TSE} = (\mathbf{B}'\mathbf{X}' - \mathbf{y}')(\mathbf{XB} - \mathbf{y})$$
$$= \mathbf{B}'\mathbf{X}'(\mathbf{XB} - \mathbf{y}) - \mathbf{y}'(\mathbf{XB} - \mathbf{y})$$
$$= \mathbf{B}'\mathbf{X}'\mathbf{XB} - \mathbf{B}'\mathbf{X}'\mathbf{y} - \mathbf{y}'\mathbf{XB} + \mathbf{y}'\mathbf{y}$$
$$= \mathbf{B}'\mathbf{X}'\mathbf{XB} - 2\mathbf{B}'\mathbf{X}'\mathbf{y} + \mathbf{y}'\mathbf{y}$$

Now we have to find the vector $\mathbf{B}$ that gives us the smallest possible value for TSE. If we perform some tricky matrix calculus calculations, it turns out that $\mathbf{B}$ must satisfy the equation

$$\mathbf{X}'\mathbf{XB} = \mathbf{X}'\mathbf{y}$$

If we multiply both sides by $(\mathbf{X}'\mathbf{X})^{-1}$ we can get the solution for $\mathbf{B}$:

$$\mathbf{B} = (\mathbf{X}'\mathbf{X})^{-1}\,\mathbf{X}'\mathbf{y}$$

This formula tells us how we can calculate the optimum value of $\mathbf{B}$ (that is, of $B_1, B_2, \ldots, B_m$). Although that equation is nice theoretically, the actual calculations are arduous.

The estimator $\hat{\mathbf{B}}$ calculated from the equation is called the *ordinary least squares estimator*, and this method is called the method of ordinary least squares.

In addition to minimizing the total squared error, $\hat{\mathbf{B}}$ also has three other properties we like estimators to have:

(1) $\hat{\mathbf{B}}$ is the maximum likelihood estimator of the true values for $\mathbf{B}$.

(2) $\hat{\mathbf{B}}$ is consistent.

(3) $\hat{\mathbf{B}}$ is an unbiased estimator of $\mathbf{B}$—in other words, $E(\hat{B}_1) = B_1$.

We can calculate the r^2 value (the coefficient of determination) just as we did earlier:

$$r^2 = 1 - \frac{SE_{av}}{TSE}$$

Here are the results for the statistics book example. B_1 is 12.2861; B_2 is -7.738; and B_3 is -2.764. The r^2 value is .9957. That means we can estimate that the demand for statistics books is:

(Number of books demanded) =
12.2861 (income) $-$ 7.738 (price) $-$ 2.764

Here is an important question we might want to ask. Does one particular independent variable (X) really have any effect on y? For example, we might wonder whether income really does have any effect on the demand for statistics books. If it does not, the true value of the coefficient B_1 is zero. Therefore, this also becomes a hypothesis-testing problem. The null hypothesis is $B_1 = 0$. The question: Do we accept or reject?

We mentioned earlier that the estimation vector $\hat{\mathbf{B}}$ is unbiased, which means that $E(\hat{B}_i) = 0$ if the true value of B_i is really zero. Next, we need to figure out the distribution of $\hat{B}_i$. From the equations

$$\hat{\mathbf{B}} = (\mathbf{X}'\mathbf{X})^{-1}\mathbf{X}'\mathbf{y}$$

and

$$\mathbf{y} = \mathbf{X}\mathbf{B} + \mathbf{e}$$

we can derive

$$\hat{\mathbf{B}} = (\mathbf{X}'\mathbf{X})^{-1}\,\mathbf{X}'\mathbf{X}\mathbf{B} + (\mathbf{X}'\mathbf{X})^{-1}\,\mathbf{X}'\mathbf{e}$$
$$= \mathbf{B} + (\mathbf{X}'\mathbf{X})^{-1}\,\mathbf{X}'\mathbf{e}$$
$$\hat{\mathbf{B}} - \mathbf{B} = (\mathbf{X}'\mathbf{X})^{-1}\,\mathbf{X}'\mathbf{e}$$

Remember that each element of $\mathbf{e}$ has a normal distribution with variance σ^2. We can use this information to establish that the variance of B is

$$Var(B_i) = \sigma^2 q_{ii}$$

In this case q_{ii} stands for the element in row i and column i of the matrix $(\mathbf{X}'\mathbf{X})^{-1}$. Note that we can calculate q_{ii}, but we don't know σ^2. However, this problem is similar to the estimation problems we did earlier. Remember, we didn't know the value of σ^2 then, either.

Suppose that the null hypothesis is true and that the true value of B_i is zero. Then

$$\frac{\hat{B}_i}{\sigma\sqrt{q_{ii}}}$$

will have a standard normal distribution. We don't know σ^2, but we can calculate the sample standard deviation s_2:

$$s_2{}^2 = \frac{e_1{}^2 + e_2{}^2 + \cdots + e_n{}^2}{n - 1}$$

We know that $(n - 1)s_2{}^2/\sigma^2$ has a χ^2 distribution with $n - 1$ degrees of freedom. Therefore,

$$\frac{\dfrac{\hat{B}_i}{\sigma\sqrt{q_{ii}}}}{\sqrt{\dfrac{(n - 1)s_2{}^2}{(n - 1)\sigma^2}}}$$

fits the definition of the t distribution, so the statistic

$$T = \frac{\hat{B}_i}{s_2\sqrt{q_{ii}}}$$

can be used to test the hypothesis that $B_i = 0$. Calculate the value of T. Then compare it with the value of a t distribution shown in Table A3-5 for the appropriate number of degrees of freedom. If the calculated value of T is too large, you can safely reject the hypothesis that X_i has no effect. In our example the t statistics for the first two coefficients are 186.659 and -58.477, so we can safely reject the hypothesis that $B_1 = 0$ or $B_2 = 0$. In other words, income and price clearly do seem to have an effect on the demand for statistics books. However, the t statistic for the constant term is only -0.06769, so we cannot reject the hypothesis that $B_3 = 0$. That means that there might be no constant term in the equation if we could specify the equation correctly.

We have now covered the last topic that we will include in this book. If you are interested in further work in this area there are many books that cover advanced topics in statistics. You have the foundation that you will need to understand how statistics works.

Now you're ready to head off on your own. You've learned all you need to know in order to start doing your own statistical calculations. Your knowledge of statistics will be helpful if you intend to study fields such as experimental science, psychology, economics, sociology, and many others. When you are confronted with a pile of raw data, you are now able to determine whether there is a meaningful story that can be learned from those data.

EXERCISES

☆ **1.** Derive the equations for m and b when you are running a linear regression with one independent variable.

❏ **2.** Write a program to perform a simple linear regression (one with only one independent variable).

❏   3. (This program will be very long.) Write a program that performs a multiple linear regression. Assume that you have m independent variables and t observations for each variable.

4. Perform a regression using the weather forecasts from the previous day as the independent variable and the actual temperatures as the dependent variable. Are the forecasts very accurate? In other words, is knowing the value of the predicted temperature very much help in knowing the value of the actual temperature the next day? (Note that this regression does not imply a causal connection between the two items.)

5. Perform a regression to investigate the connection between interest rates and housing starts in your area.

In each of the following lists, x represents an independent variable and y represents a dependent variable. Perform a regression calculation to see if there is a relation between x and y.

6. x: 52 12 96 28 22 45 16
   y: 16 13 11 17 11 14 17

7. x: 1   2   3   4   5   6   7   8
   y: 14 18 32 38 49 60 79 80

8. x: 19 11 11 48 16 18 15 12
   y: 15 19 34 59 19 46 15 44

9. x: 3.04   1.98   6.02   3.15   2.78   4.15   2.98
   y: 9.24   3.92   36.52 9.92   7.73   17.22 8.88

   x: 10.40   25.65   30.29   19.85
   y: 108.16 657.92 917.48 380.00

10. x: 10 11 9 9   8 9 8 7 7 9
    y: 5 11 5 8 10 5 4 5 4 7

    x: 4   9 6 4 7 6   9 7 4 6
    y: 6 11 4 8 3 9 11 2 3 8

11. x: 15 22 14 17 18 14 12 12 11 16
    y: 9 10   7   8 10   8   9   5   4   6

    x: 4 7 10 12 10 15 20 9 7 14
    y: 2 5   4   7   3   9 11 6 3   6

12. Calculate a regression line for the following values of an independent variable x and a dependent variable y.

    x: .12   .25   .38   .50   .64   .89   .95
    y: .0002 .0039 .0209 .0625 .1678 .6274 .8145

13. Take the logarithm of each of the values for x and y in Exercise 12 and then calculate a regression line using the values of the logarithms.

In the following exercises the X's represent independent variables and Y represents a dependent variable. Perform a multiple regression calculation to find the relationship between Y and the X's.

14.

Y	X_1	X_2	X_3
100	6.3	2	0
110	10.1	0	1
94	14.2	3	2
96	2.5	4	3
112	6.8	0	4
98	7.3	5	5
94	12.5	2	6
118	16.1	1	7

15.

Y	X_1	X_2
19	2	10
25	0	20
45	3	30
60	4	40
76	6	50
115	10	60
130	12	70
99	4	80

16.

Y	X_1	X_2
17	56	4
9	27	30
8	85	8
10	13	7
1	46	4
5	66	3
17	99	15
9	10	22

17.

Y	X_1	X_2
47	139	15
46	100	50
76	73	47
74	98	53
73	410	45
98	50	54
80	48	74
50	53	46

18.

Y	X_1	X_2
174	27	11
148	13	16
480	56	43
254	13	33
298	46	19
444	99	8
420	66	26
154	10	19

APPENDIX 1

ANSWERS TO SELECTED EXERCISES

Chapter 1

3. 1/2

4. If 2 doesn't divide $n + k$, the probability is 0. If 2 does divide $n + k$, the probability is

$$\left(\begin{array}{c} n \\ \dfrac{n + k}{2} \end{array} \right)$$

6.
```
 1 REM: FACTORIAL CALCULATION
10 INPUT N
20 Z = 1
30 IF N = 0 GOTO 70
40 FOR I = 1 TO N
50 Z = Z * I
60 NEXT I
70 PRINT Z : END
```

7. See Chapter 8, where will we answer a more general problem.

8. .112. .080.

Chapter 2

1. .039.

2. 1.4×10^{-17}

3. 100 tosses: Accept the hypothesis if there are 40 to 60 heads. 5 tosses: There is a 6 percent chance that you will get either 0 heads or 5 heads in 5 flips, so you cannot reject the hypothesis in any case. 10 flips: Accept the hypothesis if the number of heads is between 2 and 8.

4. If the total is 2, 3, 10, 11, or 12, then you will reject the hypothesis; otherwise you will have to accept the hypothesis. In this case there is no probability of a type 1 error.

Chapter 3

1. Mean = 18.81; median = 19; mode = 21.

2. Mean = 336; median = 256. Each number is a mode, since all of the numbers occur an equal number of times.

3. $\bar{x} = 5.25$. $\overline{x^2} = 47.75$. Standard deviation $= \sqrt{47.75 - 5.25^2} = \sqrt{20.19} = 4.49$

4. $\bar{x} = 4.074$ $\overline{x^2} = 16.667$; standard deviation = .265.

5. Let X represent the history scores and Y represent the English scores. Then $\bar{x} = 79.2$; $s_x = 13.40$; $\bar{y} = 81.43$; $s_y = 12.02$; $\overline{xy} = 6610.4$; correlation = .999. The correlation between the chemistry scores and history scores is also .999.

6. When a set of numbers contains a few numbers that are far above the mean, but no numbers that are far below the mean, then the mean will tend to be higher than the median.

7. $\bar{x} = 4$ $s_x = 2.582$; $\bar{y} = 22.6$; $s_y = 21.468$; $\overline{xy} = 144$; correlation = $r(x,y) = .962$.

8. $\bar{x} = 2.6$ $s_x = 2.417$; $\bar{y} = 5.2$; $s_y = 4.834$; $\overline{xy} = 25.2$; $r(x,y) = 1$.

9. $\bar{x} = 0$ $s_x = 1/\sqrt{2}$; $\bar{y} = 0$; $\overline{y^2} = 1/2$; $\overline{xy} = 0$; $r(x,y) = 0$.

12.
```
1 REM PROGRAM TO CALCULATE STANDARD DEV.
5 X1 = 0 : X2 = 0
10 FOR I = 1 TO N
20 INPUT X
30 X1 = X1 + X : X2 = X2 + X*X
40 NEXT I
50 X1 = X1/N : X2 = X2/N
60 V = X2 - X1 * X1
70 S1 = SQR(V)
80 S2 = SQR((N/(N-1)*V)
90 PRINT S1,S2 : END
```

```
13.   1 REM CORRELATION CALCULATION
      5 X1 = 0: X2 = 0: XY = 0: Y1 = 0: Y2 = 0
     10 FOR I = 1 TO N
     20 INPUT X,Y
     30 X1 = X1 + X : Y1 = Y1 + Y
     40 X2 = X1 + X * X : Y2 = Y2 + Y * Y
     50 XY = XY + X * Y
     60 NEXT I
     70 X1 = X1/N : X2 = X2/N : Y1 = Y1/N : Y2 = Y2/N
     80 XY = XY/N
     90 C = XY - X1 * Y1 ! COVARIANCE
    100 SX = SQR(X2 - X1 * X1) ! STAND DEV OF X
    110 SY = SQR(Y2 - Y1 * Y1) ! STAND DEV OF Y
    120 R = C/(SX * SY) ! CORRELATION
    130 PRINT R : END

14.   1 REM BUBBLE SORT PROGRAM
     10 REM THIS PROGRAM READS IN N NUMBERS
     11 REM AND PRINTS THEM OUT IN ORDER
     15 DIM A(50)
     20 INPUT N
     25 FOR I = 1 TO N : INPUT A(I) : NEXT I
     30 FOR I = 1 TO N
     40 FOR J = 1 TO N - I
     50 IF A(J)>A(J+1)LET T = A(J+1):A(J+1)=A(J):A(J)=T
     60 NEXT J
     70 NEXT I
     80 FOR I = 1 TO N : PRINT A(I) : NEXT I : END
```

Chapter 4

1. 1/2

2. 2/9

3. 1/38. This is a discrete probability space.

4. This is a continuous probability space. 0. 3/38.

5. $\emptyset, S$.

6. $1 = \Pr(S) = \Pr(X \cup X^c) = \Pr(X) + \Pr(X^c)$ (Since X and X^c are disjoint.) Then $\Pr(X) = 1 - \Pr(X^c)$. Since $\Pr(X^c) \geq 0$, it follows that $\Pr(X) \leq 1$.

7. See Exercise 6.

9. Let D be the event $B \cup C$. Then A and D are disjoint. $\Pr(A \cup B \cup C) = \Pr(A \cup D) = \Pr(A) + \Pr(D) = \Pr(A) + \Pr(B \cup C) = \Pr(A) + \Pr(B) + \Pr(C)$.

10. $A \cup B = A \cup (B \cap A^c)$; $A \cap (B \cap A^c) = \emptyset$; $\Pr(A \cup B) = \Pr(A) + \Pr(A^c \cap B)$. $B = (A \cap B) \cup (A^c \cap B)$. $(A \cap B) \cap (A^c \cap B) = \emptyset$. Then:
$\Pr(B) = \Pr(A \cap B) + \Pr(A^c \cap B)$. $\Pr(A^c \cap B) = \Pr(B) - \Pr(A \cap B)$.
$\Pr(A \cup B) = \Pr(A) + \Pr(A^c \cap B) = \Pr(A) + \Pr(B) - \Pr(A \cap B)$.

11. .000 000 07.

12. 3/4.

13. 7/8.

14. $1 - (5/6)^3 = .421$.

15. Probability of getting 9 is .116, probability of getting 10 is .125.

16. If you go for the two points now, you have a 50 percent chance of succeeding, in which case you win the game. If you fail, then you can go for two points next time. If you succeed the next time, you will tie; otherwise you will lose. Therefore, if you go for the two points this time you have a 50 percent chance of winning, a 25 percent chance of tying, and a 25 percent chance of losing. If you kick the extra point this time, then you have a 50 percent chance of winning and a 50 percent chance of losing.

21. $1 - (1/2)^n$

22. 1/21.

23. 1/7.

24. 1/49.

25. 1/4.

26. Let A be the event of getting hired by the first firm and B be the event of getting hired by the second firm. Then $\Pr(A \text{ or } B) = \Pr(A \cup B) = .40 + .40 - .16 = .64$.

27. 20 percent.

Chapter 5

1. $\binom{24}{3}\left(\dfrac{1}{8}\right)^3\left(\dfrac{7}{8}\right)^{21}$.

   $\binom{24}{4}\left(\dfrac{1}{8}\right)^4\left(\dfrac{7}{8}\right)^{20}$.

2. $\binom{1}{22}\binom{22}{10}$.

3. $\dfrac{32!}{8!\ 8!\ 2!\ 2!\ 2!\ 2!\ 2!\ 2!}$.

4. $\dfrac{7!}{4!\ 2!\ 1!} = 105$.

5. $\binom{12}{4} = 495$.

6. $\dfrac{52!}{48!} = 6{,}497{,}400$.

7. $\dfrac{\binom{4}{2} + \binom{3}{2} + \binom{2}{2}}{\binom{9}{2}} = \dfrac{6 + 3 + 1}{36} = \dfrac{5}{18}$.

8. $\dfrac{\binom{4}{2}}{\binom{9}{2}} = 1/6$.

9. $9!/6! = 504$.

10. $4!\ 2!\ 2! = 96$.

11. $5!\ 4!\ 2! = 5{,}760$.

12. $\binom{15}{10} = 3{,}003$.

13. $256/270{,}725$.

14. 10.

15. 56.

17. There is only one way to choose zero object from a group of n objects, so $\binom{n}{0}$ is 1.

18. There are n ways to choose one object from a group of n objects.

19. There is only one way to choose all n items.

20. There are n ways to select $n-1$ objects, since you have n choices as to which object you will not select.

21. They are equal. Choosing j objects from the group is the same as *not* choosing $n - j$ objects.

22. $26^5 = 11,881,376$.

23. $1/30^3 = 1/27,000$.

25. $2^5 \times 6 = 192$.

26. 120.

27. 4/9.

28. $6!/6^6 = 120/7776 = 5/324$.

30. 1/36.

31. $1/6^4 = 1/1296$.

32. $1 - (5/6)^n$.

33. 1/5.

34. 1/70.

35. Discard either the 5D or 5C. Then you can win with either 4H or 8H.

36. 28!

37. $1 - (1460/1461)^n$

45.
```
 1 REM PROGRAM TO CALCULATE NUMBER OF
   COMBINATIONS
 2 REM OF N THINGS TAKEN J AT A TIME
10 INPUT N, J
20 C = 1
```

```
30 B = J
40 IF J > (N - J) LET B = N - J
50 FOR I = 1 TO B
60 C = C * (N - I + 1)/I
70 NEXT I
80 PRINT C: END
```

46. 2: .005; 3: .016; 4: .031; 5: .053; 6: .079; 7: .111; 8: .147; 9: .189; 10: .237; 15: .553; 18: .804.

49. $\dfrac{8!}{\dbinom{16}{8}} = \dfrac{(8!)^3}{16!}$

52. When more people are involved in the drawing, the probability that any specified person will select his own name becomes very small. However, this is counteracted by the fact that there are more people who might possibly pick their own names.

53. The number of ways of choosing the first k_1 items is

$$\frac{n!}{k_1! \, (n - k_1)!}$$

The number of ways of choosing the next k_2 items from the remaining $(n - k_1)$ items is

$$\frac{(n - k_1)!}{k_2! \, (n - k_1 - k_2)!}$$

Keep going like that. When you multiply all of the terms together, then a lot of items cancel out, so the result is

$$\frac{n!}{k_1! \, k_2! \cdots k_s!}$$

Chapter 6

1. Let A be the event that a head appeared and B be the event that the coin was fair.

$$\Pr(B) = 1/2; \; \Pr(A|B) = 1/2; \; \Pr(A|B^c) = 1;$$

$$\Pr(B|A) = \frac{\Pr(A|B)\,\Pr(B)}{\Pr(A|B)\Pr(B) + \Pr(A|B^c)\Pr(B^c)}$$

$$= \frac{(1/2)\,(1/2)}{(1/2)(1/2) + (1)(1/2)} = 1/3.$$

2. $\dfrac{4 + 4 + 4 + 3 + 4 + 4 + 4 + 4}{50} = \dfrac{31}{50}$; yes.

3. $\dfrac{2 + 4 + 4 + 3 + 3 + 4 + 4 + 4}{46} = \dfrac{28}{46} = \dfrac{14}{23}$; yes.

4. $4!\left(\dfrac{1}{51 \times 50 \times 49 \times 48}\right) = \dfrac{1}{249,900}$.

   $2! \times \left(\dfrac{1}{49 \times 48}\right) = \dfrac{1}{1176}$.

   $1/48$.

5. Two ways: A, 2, 3, 4, 5; 2, 3, 4, 5, 6.

$$2 \times 3!\left(\dfrac{4}{50} \times \dfrac{4}{49} \times \dfrac{4}{48}\right) = \dfrac{8}{1225}.$$

7. Let A be the event of getting at least one head. B is the event of getting two heads.

$$\Pr(B|A) = \dfrac{\Pr(A \cap B)}{\Pr(A)} = 1/3.$$

8. Let A = ace; $B = AD$;

$$\Pr(B|A) = \dfrac{\Pr(A \cap B)}{\Pr(A)} = \dfrac{1/40}{4/40} = 1/4.$$

11. $3!\left(\dfrac{1}{50} \times \dfrac{1}{49} \times \dfrac{1}{48}\right) = 1/19,600.$

12. $\dfrac{1/13}{3/13} = 1/3.$

13. A = one 5; $B = 14$; $\Pr(A) = 25/72$; $\Pr(A \cap B) = 1/36$; $\Pr(B|A) = 2/25.$

14. (a) The event of getting tails on the first toss.
    (b) The event of getting heads on the second toss.
    (c) The null set $\emptyset$ is both disjoint and independent of every other event. However, there is no way for two events to be both disjoint and independent if one of them is not the null set.
    (d) The event of getting heads on both tosses.

15. $\Pr(J|C) = 2/3$; $\Pr(J|C_0) = 5/9$; $\Pr(C) = \Pr(C_0) = 1/2$; $\Pr(C_0|J) = 2/5.$

16. $\Pr(B|A) = \dfrac{\Pr(A \cap B)}{\Pr(A)}$

   $\Pr(A|B) = \dfrac{\Pr(A \cap B)}{\Pr(B)}$; $\Pr(A \cap B) = \Pr(A|B)\Pr(B)$

   $\Pr(A) = \Pr(A \cap B) + \Pr(A \cap B^c)$

   $\Pr(A \cap B^c) = \Pr(A|B^c)\,\Pr(B^c)$

   $\Pr(B|A) = \dfrac{\Pr(A|B)\,\Pr(B)}{\Pr(A|B)\,\Pr(B) + \Pr(A|B^c)\,\Pr(B^c)}.$

17. A = left handed; B = O blood type.

    $\Pr(A|B) = .05$; $\Pr(A|B^c)$ .10;

    $\Pr(B) = .40$; $\Pr(B|A) = \dfrac{(1/20)\,(2/5)}{(1/20)\,(2/5) + (1/10)\,(3/5)}$

    $\qquad\qquad\qquad\qquad = 1/4.$

18. $\Pr(RH|BE) = 7/10$; $\Pr(RH|GE) = 1/5$;

    $\Pr(RH|BE) = 1/20$; $\Pr(RE) = 3/4$;

    $\Pr(BE) = 1/5$; $\Pr(GE) = 1/20$;

    $\Pr(GE|RH) = \dfrac{(1/5)\,(1/20)}{(7/10)\,(3/4) + (1/5)\,(1/20) + (1/20)\,(1/5)}$

    $\qquad\qquad\qquad = .018.$

Chapter 7

2. X.

3.

k: 2	3	4	5	6	7	8	9	10	11	12
$f(k)$:1/36	1/18	1/12	1/9	5/36	1/6	5/36	1/9	1/12	1/18	1/36

4. $1 - 1/3 - 1/5 = 7/15.$

5. $1/12$

6. 5.

7. $f(k) = 2^{-(k + 1)}.$

9. $f(k) = 0$ for $k \geq 10$.

11. If c is constant, then $E(C) = c$, and $\operatorname{Var}(c) = E[(c - E(c)^2]$
    $= E[(c - c)^2] = 0.$

12. $E(Y) = 7/2$; $E(Y^2) = 1/6\,(1^2 + 2^2 + 3^2 + 4^2 + 5^2 + 6^2) = 91/6$; $\operatorname{Var}(Y)$
    $= 91/6 - (7/2)^2 = 35/12.$

13. $E(X + Y) = E(X) + E(Y) = 7/2 + 7/2 = 7$

    $E[(X + Y)^2]$

    $\quad = (1/36)\,2^2 + (2/36)\,3^2 + (3/36)\,4^2$

    $\qquad + (4/36)\,5^2 + (5/36)\,6^2 + (6/36)\,7^2$

    $\qquad + (5/36)\,8^2 + (4/36)\,9^2 + (3/36)\,10^2$

    $\qquad + (2/36)\,11^2 + (1/36)\,12^2$

    $\quad = 1/36\,(4 + 18 + 48 + 100 + 180 + 294$

    $\qquad + 320 + 324 + 300 + 242 + 144)$

    $\quad = 545/6$

    $\operatorname{Var}(X + Y) = E[(X + Y)^2] - [E(X) + E(Y)]^2$

    $\qquad\qquad\qquad = 35/6$ [which is equal to $\operatorname{Var}(X) + \operatorname{Var}(Y)$].

14. $E(X) = (7/2)n$. $\text{Var}(X) = (35/12)n$.

15. $1/2\,(-1) + 1/4\,(2) + 1/4\,(-3) = -3/4$.

You will lose 75 cents per game on average.

17. $E(X) = 4$; $E(X^2) = 20$; $\text{Var}(X) = 4$.

18.
$$f(k) = \begin{cases} .4 & \text{if } k = -2 \\ .45 & \text{if } k = 4.5 \\ .15 & \text{if } k = 9 \\ 0 & \text{elsewhere} \end{cases}$$

19. The set of all numbers $k/2$, where k is a positive integer.

20. 2.

21.

k:	1	1.5	2	2.5	3
$f(k)$:	1/36	1/18	1/12	1/9	5/36

k:	3.5	4	4.5	5	5.5	6
$f(k)$:	1/6	5/36	1/9	1/12	1/18	1/36

22. The numbers of the stations broadcasting in your area.

23. $E(X) = (1/13)\,[\sum\limits_{i=1}^{10} i + 30] = 85/13 = 6\ 7/13$.

24. $E(X) = .6$; $E(X^2) = .6$; $\text{Var}(X) = .24$.

25. $f(k) = \text{Pr}(Z = k) = \text{Pr}(X + Y = k)$

$= \sum\limits_{i} \text{Pr}(X = i)\text{Pr}(Y = k - i)$.

k:	2	3	4	5	6
$f(k)$:	1/36	1/18	1/12	1/9	5/36

k:	7	8	9	10	11	12
$f(k)$:	1/6	5/36	1/9	1/12	1/18	1/36

$E(Z) = 7 = 7/2 + 7/2 = E(X) + E(Y)$.

26. $E(cX) = \sum\limits_{i} ca;\ f(a_i) = c \sum\limits_{i} a_i\ f(a_i) = c\,E(X)$.

27. $\text{Var}(cX) = E[(cX)^2] - [E(cX)]^2$

$\qquad\qquad = E(c^2X^2) - [c\,E(X)]^2$

$\qquad\qquad = c^2\,E(X^2) - c^2\,[E(X)]^2$

$\qquad\qquad = c^2\,[E(X^2) - [E(X)]^2]$

$\qquad\qquad = c^2\,\text{Var}(X)$

28. Let $W = X + Y$.

$$E(X + Y + Z) = E(W + Z)$$
$$= E(W) + E(Z) = E(X + Y) + E(Z)$$
$$= E(X) + E(Y) + \cdot E(Z).$$

29.

$$f(k) = \begin{cases} .2 & \text{if } k = 1 \\ .2 & \text{if } k = 2 \\ .1 & \text{if } k = 4 \\ .3 & \text{if } k = 6 \\ .2 & \text{if } k = 7 \\ 0 & \text{elsewhere} \end{cases}$$

32. Note that $[X - E(X)]^2 \geq 0$.
Therefore, if we take the expectation of that expression, we get

$$E[(X - E(X))^2] \geq 0$$
$$E[X^2 - 2\,X\,E(X) + (E(X))^2] \geq 0$$
$$E(X^2) - 2\,E(X)\,E(X) + [E(X)]^2 \geq 0$$
$$E(X^2) - [E(X)]^2 \geq 0$$
$$E(X^2) \geq [E(X)]^2$$

33. $1 = \sum\limits_{k=1}^{\infty} f(k) = \sum\limits_{k=1}^{\infty} c2^{-k} = c\sum\limits_{k=1}^{\infty} 2^{-k} = c.$
Therefore $c = 1$.

Chapter 8

1. The number of meteorites that hit Wethersfield will have a binomial distribution with $p = .000\,000\,07$ and $n = 11,000$. The probability of two hits is 2.96×10^{-7}. Interestingly enough, the town of Wethersfield *was* hit by two meteorites in an eleven-year period.

2. $\binom{5}{3}\left(\frac{1}{2}\right)^3\left(\frac{1}{2}\right)^2 = \frac{5}{16}.$

3. $\binom{5}{4}\left(\frac{1}{2}\right)^4\left(\frac{1}{2}\right) + \binom{5}{5}\left(\frac{1}{2}\right)^5\left(\frac{1}{2}\right)^0 = \frac{3}{16}.$

4. $\binom{7}{6}\left(\frac{1}{10}\right)^6\left(\frac{9}{10}\right) + \binom{7}{7}\left(\frac{1}{10}\right)^7\left(\frac{9}{10}\right)^0 = \frac{1}{156,250}.$

5. $\binom{4}{3}\left(\frac{2}{3}\right)^3\left(\frac{1}{3}\right) + \binom{4}{4}\left(\frac{2}{3}\right)^4\left(\frac{1}{3}\right)^0 = \frac{16}{27}.$

6. $\sum\limits_{k=75}^{100} \binom{100}{k} \times \frac{1}{2^{100}}.$

8. $1 - (.9)^3 = .271.$

9. $\binom{3}{2}\left(\frac{1}{7}\right)^2\left(\frac{6}{7}\right) = \frac{18}{343}.$

10. $\binom{6}{4}\left(\frac{2}{5}\right)^4\left(\frac{3}{5}\right)^2 = \frac{432}{3125}.$

11. X_1 can be thought of as the number of successes in n_1 trials, with each trial having probability p of success; and X_2 can be thought of as the number of successes in the next n_2 trials; then $X_1 + X_2$ can be interpreted as the number of successes in $n_1 + n_2$ trials, and therefore will have a binomial distribution.

12. $\binom{3}{2}\left(\frac{9}{20}\right)^2\left(\frac{11}{20}\right) + \binom{3}{3}\left(\frac{9}{20}\right)^3\left(\frac{11}{20}\right) = .425.$

15. If you take 210 reservations, you have a 6.9 percent chance of an overflow. If you take 209 reservations, there is only a 3.8 percent chance of an overflow.

16.
```
  1 REM BINOMIAL RANDOM VARIABLE TABLE
 10 INPUT N, P
 20 T = 0
 30 FOR X = 0 TO N
 40 C = 1
 50 IF X = 0 GOTO 120
 60 IF X = N LET C = P ↑ N : GOTO 130
 70 B = X
 80 IF X > (N - X) LET B = N - X
 90 FOR I = 1 TO B
100     C = C * (N - I + 1)/I
110 NEXT I
120 C = C * P ↑ X * (1 - P) ↑ (N - X)
130 T = T + C
140 PRINT X, C, T
150 NEXT X : END
```

Chapter 9

1. Mean 7.5; variance 5.12.

2. Mean = 75; variance = 150.

3. Mean = 64; variance = 192

4. Mean = 10.

5. Mean = 180; variance = 3060.

6. $\Pr(X > 1) = 1 - (3/2)e^{-1/2}$

7. $\Pr(X = n) = e^{-\lambda} \lambda^n/n!$ where $n \leq \lambda < n + 1$.

8. $e^{-10} (680/3)$.

9. $\Pr(X \leq 4) = p + p(1 - p) + p(1 - p)^2 + p(1 - p)^3 = .802$.

10. $n = 2$.

11. $448/3^8$.

13.
$$\frac{\binom{20}{1}\binom{180}{2}}{\binom{200}{3}} = .245.$$

14.
$$\frac{\binom{2}{2}\binom{6}{1}}{\binom{8}{3}} = .107.$$

15. $e^{-3} (131/8)$.

16. $8/81 = .099$.

17. $\binom{19}{7}\left(\frac{1}{3}\right)^8\left(\frac{2}{3}\right)^{12} = 4{,}199 \left(\frac{2^{14}}{3^{19}}\right)$.

18.
$$\frac{\binom{30}{2}\binom{270}{3}}{\binom{300}{5}} = .072.$$

19. $11^{19}/12^{20}$

20.
```
1 REM: POISSON PROBABILITY TABLE
10 INPUT L
15 C = EXP (-L)
20 INPUT S !S IS THE HIGHEST VALUE FOR WHICH
21 REM     YOU WANT THE PROBABILITY PRINTED
30 FOR X = 0 TO S
```

```
40      P = C
50      IF X = 0 GOTO 90
60      FOR I = 1 TO X
70         P = P * L / I
80 NEXT I
90 PRINT X , P
100 NEXT X : END
```

22.
```
1 REM HYPERGEOMETRIC PROBABILITIES
10 REM N = NUMBER OF OBJECTS IN BOX
11 REM R = NUMBER OF OBJECTS OF DESIRED TYPE
12 REM N - R = NUMBER OF UNDESIRED OBJECTS
13 REM B = NUMBER OF OBJECTS IN SAMPLE
14 REM J = NUMBER OF OBJECTS OF DESIRED
15 REM        TYPE IN SAMPLE
20 V = N - B : U = N - R
30 P = 1
40 FOR I = 1 TO J
50      W = J - I
60      P = P * (R-W)*(B-W)/(I*(V+I))
70 NEXT I
80 FOR I = 0 TO (B - J - 1)
90      P = P * (U - I)/(N - I)
100 NEXT I
110 PRINT P : END
```

24.
$$f(k) = e^{-\lambda} \frac{\lambda^k}{k!}$$

$$\sum_{k=0}^{\infty} f(k) = \sum_{k=0}^{\infty} e^{-\lambda} \frac{\lambda^k}{k!}$$

$$= e^{-\lambda} \sum_{k=0}^{\infty} \frac{\lambda^k}{k!}$$

$$= e^{-\lambda} e^{\lambda}$$

$$= 1$$

25. Let $\lambda = np$. Then

$$f(k) = \binom{n}{k} p^k (1 - p)^{n-k}$$

$$= \frac{n!}{k!(n-k)!} \left(\frac{\lambda}{n}\right)^k (1 - p)^{n-k}$$

$$= \frac{n!}{(n-k)! n^k} \frac{\lambda^k}{k!} \frac{\left(1 - \frac{\lambda}{n}\right)^n}{\left(1 - \frac{\lambda}{n}\right)^k}$$

$$\lim_{n \to \infty} \frac{n!}{(n-k)! n^k} = \lim_{n \to \infty} \left(\frac{n}{n}\right)\left(\frac{n-1}{n}\right) \cdots \left(\frac{n-k+1}{n}\right)$$

$$= 1$$

$$\lim_{n \to \infty} \left(1 - \frac{\lambda}{n}\right)^k = 1$$

$$\lim_{n \to \infty} \left(1 - \frac{\lambda}{n}\right)^n = \exp \lim_{n \to \infty} \left[n \ln \left(1 - \frac{\lambda}{n}\right)\right]$$

$$\lim_{n \to \infty} \left[n \ln \left(1 - \frac{\lambda}{n}\right)\right] = \lim_{n \to \infty} \frac{\ln \left(1 - \frac{\lambda}{n}\right)}{1/n}$$

$$= \lim_{n \to \infty} \frac{\left(\frac{\lambda}{n^2}\right)\left(1 - \frac{\lambda}{n}\right)^{-1}}{-1/n^2} \quad \text{(by l'Hôpital's rule)}$$

$$= -\lambda$$

$$\lim_{n \to \infty} \left(1 - \frac{\lambda}{n}\right)^n = e^{-\lambda}$$

$$\lim_{n \to \infty} f(k) = e^{-\lambda} \frac{\lambda^k}{k!}, \quad \text{which is the density function for a Poisson random variable.}$$

Chapter 10

1. Height, weight, temperature.

2. F has a maximum at k only if there is no probability that the random variable will be greater than K. F has a minimum at j only if there is no probability that the random variable will be less than j.

4. $r^2/900$.

5. $f(r) = r/450$.

6. $n + 1$

7. $F(0) = 0 = F(1/2)$, $F(10) = \ln 10$.

8. $f(x) = 0$ for $x \le 0$, $f(x) = e^{-x}$ for $x > 0$.

9. (a) g decreases from 2 to 3.
(b) g is above 1 from 1 to 3.

10. 1/2.

11. $F(a) = 0$ for $a \le -\pi/3$; $F(a) = \cos a - 1/2$ for $-\pi/3 < a < 0$; $F(a) = 3/2 - \cos a$ for $0 < a < \pi/3$; $F(a) = 1$ for $a > \pi/3$.

12. $F(x) = 0$ for $x \le -1$; $F(x) = (3/4)(x - x^3/3 + 2/3)$ for $-1 \le x \le 1$; $F(x) = 1$ for $x > 1$.

14. $f(x) = 1/(b - a)$ for $a < x < b$; $f(x) = 0$ otherwise.

$$E(X) = \int_a^b x/(b - a)\, dx = 1/(b - a)x^2/2 \Big|_a^b = (a + b)/2.$$

$$E(X^2) = \int_a^b x^2 f(x)\, dx = 1/(b - a) \int_a^b x^2\, dx$$

$$= (b^3 - a^3)/[3(b - a)]$$

$$\mathrm{Var}(X) = (a^2 + ab + b^2)/3 - (a^2 + 2ab + b^2)/4 = (b - a)^2/12.$$

15. $E(X) = \displaystyle\int_{-\infty}^{\infty} x f(x)\, dx$. Let $y = x - c$. Then

$$E(X) = \int_{-\infty}^{\infty} (c + y) f(c + y)\, dy$$

$$= c \int_{-\infty}^{\infty} f(c + y)\, dy + \int_{-\infty}^{\infty} y f(c + y)\, dy$$

$$= c + \int_{-\infty}^{0} y f(c + y)\, dy + \int_{0}^{\infty} y f(c + y)\, dy$$

$$= c + \int_{-\infty}^{0} y f(c - y)\, dy + \int_{0}^{\infty} y f(c + y)\, dy$$

Let $z = -y$. Then

$$E(X) = c - \int_{0}^{\infty} z f(c + z)\, dz + \int_{0}^{\infty} y f(c + y)\, dy$$

$$= c$$

17. $a = \ln 2$.

18. 1/30.

19. $F(a) = 0$ for $a \leq 0$;

$F(a) = a^2/2$ for

$0 < a < 1$; $F(a) = 1/2a^2$ for $a > 1$.

20. $f(x) = 0$ for $x < 1$

$f(x) = (2x + 3)/2$ for $-1 < x < 0$;

$f(x) = 0$ for $0 < x$.

21. $0 \leq x \leq 1$.

22. $c = 1/18750$.

$F(a) = 0$ for $a \leq 0$

$F(a) = (30a^2 + 3600a)/18750$

for $0 \leq a \leq 5$; $F(a) = 1$ for $a \geq 5$.

Chapter 11

1. .08; .66.

2. .20; .63.

3. .07.

4. .34.

5. .31.

6. .28; .58; the normal distribution can only approximately represent this situation, since the number of glasses sold is a discrete random variable.

8. .15.

9. −2.25.

10. 35.43.

11. $F(3) = F(\mu) = \Phi(0) = .5$ which is greater than $F(4) = .4$, thereby contradicting the fact that F must be an increasing function.

12. 0.

13. 0.

14. $-9.24 < a < -3.16$.

15. Mean = 10, variance = .0064.

17. $1 - \Phi\left[\dfrac{\mu_1 - \mu_2}{\sqrt{\sigma_1^2 + \sigma_2^2}}\right]$

18. .39.

19. We know that $aX + b$ is also a normal random variable. Let $a = 1/\sigma$ and $b = -\mu/\sigma$, then $(X - \mu)/\sigma$ is also a normal random variable. $E[(X - \mu)/\sigma] = (1/\sigma)[E(X) - \mu] = 0$. $\mathrm{Var}[(X - \mu)/\sigma] = 1/\sigma^2\,\mathrm{Var}(X - \mu) = 1/\sigma^2\,\mathrm{Var}(X) = 1$.

20. $\Pr(|X - \mu| \le \sigma) = \Pr[-1 \le (X - \mu)/\sigma \le 1] = \Phi(1) - \Phi(-1) = 2\Phi(1) - 1 = .68$.

22. The mean.

23. The mean.

24. If X, Y, and Z are normal random variables, let $W = X + Y + Z$, and $U = X + Y$. Then U is a normal random variable, and so is $W = U + Z = X + Y + Z$.

25.
```
 1 REM PROGRAM TO PRINT TABLE OF
 2 REM STANDARD NORMAL DISTRIBUTION
10 A = 0 : P = SQR(2 * 3.14159)
20 FOR I = 1 TO 350
30 X = I/100 - .005
40 Y = EXP(-X * X/2)
45 A = A + Y
50 B = .5 + A/(100 * P) + .00005
60 Z = I/100
70 PRINT USING ".";Z;USING".";B
80 NEXT I : END
```

26. Let X be a normal random variable with parameters μ and σ^2.

$$E(X) = \frac{1}{\sigma\sqrt{2\pi}} \int_{-\infty}^{\infty} x e^{-(x-\mu)^2/2\sigma^2}\, dx$$

$$= \frac{1}{\sigma\sqrt{2\pi}} \int_{-\infty}^{\infty} (x-\mu) e^{-(x-\mu)^2/2\sigma^2}\, dx + \frac{1}{\sigma\sqrt{2\pi}} \int_{-\infty}^{\infty} \mu e^{-(x-\mu)^2/2\sigma^2}\, dx$$

Letting $t = x - \mu$,

$$\frac{1}{\sigma\sqrt{2\pi}} \int_{-\infty}^{\infty} (x - \mu) e^{-(x-\mu)^2/2\sigma^2}\, dx = \frac{1}{\sigma\sqrt{2\pi}} \int_{-\infty}^{\infty} t e^{-t^2/2\sigma^2}\, dt$$

$$= \frac{\sigma}{\sqrt{2\pi}}\left(-e^{-t^2/2\sigma^2}\right)\Bigg|_{t=-\infty}^{t=\infty}$$

$$= 0$$

$$\frac{1}{\sigma\sqrt{2\pi}} \int_{-\infty}^{\infty} \mu e^{-(x-\mu)^2/2\sigma^2} \, dx = \mu \int_{-\infty}^{\infty} f_X(x) \, dx$$

$$= \mu$$

$$E(X) = 0 + \mu$$

$$= \mu$$

27. $Var(X) = E((X - \mu)^2)$

$$= \frac{1}{\sigma\sqrt{2\pi}} \int_{-\infty}^{\infty} (x - \mu)^2 \, e^{-(x-\mu)^2/2\sigma^2} \, dx$$

$$= \frac{1}{\sigma\sqrt{2\pi}} \int_{-\infty}^{\infty} t^2 e^{-t^2/2\sigma^2} \, dt \qquad \text{(letting } t = x - \mu)$$

$$= \frac{1}{\sigma\sqrt{2\pi}} (t)(-\sigma^2 e^{-t^2/2\sigma^2}) \Big|_{t=-\infty}^{t=\infty} + \frac{\sigma^2}{\sigma\sqrt{2\pi}} \int_{-\infty}^{\infty} e^{-t^2/2\sigma^2} \, dt$$

Using integration by parts,

$$Var(X) = 0 + \sigma^2 \int_{-\infty}^{\infty} f_Y(t) \, dt$$

$$= \sigma^2$$

where Y is a normal random variable with parameters $\mu = 0$, σ^2.

28. Let $I = \int_{-\infty}^{\infty} e^{-x^2/2} \, dx$

$$I^2 = \int_{-\infty}^{\infty} e^{-x^2/2} dx \int_{-\infty}^{\infty} e^{-y^2/2} \, dy$$

$$= \int_{-\infty}^{\infty} \int_{-\infty}^{\infty} e^{-(x^2+y^2)/2} \, dx \, dy$$

$$= \int_{0}^{2\pi} \int_{0}^{\infty} e^{-r^2/2} r \, dr \, d\theta$$

Shifting to polar coordinates,

$$I^2 = \int_{0}^{2\pi} d\theta$$

$$= 2\pi$$

$$I = \sqrt{2\pi}$$

$$\frac{1}{\sqrt{2\pi}} \int_{-\infty}^{\infty} e^{-x^2/2} \, dx = 1 = \text{the area under the standard}$$

$$\text{normal density function } \frac{1}{\sqrt{2\pi}} e^{-x^2/2}$$

Chapter 12

1. A bit less than .25.

2. About .10.

3. About .30.

4. About .15.

5. There is a probability of about .2 that this random variable might be as big as 16, so you can believe the person.

6. There is less than a .005 probability that this random variable will be less than 5, so you should not believe this claim.

7. There is only a .05 probability that this random variable will be smaller than -2.3, so this value is implausible but you cannot reject it with certainty.

8. Yes.

9. F distribution with 1 and n degrees of freedom.

10.
```
  1 REM PROGRAM TO PRINT CHI-SQUARE TABLE
 80 INPUT M ! M IS THE DEGREES OF FREEDOM
110 IF INT(M/2) = M/2 GOTO 170
115 J = .5 : C = SQR(3.14159)
120 K = (M - 1)/2
125 FOR I = 1 TO K
130 C = C * J
135 J = J + 1
140 NEXT I
150 C = 1/(C * 2 (M/2))
160 GOTO 200
165 !
170 K = M/2 - 1
180 FOR I = 1 TO K
185 C = C * I
190 NEXT I
195 C = 1/(C * 2 ↑ (M/2))
200 REM --------------------
210 DIM L(10)
```

```
220 FOR I = 1 TO 10 : READ L(I) : NEXT I
230 DATA .005, .01, .05, .25, .5, .75, .9, .95, .975, .99
240 J = 1 : K = L(J)
245 D = M/100 ! D IS THE WIDTH OF EACH RECTANGLE
250 A = 0 : C = C * D : X = -D/2
260 FOR I = 1 TO 980
270 F = C * X ↑ (M/2 - 1) * EXP(-X/2)
280 A = A + F
290 IF A > K GOSUB 300
292 O = A
295 NEXT I
296 GOTO 399 ! END
300 Z = D * (A - K)/(A - O)
310 U = X + D/2 - Z + .0005
320 PRINT USING ".";U;K
330 J = J + 1
340 IF J = 10 GOTO 399
350 K = L(J)
360 RETURN
399 END
```

```
11.    1 REM PROGRAM TO PRINT TABLE OF T DISTRIBUTION
      80 INPUT M ! M IS THE DEGREES OF FREEDOM
      90 C = 1
     100 IF (M/2) = INT(M/2) GOTO 180
     110 J = (M - 1)/2
     130 FOR I = 1 TO J
     140 C = C * I/(M/2 - I)
     150 NEXT I
     160 C = C/(SQR(M) * 3.14159)
     170 GOTO 200
     180 J = M/2 - 1 : K (M + 1)/2
     190 FOR I = 1 TO J
     200 C = C * (K - I)/I
     210 NEXT I
```

```
220 C = C * .5/SQR(M)
200 REM --------
210 DIM L(5)
220 FOR I = 1 TO 5 : READ L(I) : NEXT I
230 DATA .75, .9, .95, .975, .99
240 B = -(M + 1)/2 : A = .5 : J = 0 : C = C/100
245 J = 1 : K = L(J)
248 X = -.005
250 FOR I = 1 TO 500 : X = X + .01
260    F = (1 + X * X/M) ↑ B
270    A = A + C * F
295    IF A > K GOSUB 400
300    O = A
310 NEXT I
400 U = X - .005
405 Z = ((K - O)/(A - O))/100 + U + .0005
415 PRINT USING ".";Z; K
420 J = J + 1
430 IF J = 6 GOTO 499
440 K = L(J)
450 RETURN
499 END
```

12. $E(X) = \displaystyle\int_0^\infty \lambda x e^{-\lambda x}\, dx$

$$= -x e^{-\lambda x}\Big|_{x=0}^{x=\infty} + \int_0^\infty e^{-\lambda x}\, dx \qquad \text{(integrating by parts)}$$

$$= 0 + \frac{1}{\lambda}$$

$$= \frac{1}{\lambda}$$

$E(X^2) = \displaystyle\int_0^\infty \lambda x^2 e^{-\lambda x}\, dx$

$$= -\lambda^2 e^{-\lambda x}\Big|_{x=0}^{x=\infty} + 2\int_0^\infty x e^{-\lambda x} \qquad \text{(integrating by parts)}$$

$$= 0 + \frac{2}{\lambda} E(X)$$

$$= \frac{2}{\lambda^2}$$

$$\text{Var}(X) = E(X^2) - [E(X)]^2$$

$$= \frac{2}{\lambda^2} - \frac{1}{\lambda^2}$$

$$= \frac{1}{\lambda^2}$$

13.
$$F(a) = \int_0^a \lambda e^{-\lambda x}\, dx$$

$$= -e^{-\lambda x}\Big|_{x=0}^{x=a}$$

$$= 1 - e^{-\lambda a} \text{ for } a \geq 0.$$

14. $\frac{\lambda}{\lambda - t}$ for $t < \lambda$.

15.
$$\Pr(X > s) = 1 - F(s)$$

$$= e^{-\lambda s}$$

$$\Pr(X > a + b) = e^{-\lambda(a+b)}$$

$$= e^{-\lambda a} e^{-\lambda b}$$

$$= \Pr(X > a)\,\Pr(X > b)$$

16.
$$F(y) = \Pr(Y < y)$$

$$= \Pr(Z^2 < y)$$

$$= \Pr(-\sqrt{y} < Z < \sqrt{y})$$

$$= \Phi(\sqrt{y}) - \Phi(-\sqrt{y})$$

$$f(y) = \Phi'(\sqrt{y})\left(\frac{1}{2\sqrt{y}}\right) - \Phi'(-\sqrt{y})\left(\frac{-1}{2\sqrt{y}}\right)$$

$$= \frac{1}{2\sqrt{y}}\left(\Phi'(\sqrt{y}) + \Phi'(-\sqrt{y})\right)$$

$$\Phi'(x) = \frac{1}{\sqrt{2\pi}}\left(e^{-x^2/2}\right)$$

$$f(y) = \frac{1}{\sqrt{2\pi}}\left(\frac{1}{2\sqrt{y}}\right)(2e^{-y/2})$$

$$= \frac{e^{-y/2}}{\sqrt{2\pi y}}$$

18. Let X be a chi-squared random variable with m degrees of freedom.

$$f_X(x) = \frac{x^{\frac{m-2}{2}} e^{-x/2}}{2^{m/2}\Gamma\left(\frac{m}{2}\right)} \quad \text{for } x > 0$$

$$\psi_X(t) = E(e^{tx})$$

$$= \frac{1}{2^{m/2}\Gamma\left(\frac{m}{2}\right)} \int_0^\infty e^{tx} x^{\frac{m-2}{2}} e^{-x/2} \, dx$$

Let $u = (1 - 2t)x$ with $t < 1/2$; then

$$\psi_X(t) = \frac{1}{2^{m/2}\Gamma\left(\frac{m}{2}\right)} \int_0^\infty \frac{u^{(m-2)/2} e^{-u/2}}{(1 - 2t)^{m/2}} \, du$$

$$= (1 - 2t)^{-m/2} \int_0^\infty f_X(u) \, du$$

$$= (1 - 2t)^{-m/2}$$

19.

$$\psi_{Y_1+Y_2}(t) = \psi_{Y_1}(t)\,\psi_{Y_2}(t)$$

$$= (1 - 2t)^{-n_1/2}(1 - 2t)^{-n_2/2}$$

$$= (1 - 2t)^{-(n_1+n_2)/2}$$

and $Y_1 + Y_2$ has a chi-squared distribution with $n_1 + n_2$ degrees of freedom.

20. Let X_n be a random variable with a t distribution with n degrees of freedom.

$$f_{X_n}(x) = \frac{c_n}{\left(1 + \frac{x^2}{n}\right)^{\frac{n+1}{2}}}, \text{ where } c_n = \frac{\Gamma\left(\frac{n+1}{2}\right)}{\sqrt{n\pi}\,\Gamma\left(\frac{n}{2}\right)}$$

Assume that $\lim\limits_{n\to\infty} c_n = \dfrac{1}{\sqrt{2\pi}}$.

$$\lim_{n\to\infty}\left(1 + \frac{x^2}{n}\right)^{-(n+1)/2} = \lim_{n\to\infty} \exp\left[\frac{-(n + 1)}{2}\ln\left(1 + \frac{x^2}{n}\right)\right]$$

$$= \exp \lim_{n\to\infty}\left[\frac{-(n + 1)}{2}\ln\left(1 + \frac{x^2}{n}\right)\right]$$

$$\lim_{n\to\infty}\left[\frac{-(n+1)}{2}\ln\left(1+\frac{x^2}{n}\right)\right] = \lim_{n\to\infty}\frac{-\ln\left(1+\frac{x^2}{n}\right)}{2/(n+1)}$$

$$= \lim_{n\to\infty}\frac{\left(\frac{x^2}{n^2}\right)\left(1+\frac{x^2}{n}\right)^{-1}}{-2/(n+1)^2} \quad \text{(by l'Hôpital's rule)}$$

$$= \lim_{n\to\infty}\left(\frac{n+1}{n}\right)^2\left[\frac{-x^2}{2\left(1+\frac{x^2}{n}\right)}\right]$$

$$= -\frac{x^2}{2}$$

$$\lim_{n\to\infty}\left(1+\frac{x^2}{n}\right)^{-(n+1)/2} = e^{-x^2/2}$$

$$\lim_{n\to\infty}f_{X_n}(x) = \frac{1}{\sqrt{2\pi}}e^{-x^2/2}$$

and as $n\to\infty$ the distribution of X_n approaches that of a standard normal random variable.

Chapter 13

1.

X	Y=2	Y=3	Y=4	Y=5	Y=6	Y=7	Y=8	Y=9	Y=10	Y=11	Y=12
2	1/216	1/216	1/216	1/216	1/216	1/216	0	0	0	0	0
3	1/216	2/216	2/216	2/216	2/216	2/216	1/216	0	0	0	0
4	1/216	2/216	3/216	3/216	3/216	3/216	2/216	1/216	0	0	0
5	1/216	2/216	3/216	4/216	4/216	4/216	3/216	2/216	1/216	0	0
6	1/216	2/216	3/216	4/216	5/216	5/216	4/216	3/216	2/216	1/216	0
7	1/216	2/216	3/216	4/216	5/216	6/216	5/216	4/216	3/216	2/216	1/216
8	0	1/216	2/216	3/216	4/216	5/216	5/216	4/216	3/216	2/216	1/216
9	0	0	1/216	2/216	3/216	4/216	4/216	4/216	3/216	2/216	1/216
10	0	0	0	1/216	2/216	3/216	3/216	3/216	3/216	2/216	1/216
11	0	0	0	0	1/216	2/216	2/216	2/216	2/216	2/216	1/216
12	0	0	0	0	0	1/216	1/216	1/216	1/216	1/216	1/216

2.

	1	2	3	4	5	6
2	1/36	0	0	0	0	0
3	1/36	1/36	0	0	0	0
4	1/36	1/36	1/36	0	0	0
5	1/36	1/36	1/36	1/36	0	0
6	1/36	1/36	1/36	1/36	1/36	0
7	1/36	1/36	1/36	1/36	1/36	1/36
8	0	1/36	1/36	1/36	1/36	1/36
9	0	0	1/36	1/36	1/36	1/36
10	0	0	0	1/36	1/36	1/36
11	0	0	0	0	1/36	1/36
12	0	0	0	0	0	1/36

3. $p_X(x) \geq p_{X,Y}(x,y)$

4. 3

5.
x:	-2	4	5	
$f(x)$:	.4	.2	.4	
y:	0	2	4	6
$f(y)$:	.2	.1	.2	.5

The covariance and correlation are 0.

6.
x:	-2	-1	0	1	2
$f(x)$:	.2	.25	.1	.35	.1

y:	3	5	9
$f(y)$:	.35	.25	.4

$\text{Cov}(X,Y) = .49$; $r(XY) = .139$.

7.
x:	0	5	9	11	13
$f(x)$:	.2	.25	.05	.35	.15

y:	1	4	5	6	9
$f(y)$:	.25	.45	.1	.05	.15

$\text{Cov}(X,Y) = -6.28$; $r(X,Y) = -.920$.

8.
x:	-3	2	4	5	7
$f(x)$:	.25	.05	.15	.05	.50

y:	-9	-4	-3	-1	0
$f(y)$:	.05	.35	.15	.1	.35

$\text{Cov}(X,Y) = -.17$; $r(X,Y) = -.018$.

9.
x:	1	2	3	4
$f(x)$:	.4	0	.4	.2

y:	1	2	3	4
$f(y)$:	.2	.2	.3	.3

11. If y is between 1 and 31, then $f(x,y) = 1/365$ if x is 1, 3, 5, 7, 8, 10, or 12. If y is between 1 and 30, and x is 4, 6, 9, or 11, then $f(x,y) = 1/365$. Finally, if y is between 1 and 28, and x is 2, then $f(x,y) = 1/365$. $f(x,y) = 0$ for all other values of x and y.

13. 7.

15.

	$y < 7$	$7 \leq y < 10$	$10 \leq y < 13$	$13 \leq y < 14$	$14 \leq y$
$x < 1$	0	0	0	0	0
$1 \leq x < 2$	0	.1	.1	.2	.2
$2 \leq x < 5$	0	0	.1	.2	.35
$5 \leq x < 9$	0	0	.35	.45	.7
$9 \leq x$	0	.2	.55	.75	1

16. Because the sum of the values is greater than 1.

17. Cov(X,Y) = −2.917; $r(X,Y)$ = −1.

18. Cov(X,Z) = 0; $r(X,Z)$ = 0.

Chapter 14

1. 0.

2. .68.

3. .02.

4. .32.

7. .94.

8. 1/4.

9. 1/16.

12. It will have a normal distribution.

13. Suppose that X is a discrete random variable. (The proof is very similar for a continuous random variable.) Let $f(x)$ be the density function of X. Then we can write out the definition of expectation:

$$E(X) = x_1f(x_1) + x_2f(x_2) + \cdots + x_nf(x_n)$$

Let's say that $x_1, x_2, \cdots x_{a^*}$ are all of the possible values of X that are less than a, and that $x_k, x_{k+1}, \cdots x_n$ are the possible values of X that are greater than a.

Then we can break the expectation into two parts, like this:

$$E(X) = [x_1f(x_1) + x_2f(x_2) + \cdots + x_{a^*}f(x_{a^*})]$$
$$+ [x_kf(x_k) + x_{k+1}f(x_{k+1}) + \cdots + x_nf(x_n)]$$

We know that the first term is positive, so we have

$$E(X) = \text{(something positive)} + [x_kf(x_k) + x_{k+1}f(x_{k+1}) + \cdots + x_nf(x_n)]$$

We're just going to ignore the first term, and change the equal sign into an inequality:

$$E(X) \geq x_kf(x_k) + x_{k+1}f(x_{k+1}) + \cdots + x_nf(x_n)$$

(There's no reason why we can't do this, although if the term we're ignoring is very large, $E(X)$ will be much bigger than the right hand side.)

Every value of x that appears in the right hand side is bigger than a, so we also have this inequality:

$$x_k f(x_k) + x_{k+1} f(x_{k+1}) + \cdots + x_n f(x_n)$$
$$\geq a f(x_k) + a f(x_{k+1}) + \cdots + a f(x_n)$$

Putting these two inequalities together,

$$E(X) \geq \sum_{i=k}^{n} x_i f(x_i) \geq \sum_{i=k}^{n} a f(x_i)$$

Now we're going to ignore the middle expression:

$$E(X) \geq a f(x_k) + a f(x_{k+1}) + \cdots + a f(x_n)$$
$$E(X) \geq a[f(x_k) + f(x_{k+1}) + \cdots + f(x_n)]$$

The term in the brackets is equal to $\Pr(X \geq a)$. Therefore,

$$E(X) \geq a \Pr(X \geq a)$$

We can rewrite that:

$$\Pr(X \geq a) \leq \frac{E(X)}{a}$$

And Markov's inequality has been proved.

Chapter 15

1. $\Pr(6 < \bar{x} < 8) = .7062$.
   $\Pr(8 < \bar{x} < 9) = .1295$.
   $\Pr(9 < \bar{x} < 10) = .0166$.

2. Mean 19.53.
   Variance 13.85.

3. Mean 10.33.
   Variance 6.89.

4. Mean 14.53.
   Variance 12.52.

Chapter 16

2. 17.39 to 21.66.

3. 8.82 to 11.83.

4. 12.50 to 16.56.

8. 8.14 to 16.57.

9. 9.80 to 16.19.

10. 11.58 to 16.77

11. 10.80 to 15.55

13. $E(X^2) - [E(X)]^2$

15.

```
  1 REM PROGRAM TO CALCULATE CONFIDENCE
  2 REM INTERVALS USING THE T DISTRIBUTION
 10 INPUT "N:";N
 20 INPUT "VALUE FROM T TABLE:";A
 30 T = 0 : U = 0
 40 FOR I = 1 TO N
 50    INPUT X
 60    T = T + X
 70    U = U + X * X
 80 NEXT I
 90 T = T/N : U = U/N
100 S = SQR((U - T * T)*(N/(N - 1)))
110 C = S * A/(SQR(N))
120 E = T - C : F = T + C
130 PRINT "CONFIDENCE INTERVAL:"
140 PRINT "FROM ";E;" TO ";F
150 END
```

Chapter 17

1. Test statistic: .383; accept.

2. Test statistic: .380; accept.

3. Test statistic: −3.15; reject.

4. Test statistic: −.101; accept.

Chapter 18

k	Probability that the number of people in the sample on your side will equal k
5. 1	.093
2	.326
3	.392
4	.163
6. 1	.495
2	.220
3	.022
4	.000
7. 1	.017
2	.149
3	.400
4	.350
8. 1	.052
2	.207
3	.367
4	.288
9. 4	.075
5	.188
6	.285
7	.258
10. 9	.020
10	.071
11	.162
12	.243
11. 8	.097
9	.227
10	.300
11	.227
12	.097
12. 8	.119
9	.193
10	.227
11	.193
12	.119
13. 8	.122
9	.175
10	.197
11	.175
12	.122

Chapter 19

1. The expression for TSE is:

$$\text{TSE} = \sum_{i=1}^{n} (mx_i + b - y_i)^2$$

We can rewrite the equation for TSE like this:

$$\text{TSE} = \sum_{i=1}^{n} [(mx_i + b)^2 - 2(mx_i + b)y_i + y_i^2]$$

$$= \sum_{i=1}^{n} [m^2x_i^2 + 2bmx_i + b^2 - 2mx_iy_i - 2by_i + y_i^2]$$

$$= m^2 \sum_{i=1}^{n} x_i^2 + 2bm \sum_{i=1}^{n} x_i + nb^2$$

$$- 2m \sum_{i=1}^{n} x_iy_i - 2b \sum_{i=1}^{n} y_i + \sum_{i=1}^{n} y_i^2$$

We can simplify this expression by using $\bar{x}$ to represent the average value of x, $\left[\bar{x} = (1/n) \times \sum_{i=1}^{n} x_i\right]$, $\bar{y}$ to represent the average value of y, $\overline{x^2}$ to represent the average value of x^2, $\overline{y^2}$ to represent the average value of y^2, and $\overline{xy}$ to represent the average value of xy.

$$\text{TSE} = m^2n\overline{x^2} + 2bmn\bar{x} + nb^2 - 2mn\overline{xy} - 2bn\bar{y} + n\overline{y^2}$$

Finding the values of b and m that minimize this expression requires a little bit of calculus. Take the derivatives of TSE with respect to m and with respect to b and then set both derivatives equal to zero. Then optimum values of m and b must satisfy these two equations:

$$2nm\bar{x} + 2nb - 2n\bar{y} = 0$$
$$2nm\overline{x^2} + 2nb\bar{x} - 2n\overline{xy} = 0$$

We can divide both of these equations by $2n$:

$$m\bar{x} + b - \bar{y} = 0$$
$$m\overline{x^2} + b\bar{x} - \overline{xy} = 0$$

Now we can use these two equations to find the value for the slope:

$$m = \frac{\overline{xy} - \bar{x}\,\bar{y}}{\overline{x^2} - \bar{x}^2}$$

Once we know m, we can calculate b:

$$b = \bar{y} - m\bar{x}$$

2.

```
1 REM PROGRAM TO PERFORM SIMPLE LINEAR
    REGRESSION
10 X1 = 0 : Y1 = 0 : X2 = 0 : Y2 = 0 : Z = 0
20 FOR I = 1 TO N
30      INPUT X
40      INPUT Y
50      X1 = X1 + X
60      X2 = X2 + X * X
70      Y1 = Y1 + Y
80      Y2 = Y2 + Y * Y
90      Z = Z + X * Y
100 NEXT I
110 X1 = X1/N : Y1 = Y1/N : X2 = X2/N : Y2 = Y2/N : Z = Z/N
120 C = Z - X1 * Y1
130 S1 = X2 - X1 * X1
140 S2 = Y2 - Y1 * Y1
150 M = C/S1
160 B = Y1 - M * X1
170 R = C * C/(S1 * S2)
180 PRINT "SLOPE:" ; M
190 PRINT "INTERCEPT:" ; B
200 PRINT "R SQUARED:"; R
210 END
```

3.

```
LIST
00001 REM     MULTIPLE LINEAR REGRESSION PROGRAM
00002 REM      THIS BASIC PROGRAM PERFORMS A REGRESSION
00003 REM      CALCULATION.
00004 REM      X IS AN ARRAY WITH T ROWS AND M COLUMNS
00005 REM       CONSISTING OF T OBSERVATIONS EACH FOR
00006 REM       M-1 INDEPENDENT VARIABLES.
00007 REM      Y IS AN ARRAY WITH T ROWS CONSISTING OF
00008 REM       OBSERVATIONS OF THE DEPENDENT VARIABLE.
00009 REM       IN THIS EXAMPLE, T IS 8 AND M IS 3.
00010 M = 3 % T = 8
00015 !
00016 !
```

```
00017 REM    READ IN THE VALUES FOR X
00018 REM
00020 DIM X(8,3)
00021 FOR I = 1 TO T % FOR J = 1 TO M % READ X(I,J)
00022    NEXT J % NEXT I
00024 DATA    27,   11,   1
00025 DATA    13,   16,   1
00026 DATA    56,   43,   1
00027 DATA    13,   33,   1
00028 DATA    46,   19,   1
00029 DATA    99,    8,   1
00030 DATA    66,   26,   1
00031 DATA    10,   19,   1
00040 !
00041 !
00042 REM  READ IN THE VALUES FOR Y
00043 !
00050 DIM Y(8)
00055 FOR I = 1 TO T % READ Y(I) % NEXT I
00056 DATA 174, 148, 480, 254, 298, 444, 420, 154
00057 !
00058 !
00059 REM DIM E(T), Y2(T), D(M,T), C(M,M), Z(2*M,M), B(M), T3(M)
00060     DIM E(8), Y2(8), D(3,8), C(3,3), Z(  6,3), B(3), T3(3)
00061 !
00062 !
00198 REM    BEGIN CALCULATION
00199 !
00200 FOR I = 1 TO M
00210    FOR J = 1 TO M
00220         Z2 = 0
00230             FOR K = 1 TO T
00240                  Z2 = Z2 + X(K,I) * X(K,J)
00250             NEXT K
00260         Z(I,J) = Z2
00270     NEXT J
00280  NEXT I
00290 !
00291 !
00300  FOR I = (M + 1) TO 2 * M
00310      FOR J = 1 TO M
00320       Z(I,J) = 0
00330      NEXT J
00340  NEXT I
00345 !
00350  FOR I = 1 TO M
00360     Z((M + I),I) = 1
00370  NEXT I
00380 !
00382 !
00400  FOR J = 1 TO M
00401   Z5 = Z(J,J)
00410     FOR I = 1 TO 2 * M
```

```
00420     Z(I,J) = Z(I,J)/Z5
00430     NEXT I
00435 !
00440   FOR K = 1 TO M
00445      Z6= Z(J,K)
00450        IF K = J THEN GOTO 490
00460          FOR I = 1 TO 2 * M
00470             Z(I,K) = Z(I,K) - Z(I,J) * Z6
00480          NEXT I
00490      NEXT K
00500   NEXT J
00505 !
00510   FOR I = 1 TO M
00520      FOR J = 1 TO M
00530         C(I,J) = Z((M+I),J)
00540      NEXT J
00550   NEXT I
00580 !
00590 !
00600   FOR I = 1 TO M
00610      FOR J = 1 TO T
00620         Z2 = 0
00630      FOR K = 1 TO·M
00640             Z2 = Z2 + C(I,K) * X(J,K)
00650         NEXT K
00660         D(I,J) = Z2
00670      NEXT J
00680   NEXT I
00681 !
00682   FOR J = 1 TO M
00683      B(J) = 0
00684      FOR I = 1 TO T
00685         B(J) = B(J) + D(J,I) * Y(I)
00686      NEXT I
00687    NEXT J
00688  !
00689 !
00690 !
00691 !
00700   S2 = 0
00710   FOR I = 1 TO T
00720      Z2 = 0
00730      FOR J = 1 TO M
00740          Z2 = Z2 + X(I,J) * B(J)
00750      NEXT J
00760      Y2(I) = Z2      ! ESTIMATED VALUE FOR Y
00770      E(I) = Y(I) - Y2(I) ! ESTIMATED VALUE FOR ERROR
00780       S2 = S2 + E(I) * E(I)
00790    NEXT I
00800   S = S2/(T - M)  ! ESTIMATE OF STANDARD DEVIATION
00810   Y3 = 0
00820    FOR I = 1 TO T
00830        Y3 = Y3 + Y(I)
```

```
00840      NEXT I
00850      Y3 = Y3/T      ! AVERAGE VALUE FOR Y
00860      S4 = 0
00870    FOR I = 1 TO T
00880         S4 = S4 + (ABS(Y(I) - Y3))**2
00885 NEXT I
00890     R2 = 1 - S2/S4   ! R SQUARED COEFFICIENT
00900    FOR I = 1 TO M
00910        T3(I) = B(I)/(S * C(I,I))  ! T STATISTIC
00920    NEXT I
00990 !
00991 !
01000 REM ******* OUTPUT **************
01010  PRINT "R SQUARED:";R2
01030  FOR I = 1 TO M
01040       PRINT "COEFFICIENT ";I
01050       PRINT B(I)
01060       PRINT "T STATISTIC "
01070       PRINT T3(I)
01080        PRINT " "
01090    NEXT I
01100    END
Ready
RUN
EX-00 Execution begins...
R SQUARED: .999872
COEFFICIENT  1
 3.97935
T STATISTIC
 8245.56514

COEFFICIENT  2
 5.995739
T STATISTIC
 1692.904523

COEFFICIENT  3
 1.195036
T STATISTIC
 .372305
```

	Slope	Intercept	r^2
6.	−0.033	15.418	.136
7.	10.262	0.071	.979
8.	0.842	15.585	.373
9.	8.317	−15.288	.977
10.	0.48	2.87	.112

11.	0.50	0.19	.721
12.	0.979	−0.279	.830
13.	4.02	0.007	.999

This result suggests that the true relation between y and x is of the form $y = x^4$.

	Coefficient 1	Coefficient 2	coefficient 3	Constant	r^2
14.	−0.254	−4.051	1.316	109.16	.620
15.	5.129	0.968		1.26	.994
16.	0.062	0.160		4.54	.146
17.	0.017	0.677		33.38	.326
18.	3.980	5.996		1.20	.999

APPENDIX 2

SUMMARY OF BASIC PROGRAMMING LANGUAGE

Symbols

letters: A, B, C, D, E, F, G, H, I, J, K, L, M, N, O, P, Q, R, S, T, U, V, W, X, Y, Z

digits: 0, 1, 2, 3, 4, 5, 6, 7, 8, 9

operations: + (addition), − (subtraction), * (multiplication), / (division), ↑ or ** (exponentiation)

other symbols:

= equals: in assignment statement or condition
( ) parentheses for grouping
, separator
; separator
" quotation mark—to enclose character strings
: to separate two statements on the same line
\$ symbol for character string variables
< less than
> greater than
>= greater than or equal
<= less than or equal
<> not equal
% used to separate two statements on the same line in some systems.

exponential notation:

5.4 E 6 (for example) means $5.4 \times 10^6 = 5,400,000$

Commands

Items in italics can be replaced by appropriate items of your choosing. *x* and *y* stand for variable names; *n* stands for numbers. Items in capital letters need to be typed exactly as shown. Only commands

255

which are standard in almost all systems are included. In particular, character string functions will depend a lot on the specific computer being used, so check a manual for your computer.

ABS(*x*)   built-in function: absolute value

ASN(*x*)   built-in function: arcsine

ATN(*x*)   built-in function: arctangent

COS(*x*)   built-in function: cosine

DATA *n1, n2, . . .*   creates a data stack of the values of *n1, n2, . . .* The values in the stack will be assigned to variables by the use of the READ command.

DEF FN*x*(*y*) = *expression*

The DEF command creates a user-defined function with the name FN*x*(*y*).

DIM *x*(*n*)   declares that *x* will be a 1-dimensional array with *n* elements.

DIM *x*(*n1, n2*)   declares that *x* will be a 2-dimensional array with *n1* rows and *n2* columns.

END   the statement at the end of the program that tells the computer that the program is completed.

EXP(*x*)   built in function: e^x

FOR . . .   the first statement in a loop.

GOSUB *sn*   tells the computer to start executing subroutine that starts at statement number *sn*.

GOTO *sn*   The next statement that will be executed is the statement with the number *sn*.

IF *condition* GOTO *sn*

If the *condition* is true, the next statement executed will be number *sn*. If the *condition* is false, the statement immediately following the IF statement will be executed next.

IF *condition* LET *x* = *expression*

IF *condition* PRINT *item*

In both cases the second part of the statement will be executed only if the *condition* is true.

INPUT *x*   causes the computer to stop, display a question mark, and then wait for the user to type in a value, and then assign that value to the variable *x*.

INPUT *x, y*   same as above, except two values need to be typed in.

INPUT "*message*"; *x*   same as INPUT *x*, except *message* will be displayed instead of the question mark.

INT(*x*)   built-in function: greatest integer smaller than *x*

LET *x* = *expression*

calculates the value of *expression* and then assigns that value to *x*. (The use of LET is optional.)

LN(*x*)   built-in function: logarithm to the base *e*.

LOG(*x*)   built-in function: logarithm to the base 10. (On some computers LOG(*x*) will be the log to the base *e*.)

NEXT *x* the last statement in a loop.

PRINT *x* causes the value of *x* to be printed (or displayed on the screen if you are using a television terminal).

PRINT *"chars"* causes the characters *chars* to be printed

PRINT *item1*, *item2* causes the two items to be printed, separated by a standard amount.

PRINT *item1*; *item2* causes the two items to be printed right next to each other.

READ *x* causes the top value of the data stack to be assigned to the variable *x*. (Data stacks are created with DATA statements.)

REM causes the computer to ignore the rest of that line, allowing a message for the programmers to be included in the program.

RETURN the statement at the end of a subroutine.

SGN(*x*) built-in function:
SGN(*x*) is 1 if $x > 0$
SGN(*x*) is 0 if $x = 0$
SGN(*x*) is -1 if $x < 0$

SIN(*x*) built-in function: sine of *x*

STEP used with FOR/NEXT loop.

SQR(*x*) built in function: square root of *x*

TAB used as follows:
PRINT TAB(*x*); *item*
causes item to be printed starting at column *x* of the screen.

TAN(*x*) built in function: tangent of *x*

TO used with FOR/NEXT loop.

USING used as follows:
PRINT USING*"###.##"*;*x*
means that *x* is to be printed with two digits to the right of the decimal point and three digits to the left.

APPENDIX 3

TABLES

TABLE A3-1: The Standard Normal Distribution

If Z has a standard normal distribution, the table gives the value of $\Pr(Z < z)$

z	$\Pr(Z < z)$	z	$\Pr(Z < z)$	z	$\Pr(Z < z)$	z	$\Pr(Z < z)$
0.01	.5040	0.29	.6141	0.57	.7157	0.85	.8023
0.02	.5080	0.30	.6179	0.58	.7190	0.86	.8051
0.03	.5120	0.31	.6217	0.59	.7224	0.87	.8079
0.04	.5160	0.32	.6255	0.60	.7257	0.88	.8106
0.05	.5199	0.33	.6293	0.61	.7291	0.89	.8133
0.06	.5239	0.34	.6331	0.62	.7324	0.90	.8159
0.07	.5279	0.35	.6368	0.63	.7357	0.91	.8186
0.08	.5319	0.36	.6406	0.64	.7389	0.92	.8212
0.09	.5359	0.37	.6443	0.65	.7422	0.93	.8238
0.10	.5398	0.38	.6480	0.66	.7454	0.94	.8264
0.11	.5438	0.39	.6517	0.67	.7486	0.95	.8289
0.12	.5478	0.40	.6554	0.68	.7517	0.96	.8315
0.13	.5517	0.41	.6591	0.69	.7549	0.97	.8340
0.14	.5557	0.42	.6628	0.70	.7580	0.98	.8365
0.15	.5596	0.43	.6664	0.71	.7611	0.99	.8389
0.16	.5636	0.44	.6700	0.72	.7642	1.00	.8413
0.17	.5675	0.45	.6736	0.73	.7673	1.01	.8438
0.18	.5714	0.46	.6772	0.74	.7704	1.02	.8461
0.19	.5753	0.47	.6808	0.75	.7734	1.03	.8485
0.20	.5793	0.48	.6844	0.76	.7764	1.04	.8508
0.21	.5832	0.49	.6879	0.77	.7794	1.05	.8531
0.22	.5871	0.50	.6915	0.78	.7823	1.06	.8554
0.23	.5910	0.51	.6950	0.79	.7852	1.07	.8577
0.24	.5948	0.52	.6985	0.80	.7881	1.08	.8599
0.25	.5987	0.53	.7019	0.81	.7910	1.09	.8621
0.26	.6026	0.54	.7054	0.82	.7939	1.10	.8643
0.27	.6064	0.55	.7088	0.83	.7967	1.11	.8665
0.28	.6103	0.56	.7123	0.84	.7995	1.12	.8686

TABLE A3-1: The Standard Normal Distribution

z	Pr(Z < z)	z	Pr(Z < z)	z	Pr(Z < z)	z	Pr(Z < z)
1.13	.8708	1.44	.9251	1.75	.9599	2.06	.9803
1.14	.8729	1.45	.9265	1.76	.9608	2.07	.9808
1.15	.8749	1.46	.9279	1.77	.9616	2.08	.9812
1.16	.8770	1.47	.9292	1.78	.9625	2.09	.9817
1.17	.8790	1.48	.9306	1.79	.9633	2.10	.9821
1.18	.8810	1.49	.9319	1.80	.9641	2.11	.9826
1.19	.8830	1.50	.9332	1.81	.9649	2.12	.9830
1.20	.8849	1.51	.9345	1.82	.9656	2.13	.9834
1.21	.8869	1.52	.9357	1.83	.9664	2.14	.9838
1.22	.8888	1.53	.9370	1.84	.9671	2.15	.9842
1.23	.8907	1.54	.9382	1.85	.9678	2.16	.9846
1.24	.8925	1.55	.9394	1.86	.9686	2.17	.9850
1.25	.8944	1.56	.9406	1.87	.9693	2.18	.9854
1.26	.8962	1.57	.9418	1.88	.9699	2.19	.9857
1.27	.8980	1.58	.9429	1.89	.9706	2.20	.9861
1.28	.8997	1.59	.9441	1.90	.9713	2.25	.9878
1.29	.9015	1.60	.9452	1.91	.9719	2.30	.9893
1.30	.9032	1.61	.9463	1.92	.9726	2.35	.9906
1.31	.9049	1.62	.9474	1.93	.9732	2.40	.9918
1.32	.9066	1.63	.9484	1.94	.9738	2.50	.9938
1.33	.9082	1.64	.9495	1.95	.9744	2.60	.9953
1.34	.9099	1.65	.9505	1.96	.9750	2.70	.9965
1.35	.9115	1.66	.9515	1.97	.9756	2.80	.9974
1.36	.9131	1.67	.9525	1.98	.9761	2.90	.9981
1.37	.9147	1.68	.9535	1.99	.9767	3.00	.9987
1.38	.9162	1.69	.9545	2.00	.9773	3.10	.9990
1.39	.9177	1.70	.9554	2.01	.9778	3.20	.9993
1.40	.9192	1.71	.9564	2.02	.9783	3.30	.9995
1.41	.9207	1.72	.9573	2.03	.9788	3.40	.9997
1.42	.9222	1.73	.9582	2.04	.9793	3.50	.9998
1.43	.9236	1.74	.9591	2.05	.9798		

TABLE A3-2: The Standard Normal Distribution

z	Pr(−z < Z < z)	z	Pr(−z < Z < z)
0.10	.0796	1.30	.8064
0.20	.1586	1.40	.8384
0.30	.2358	1.50	.8664
0.40	.3108	1.60	.8904
0.50	.3830	1.70	.9108
0.60	.4514	1.80	.9282
0.70	.5160	1.90	.9426
0.80	.5762	1.96	.9500
0.90	.6318	2.00	.9546
1.00	.6826	2.50	.9876
1.10	.7286	3.00	.9974
1.20	.7698		

TABLE A3-3: The Chi-square Cumulative Distribution Function

If X has a chi-square distribution with n degrees of freedom, the table gives the value x such that $\Pr(X < x) = p$. For example, if X has a chi-square distribution with 10 degrees of freedom, there is a probability of .95 that X will be less than 18.3.

n	$p=.005$	$p=.01$	$p=.05$	$p=.25$	$p=.50$	$p=.75$	$p=.90$	$p=.95$	$p=.975$	$p=.99$
2	0.01	.02	.10	.57	1.38	2.77	4.60	5.99	7.37	9.21
3	0.07	.11	.35	1.21	2.36	4.10	6.24	7.80	9.33	11.31
4	0.20	.29	.71	1.92	3.35	5.38	7.77	9.48	11.14	13.27
5	0.41	.55	1.14	2.67	4.35	6.62	9.23	11.07	12.83	15.08
6	0.67	.87	1.63	3.45	5.34	7.84	10.64	12.59	14.44	16.81
7	0.98	1.24	2.17	4.26	6.35	9.04	12.02	14.07	16.01	18.48
8	1.34	1.65	2.73	5.07	7.34	10.22	13.36	15.51	17.54	20.09
9	1.73	2.09	3.33	5.90	8.34	11.39	14.68	16.92	19.02	21.67
10	2.16	2.56	3.94	6.74	9.3	12.5	15.9	18.3	20.5	23.2
11	2.60	3.05	4.57	7.58	10.3	13.7	17.3	19.7	21.9	24.7
12	3.07	3.57	5.23	8.44	11.3	14.8	18.6	21.0	23.3	26.2
13	3.56	4.11	5.89	9.30	12.3	16.0	19.8	22.4	24.7	27.7
14	4.08	4.66	6.57	10.17	13.3	17.1	21.1	23.7	26.1	29.1
15	4.60	5.23	7.26	11.04	14.3	18.2	22.3	25.0	27.5	30.6
16	5.14	5.81	7.96	11.91	15.3	19.4	23.5	26.3	28.8	32.0
17	5.70	6.41	8.67	12.79	16.3	20.5	24.8	27.6	30.2	33.4
18	6.26	7.02	9.39	13.68	17.3	21.6	26.0	28.9	31.5	34.8
19	6.85	7.63	10.12	14.56	18.3	22.7	27.2	30.1	32.9	36.2
20	7.43	8.26	10.85	15.45	19.3	23.8	28.4	31.4	34.2	37.6
21	8.03	8.90	11.59	16.34	20.3	24.9	29.6	32.7	35.5	38.9
22	8.64	9.54	12.34	17.24	21.3	26.0	30.8	33.9	36.8	40.3
23	9.26	10.19	13.09	18.14	22.3	27.1	32.0	35.2	38.1	41.6
24	9.89	10.86	13.85	19.04	23.3	28.2	33.2	36.4	39.4	43.0
25	10.52	11.52	14.61	19.94	24.3	29.3	34.4	37.7	40.7	44.3
30	13.79	14.95	18.49	24.48	29.3	34.8	40.3	43.8	47.0	50.9
40	20.70	22.16	26.51	33.66	39.3	45.6	51.8	55.7	59.3	63.7
50	27.99	29.70	34.76	42.94	49.3	56.3	63.2	67.5	71.4	76.2
60	35.53	37.48	43.19	52.29	59.3	67.0	74.4	79.1	83.3	88.4
70	43.27	45.44	51.74	61.70	69.3	77.6	85.5	90.5	95.0	100.4
80	51.18	53.54	60.38	71.15	79.3	88.1	96.6	101.9	106.6	112.3
90	59.19	61.74	69.12	80.62	89.3	98.7	107.6	113.2	118.1	124.1

TABLE A3-4: The *t* Distribution

If X has a t distribution with n degrees of freedom, the table gives the value of x such that $\Pr(X < x)$ $= p$. For example, if X has a t distribution with 15 degrees of freedom there is a 95 percent chance X will be less than 1.753.

n	p = .750	p = .900	p = .950	p = .975	p = .990	p = .995
1	1.000	3.078	6.314	12.706	31.821	63.657
2	0.817	1.886	2.920	4.303	6.965	9.925
3	0.765	1.638	2.353	3.182	4.541	5.841
4	0.741	1.533	2.132	2.776	3.747	4.604
5	0.727	1.476	2.015	2.571	3.365	4.032
6	0.718	1.440	1.943	2.447	3.143	3.707
7	0.711	1.415	1.895	2.365	3.000	3.499
8	0.706	1.397	1.860	2.306	2.896	3.355
9	0.703	1.383	1.833	2.262	2.821	3.250
10	0.700	1.372	1.812	2.228	2.764	3.169
11	0.697	1.363	1.796	2.201	2.718	3.106
12	0.695	1.356	1.782	2.179	2.681	3.055
13	0.694	1.350	1.771	2.160	2.650	3.012
14	0.692	1.345	1.761	2.145	2.600	2.977
15	0.691	1.341	1.753	2.131	2.600	2.947
16	0.690	1.337	1.746	2.120	2.584	2.921
17	0.689	1.333	1.740	2.110	2.567	2.898
18	0.688	1.330	1.734	2.101	2.552	2.878
19	0.688	1.328	1.729	2.093	2.539	2.861
20	0.687	1.325	1.725	2.086	2.528	2.845
21	0.686	1.323	1.721	2.080	2.518	2.831
22	0.686	1.321	1.717	2.074	2.508	2.819
23	0.685	1.319	1.714	2.069	2.500	2.807
24	0.685	1.318	1.711	2.064	2.492	2.797
25	0.684	1.316	1.708	2.060	2.485	2.787
26	0.684	1.315	1.706	2.056	2.479	2.779
27	0.684	1.314	1.703	2.052	2.473	2.771
28	0.683	1.313	1.701	2.048	2.467	2.763
29	0.683	1.311	1.699	2.045	2.462	2.756
30	0.683	1.310	1.697	2.042	2.457	2.750
35	0.682	1.306	1.690	2.030	2.438	2.724
40	0.681	1.303	1.684	2.021	2.423	2.704
50	0.679	1.299	1.676	2.009	2.400	2.678
60	0.679	1.296	1.671	2.000	2.400	2.660
100	0.677	1.290	1.660	1.984	2.364	2.626
120	0.677	1.289	1.658	1.980	2.358	2.617

TABLE A3-5: The t Distribution

If X has a t distribution with n degrees of freedom, the table gives the value of x such that $Pr(-x < X < x) = p$.

n	$p = .95$	$p = .99$	n	$p = .95$	$p = .99$
1	12.706	63.657	20	2.086	2.845
2	4.303	9.925	21	2.080	2.831
3	3.182	5.841	22	2.074	2.819
4	2.776	4.604	23	2.069	2.807
5	2.571	4.032	24	2.064	2.797
6	2.447	3.707	25	2.060	2.787
7	2.365	3.499	26	2.056	2.779
8	2.306	3.355	27	2.052	2.771
9	2.262	3.250	28	2.048	2.763
10	2.228	3.169	29	2.045	2.756
11	2.201	3.106	30	2.042	2.750
12	2.179	3.055	35	2.030	2.724
13	2.160	3.012	40	2.021	2.704
14	2.145	2.977	50	2.009	2.678
15	2.131	2.947	60	2.000	2.660
16	2.120	2.921	100	1.984	2.626
17	2.110	2.898	120	1.980	2.617
18	2.101	2.878			
19	2.093	2.861			

TABLE A3-6: The F-distribution

If F has an F distribution with m and n degrees of freedom, then the table gives the value of x such that $Pr(F < x) = .95$

n	$m = 2$	$m = 3$	$m = 4$	$m = 5$	$m = 10$	$m = 15$	$m = 20$	$m = 30$	$m = 60$	$m = 120$
2	19.00	19.16	19.25	19.30	19.40	19.43	19.45	19.46	19.48	19.49
3	9.55	9.28	9.12	9.01	8.79	8.70	8.66	8.62	8.57	8.55
4	6.94	6.59	6.39	6.26	5.96	5.86	5.80	5.75	5.69	5.66
5	5.79	5.41	5.19	5.05	4.74	4.62	4.56	4.50	4.43	4.40
6	5.14	4.76	4.53	4.39	4.06	3.94	3.87	3.81	3.74	3.70
7	4.74	4.35	4.12	3.97	3.64	3.51	3.44	3.38	3.30	3.27
8	4.46	4.07	3.84	3.69	3.35	3.22	3.15	3.08	3.01	2.97
9	4.26	3.86	3.63	3.48	3.14	3.01	2.94	2.86	2.79	2.75
10	4.10	3.71	3.48	3.33	2.98	2.85	2.77	2.70	2.62	2.58
15	3.68	3.29	3.06	2.90	2.54	2.40	2.33	2.25	2.16	2.11
20	3.49	3.10	2.87	2.71	2.35	2.20	2.12	2.04	1.95	1.90
30	3.32	2.92	2.69	2.53	2.16	2.01	1.93	1.84	1.74	1.68
60	3.15	2.76	2.53	2.37	1.99	1.84	1.75	1.65	1.53	1.47
120	3.07	2.68	2.45	2.29	1.91	1.75	1.66	1.55	1.43	1.35

INDEX

MAXIMIZE YOUR MATH SKILLS!

BARRON'S EASY WAY SERIES

Specially structured to maximize learning with a minimum of time and effort, these books promote fast skill building through lively cartoons and other fun features.

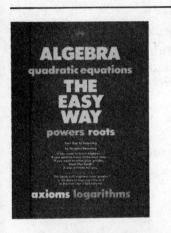

ALGEBRA THE EASY WAY
Douglas Downing
In this one-of-a-kind algebra text, all the fundamentals are discovered through the fascinating adventures that took place in a faraway land! Written as a fantasy novel, this book includes plenty of exercises with solutions, and over 100 illustrations. 352 pp. (2716-7) $8.95, Can. $12.95

CALCULUS THE EASY WAY, *Revised*
Douglas Downing
Here, a journey through a fantasy land leads to calculus mastery. All principles are taught in an easy-to-follow adventure tale. Included are numerous exercises, diagrams, and cartoons which aid comprehension. 228 pp. (4078-3) $9.95, Can. $13.95

GEOMETRY THE EASY WAY
Lawrence Leff
While other geometry books simply summarize basic principles, this book focuses on the "why" of geometry: why you should approach a problem a certain way, and why the method works. Each chapter concludes with review exercises. 288 pp. (2718-3) $8.95, Can. $12.95

TRIGONOMETRY THE EASY WAY
Douglas Downing
In this adventure story, the inhabitants of a faraway kingdom use trigonometry to solve their problems. Covered is all material studied in high school or first-year college classes. Practice exercises, explained answers, and illustrations enhance understanding. 288 pp. (2717-5) $8.95, Can. $12.95

FM: FUNDAMENTALS OF MATHEMATICS
Cecilia Cullen and Eileen Petruzillo, editors
Volume 1 (2501-6) — Formulas; Introduction to Algebra; Metric Measurement; Geometry; Managing Money; Probability and Statistics.
Volume 2 (2508-3) — Solving Simple Equations; Tables, Graphs and Coordinate Geometry; Banking; Areas; Indirect Measurement and Scaling; Solid Geometry. The ideal text/workbooks for pre-algebra students and those preparing for state minimum competency exams. They conform with the New York State curriculum, and follow units recommended by the New York City Curriculum Guide. Each book 384 pp., $12.95, Can. $17.95

SURVIVAL MATHEMATICS
Edward Williams
Presented here are refreshing, practical new math concepts for basic computational skills. The clear text includes numerous practice exercises that build basic competency skills. 416 pp., $9.95, Can. $13.95 (2012-X)

Books may be purchased at your bookstore, or by mail from Barron's. Enclose check or money order for total amount plus sales tax where applicable and 10% for postage (minimum charge $1.50). All books are paperback editions. Prices subject to change without notice.

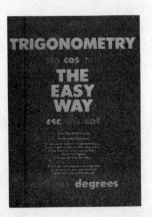

Barron's Educational Series, Inc.
250 Wireless Boulevard
Hauppauge, New York 11788
In Canada:
Georgetown Book Warehouse
34 Armstrong Ave.
Georgetown, Ontario L7G 4R9

More selected BARRON'S titles:

DICTIONARY OF ACCOUNTING TERMS
Joel Siegel and Jae Shim
Approximately 2500 terms are defined for accountants, business managers, students, and small business persons.
Paperback, $8.95, Canada $12.95/ISBN 3766-9

DICTIONARY OF ADVERTISING AND DIRECT MAIL TERMS
Jane Imber and Betsy-Ann Toffler
Approximately 3000 terms are defined as reference for ad industry professionals, students, and consumers.
Paperback, $8.95, Canada $12.95/ISBN 3765-0

DICTIONARY OF BUSINESS TERMS
Jack P. Friedman, general editor
Over 6000 entries define a wide range of terms used throughout business, real estate, taxes, banking, investment, more.
Paperback, $8.95, Canada $12.95/ISBN 3775-8

DICTIONARY OF COMPUTER TERMS
Douglas Downing and Michael Covington
Over 600 key computer terms are clearly explained, and sample programs included. Paperback, $8.95, Canada $12.95/ISBN 2905-4

DICTIONARY OF INSURANCE TERMS, *by Harvey W. Rubin*
Approximately 2500 insurance terms are defined as they relate to property, casualty, life, health, and other types of insurance.
Paperback, $8.95, Canada $12.95/ISBN 3722-3, 448 pages

BARRON'S BUSINESS REVIEW SERIES
Self-instruction guides cover topics taught in a college-level business course, presenting essential concepts in an easy-to-follow format.
Each book paperback $9.95, Canada $13.95, approx. 228 pages
ACCOUNTING, *by Peter J. Eisen*/ISBN 3574-7
BUSINESS LAW, *by Hardwicke and Emerson*/ISBN 3495-3
BUSINESS STATISTICS, *by Downing and Clark*/ISBN 3576-3
ECONOMICS, *by Walter J. Wessels*/ISBN 3560-7
FINANCE, *by A. A. Groppelli and Ehsan Nikhbakht*/ISBN 3561-5
MANAGEMENT, *by Montana and Charnov*/ISBN 3559-3
MARKETING, *by Richard L. Sandhusen*/ISBN 3494-5
QUANTITATIVE METHODS, *by Downing and Clark.* $10.95, Canada $15.95/ISBN 3947-5

TALKING BUSINESS SERIES: BILINGUAL DICTIONARIES
Five bilingual dictionaries translate about 3000 terms not found in most foreign phrasebooks. Includes words related to accounting, sales, banking, computers, export/import and finance.
Each book paperback, $6.95, Canada $9.95, approx. 256 pages
TALKING BUSINESS IN FRENCH, *by Beppie Le Gal*/ISBN 3745-6
TALKING BUSINESS IN GERMAN, *by Henry Strutz*/ISBN 3747-2
TALKING BUSINESS IN ITALIAN, *by Frank Rakus*/ISBN 3754-5
TALKING BUSINESS IN JAPANESE, *by C. & N. Akiyama*/3848-7
TALKING BUSINESS IN KOREAN, *by Un Bok Cheong*/ISBN 3992-0
TALKING BUSINESS IN SPANISH, *by Fryer and Faria*/ISBN 3769-3